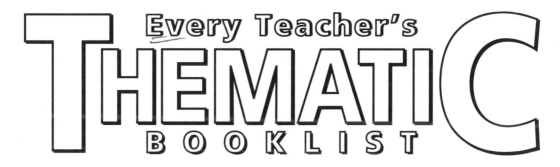

Every Teacher's
THEMATIC
BOOKLIST

By William J. Devers III and James Cipielewski

SCHOLASTIC
PROFESSIONAL BOOKS

New York • Toronto • London • Auckland • Sydney

Copyright ©1993 by William J. Devers, III, and James F. Cipielewski

ISBN 0-590-49170-9

Cover and interior design by Vincent Ceci
Cover and interior illustration by Mona Mark

TABLE OF CONTENTS

INTRODUCING
BILL DEVERS AND JIM CIPIELEWSKI

The enthusiasm with which teachers Jim Cipielewski and Bill Devers present literature to their students is catching—and enthusiasm is always best "caught, not taught" to children, especially youngsters in their formative years. Reading enjoyment is most effectively conveyed through adults' genuine delight in literature, along with a well-grounded understanding of the writing-reading process, and respect for and curiosity about differences in human growth and development, differences in social, economic, and ethnic backgrounds, and differences in individual interests, tastes, and needs. Instead of being overwhelmed by the diversity represented in today's classrooms, Cipielewski and Devers are challenged by it—and are willing and eager to respond to their students' uniqueness. They are each in their own way remarkable teachers.

In my undergraduate and graduate children's literature courses at Oakland University, I have become aware of several practices that I either observed in Jim or Bill's classrooms or know to be taking place there. For example, some years ago, Jim was teaching in an independent school which had little in the way of library resources. He was (and still is) an avid reader, and he wanted desperately to make good books—and lots of them—available to his middle school students. He built a library for them by buying books from used book stores, public library book sales, wholesale book dealers, children's book stores, mail order catalogs—most often using his own resources.

Jim uses many techniques to "catch" his listeners. He tells folktales, jokes, and riddles, and uses poetry with great delight. His lively classes reflect the joy he finds in giving the best of himself and the things he loves most, one of which is his love of story. (Both Jim and Bill are devotees of the King Arthur stories. I hope they all get to meet someday. It would be a meeting of long-time friends.)

Never content with the status quo, Jim has taken children's literature courses, researched special topics he knew his students were especially interested in, attended local, state, and national conferences—and, always, he has engaged in book discussions with students and colleagues. As a normal part of his daily routine, Jim talks about books with a variety of people—elementary students, college students, doctoral students, university professors, and those many colleagues he meets via Internet on his computer.

Throughout his career, Jim has made a point of reading and discussing all types of literature, including biographies, autobiographies, fiction, poetry, and essays by a variety of authors. He makes certain he is knowledgeable about a variety of genres and topics so that he can recommend appropriate resources for the wide range of people with which he works. He eagerly shares stories, poems, informational books which have especially delighted him, but he's always careful not to "say too much."
He likes to leave his listeners wondering and considering if they, too, might like reading what he has found so enjoyable.

I have often pointed out to my university students that if each teacher took just a few minutes each school day to acquaint his or her students with a particularly interesting or notable book, our children could be exposed to as many as 2,000 books during their 13 in-school years—about 180 per school year. If children read on their own only one book each week they would have read nearly 700 books between grades K—12. While it is common that teachers in grades K—2 read aloud one or more books a day to their pupils, if each of those teachers read three books a day for an entire school year, the children would have heard almost 800 books! And if the books were books of high quality, what a difference it would make in children's lives—and how differently they would think about reading. Bruno Bettelheim has aptly pointed out that if the books we present to children add little or nothing of significance to their lives, they have little or no reason to want to learn to read. Both of these teachers, Cipielewski and Devers, fully realize the importance of both the quantity and the quality of the literature they present.

Like Jim Cipieliewski, Bill Devers offers challenges to his students. For example, he encourages them to both ask and answer questions that are significant—questions basic to what it means to be human, to live in an ethnically diverse America, to live as part of a global community, and to live hopefully into the future. He especially stresses questions and answers about the past (which often grow out of biographies and historical fiction). These are then deliberated, discussed in a lively manner, and explored in terms of the present.

Bill is sensitive to the interests and needs of his fifth-graders, keeping in mind their love of mystery and of humor. He loves language, and shares especially well-written passages with his students by reading aloud, always stressing the beauty of the passage and its importance, and revealing his own delight in the material. What a difference this attitude toward literature and life can make in a classroom.

Bill builds much of his teaching on his own genuine love of history and of heroes. Student projects grow out of such concerns that provide a hearty foundation for many facets of learning. Bill's students are fortunate indeed to have him as their teacher and their guide to thought-provoking literature that opens up old, but ever new, windows on living.

Both Bill and Jim use interactive questioning extensively in their classrooms. They set aside time each day for small-group book discussions, so crucial to developing enthusiastic readers and critical thinkers. Students are helped to learn how to summarize, how to compare and contrast what they have read with other pieces of literature, as well as with their own experiences, and they are encouraged to reflect on how their reading has affected their emotions, intellect, tastes—and their hope for the future. Such discussions are basic to developing an appreciation and enthusiasm for books.

As is evident from Jim and Bill's selective but wide-ranging book lists, it is clear that they are not afraid to cross all sorts of "restrictive" lines. For example, they use picture books with older children. Today's picture books cover a wide range of topics and some are surprisingly complex—and Jim and Bill are not afraid to introduce to older children what some might (wrongfully) consider "baby books." Many picture books are appropriate for older children and provide them with real substance, usually presented in a stimulating visual setting, which for many children is their introduction to various artistic styles and media.

In addition to using lively and constructive classroom practices, both Jim Cipielewski and Bill Devers are avid readers of criticism of new books from a variety of sources. They consciously strive to become acquainted with many points of view. With each review, they hone or reinforce their own views, considering their own likes and dislikes, strengths and weaknesses.

This book, this sharing of the "list of books" that they have used successfully with their own students is just one example of their willingness to be vulnerable, to make errors of judgement, and even to change their minds if necessary in order to grow in wisdom and understanding. Perhaps that is at the root of why they are both such outstanding teachers.

I do hope that you will see this list of books as a beginning of a conversation with two teachers who approach teaching literature as well as teaching children with intellectual rigor, moral integrity, and infectious enthusiasm.

Jane M. Bingham
Professor of Children's Literature
Oakland University
Rochester, Michigan

WHAT'S THIS ALL ABOUT?

These lists of children's books began in discussions between two people who had an interest in children, books, and bringing the two together. As elementary classroom teachers, we have seen the interest and enthusiasm real books generate in children. As doctoral students studying reading, we have had many opportunities to review research attesting to the benefits of children's books being used, and being used often, in the classroom. We have been fortunate to attend Oakland University where the philosophy of an integrated language arts curriculum that included children's literature was considered the only rational curriculum. It is in this environment and from our own teaching experiences that our interest in children's literature has thrived.

As classroom teachers, we find ourselves using children's trade books more and more. We find ourselves being asked by fellow teachers for ideas on books that they could use in their own classrooms. With literally thousands of books being published each year, we never feel as though we have enough books to fuel the projects going on in our classrooms and those of our colleagues. We've found book selection guides and journals helpful, but what we really wanted to know was—what books would work well in our classrooms? This book is the result of our having asked ourselves that question.

This book is a list of books that we have used or would like to use in an elementary classroom, covering a range of topics and interests. Each subject may include both narrative and expository books, chapter books and picture books. The subject lists are deliberately not categorized by reading levels, as we believe every classroom should have a range of levels and types of books. We sincerely feel that the subject of the book plays as important a role as reading level in how easily and eagerly a book will be read.

These lists are very personal. In a few months, we will have added many new favorites to these lists. We may replace some books with others that are more current or that reflect newer thinking concerning a subject. Dinosaurs, for instance, are constantly changing even though they've been dead for 65 million years. We hope that this book is true to its goal—to be a current listing of the books we would like to use in an elementary classroom, at this moment in time.

We tried to make this book easy to use by both teachers and students. There are three indexes to the children's books: Author, Title, and Subject. The subject list is broken into approximately 175 categories. These categories are not exhaustive; they just reflect our current thinking. (We're certain that there are many more topics to explore.) The subject lists were drawn from our own experiences as teachers as well as from suggestions of fellow teachers.

In addition to the different lists, there is a bibliography containing all the children's books. Each entry contains all the information necessary to find the book in a library or to order from your favorite bookseller. In addition, there is a very short description of each book. And finally, there are lists of award-winning children's books, and teacher resources.

If you know the author you can go to the author index, find the title you wish, and then go to the annotated entry indicated by the record number. The same procedure is true of a book for which you know the title. Find the title in the title index and then go to the corresponding annotated entry in the bibliography using the record number. The subject categories are meant to allow you to find a book by looking in several places. Most books are categorized under two or more subjects. Again, once you have found a book under a subject of interest to you, use the record number to find the annotated entry in the bibliography.

We hope that you find this book helpful. We plan to continue updating our lists of books. If you have suggestions or comments, please direct them to Jim Cipielewsk at, Reading/Language Arts, Oakland University, Rochester, MI 48309 (e-mail CIPIELEW @ Argo.ACS.Oakland.EDU) or William Devers, III, at Scholastic Professional Books, 730 Broadway, NY, NY, 10003 (e-mail WJDEVERS @Argo.ACS.Oakland.EDU)

The Index of THEMES

Mathis, Sharon Bell,
The Hundred Penny Box.
No.537

McKissack, Patricia,
Mirandy and Brother Wind.
No.565

Mendez, Phil,
The Black Snowman.
No.572

AFRICAN-AMERICAN-FOLK TALE

Bang, Molly,
Wiley and the Hairy Man.
No.49

Bryan, Ashley,
The Cat's Purr.
No.99

Durell, Ann,
The Diane Goode Book of American Folk Tales & Songs.
No.231

Hamilton, Virginia,
The People Could Fly: American Black Folk tales.
No.351

Jaquith, Priscilla (reteller),
Bo Rabbit Smart for True: Folk tales from the Gullah.
No.399

Lester, Julius,
The Knee-High Man and Other Tales.
No.474

Lester, Julius,
More Tales of Uncle Remus: Further Adventures of Brer Rabbit, His Friends, Enemies, and Others.
No.475

San Souci, Robert,
The Talking Eggs.
No.669

Winter, Jeanette,
Follow the Drinking Gourd.
No.811

AFRICAN-AMERICAN-INFORMATIONAL

Aliki,
A Weed is a Flower: The Life of George Washington Carver.
No.19

Davidson, Margaret,
Frederick Douglass Fights for Freedom.
No.198

Denenberg, Barry,
Stealing Home: The Story of Jackie Robinson.
No.213

Griffin, Judith Berry,
Phoebe The Spy.
No.331

Haskins, Jim,
The Day Martin Luther King Jr. Was Shot.
No.354

Lester, Julius,
To Be A Slave.
No.476

McKissack, Patricia,
Jesse Jackson.
No.564

Peck, Ira,
The Life and Words of Martin Luther King, Jr.
No.631

Sterling, Dorothy,
Freedom Train The Story of Harriet Tubman.
No.743

ALPHABET BOOK

Aylesworth, Jim,
Old Black Fly.
No.36

Base, Graeme,
Animalia.
No.58

Bayer, Jane,
A, My Name is Alice.
No.62

Dragonwagon, Crescent,
Alligator Arrived with Apples: A Potluck Alphabet Feast. No.229

Ehlert, Lois,
Eating the Alphabet: Fruits and Vegetables From A to Z.
No.239

Ehlert, Lois,
Planting a Rainbow.
No.242

Eichenberg, Fritz,
Ape in a Cape: An Alphabet of Odd Animals.
No.244

Feelings, Murial,
Jambo Means Hello: Swahili Alphabet Book. No.260

Gág, Wanda,
The ABC Bunny.
No.291

Hall, Nancy Christensen,
Macmillan Fairy Tale Book.
No.346

Hepworth, Cathi,
Antics!
No.367

Jonas, Ann,
Aardvarks, Disembark!
No.409

Kellog, Steven,
Aster Aardvark's Alphabet Adventures.
No.422

Kitamura, Satoshi,
From Acorn to Zoo and Everything in Between in

Alphabetical Order.
No.433

Kitamura, Satoshi,
What's Inside: The Alphabet Book.
No.434

Lear, Edward,
An Edward Lear Alphabet.
No.462

Musgrove, Margaret,
Ashanti to Zulu: African Traditions.
No.593

Pallotta, Jerry,
The Ocean Alphabet Book.
No.616

Polette, Nancy,
The Hole by the Apple Tree.
No.639

Snow, Nicholas,
The Monster Book of ABC Sounds.
No.719

AMERICAN-FOLK TALE

Chase, Richard,
Grandfather Tales: American-English Folk Tales.
No.141

Chase, Richard,
Jack and the Three Sillies.
No.142

Chase, Richard,
The Jack Tales.
No.143

Cohen, Daniel,
Southern Fried Rat and Other Gruesome Tales.
No.163

DeFelice, Cynthia C.,
The Dancing Skeleton.
No.209

Goldin, Augusta,
Spider Silk.
No.324

Gomi, Taro,
Hi, Butterfly!
No.325

Goor, Ron; Nancy Goor,
Insect Metamorphosis.
No.327

Hawes, Judy,
Bees and Beelines.
No.356

Hepworth, Cathi,
Antics!
No.367

Horton, Casey,
Insects.
No.387

Huntington, Harriet,
Let's Look at Insects.
No.393

Jeunesse, Galimard;
Pascale de Bourgoing,
*The Ladybug and Other
Insects.*
No.405

Pringle, Laurence,
*Twist, Wiggle, and Squirm: A
Book about Earthworms.*
No.647

Ryder, Joanne,
Where Butterflies Grow.
No.662

Simon, Seymour,
Little Giants.
No.710

ANIMALS-DOMESTIC

Campbell, Joanna,
A Horse Called Wonder.
No.124

Carle, Eric,
Have you seen my cat?
No.127

Farley, Walter,
The Black Stallion.
No.258

Farm Animals.
No.259

Goble, Paul,
The Gift of theSacred Dog.
No.318

Goble, Paul,
*The Girl Who
Loved Wild Horses.*
No.319

Hale, Sarah Josepha,
Mary Had a Little Lamb.
No.342

Heller, Ruth,
*Chickens Aren't
the Only Ones.*
No.360

Herriot, James,
The Christmas Day Kitten.
No.368

Herriot, James,
Moses the Kitten.
No.369

Herriot, James,
Oscar, Cat-About-Town.
No.370

Jeunesse, Galimard;
Pascale de Bourgoing,
The Egg.
No.403

Kaizuki, Kiyonori,
A Calf Is Born.
No.411

Larrick, Nancy,
Cats Are Cats.
No.448

Lindbergh, Reeve,
The Midnight Farm.
No.482

Locker, Thomas,
Family Farm.
No.501

Morey, Walt,
Kavik the Wolf Dog.
No.582

Hall, Lynn,
Danza.
No.594

Ness, Evaline,
Sam, Bangs & Moonshine.
No.595

Paulsen, Gary,
Woodsong.
No.630

Sewell, Anna; adapted by
Robin McKinley,
Black Beauty.
No.698

Thomas, Jane Resh,
The Comeback Dog.
No.760

Viorst, Judith,
*The Tenth Good Thing
about Barney.*
No.781

William, Sue,
I Went Walking.
No.809

ANIMALS-FANTASTIC

Aardema, Verna (reteller),
*Rabbit Makes a Monkey
of the Lion.*
No.2

Aardema, Verna,
*Why Mosquitoes Buzz in
People's Ears.*
No.3

Arnold, Tedd,
No Jumping on the Bed!
No.31

Baker, Keith,
Who Is the Beast?
No.44

Barracca, Debra and Sal,
The Adventures of Taxi Dog.
No.53

Base, Graeme,
The Eleventh Hour.
No.59

Bodsworth, Nan,
A Nice Walk in the Jungle.
No.81

Brown, Marc,
*Arthur's Tooth: An Arthur
Adventure.*
No.97

Bryan, Ashley,
The Cat's Purr.
No.99

Bryan, Ashley,
*Lion and the Ostrich Chicks
& Other African Folk Tales.*
No.100

Bryan, Ashley,
Turtle Knows Your Name.
No.101

Bunting, Eve,
Terrible Things.
No.107

Burningham, John,
Mr. Gumpy's Outing.
No.112

Butterworth, Nick,
One Snowy Night.
No.118

Calhoun, Mary,
Cross-Country Cat.
No.122

Numeroff, Laura Joffe,
If You Give a Moose a Muffin.
No.601

Pfister, Marcus,
Penguin Pete's New Friends.
No.633

Ryder, Joanne,
White Bear, Ice Bear.
No.663

Sadler, Marilyn,
Elizabeth and Larry.
No.667

Shaw, Nancy,
Sheep in a Jeep.
No.700

Shaw, Nancy,
Sheep in a Shop.
No.701

Shaw, Nancy,
Sheep on a Ship.
No.702

Snape, Juliet; Charles Snape,
Frog Odyssey.
No.717

Steig, William,
Amos & Boris.
No.737

Steig, William,
Sylvester and the Magic Pebble.
No.740

Turkle, Brinton,
Deep in the Forest.
No.769

Van Laan, Nancy,
Possum Come a-Knockin'.
No.777

Vyner, Sue,
The Stolen Egg.
No.783

White, E. B.,
Charlotte's Web.
No.797

White, E. B.,
The Trumpet of the Swan.
No.798

Wildsmith, Brian,
The Lazy Bear.
No.804

Wood, Audrey,
Little Penguin's Tale.
No.815

Zolotow, Charlotte,
The Bunny Who Found Easter.
No.840

ANIMALS-FICTION

Byars, Betsy,
The Midnight Fox.
No.120

Campbell, Joanna,
A Horse Called Wonder.
No.124

Eckert, Allan W.,
Incident at Hawk's Hill.
No.236

Farley, Walter,
The Black Stallion.
No.258

Freeman, Don,
The Seal and the Slick.
No.282

George, Jean Craighead,
Julie of the Wolves.
No.301

Herriot, James,
The Christmas Day Kitten.
No.368

Herriot, James,
Moses the Kitten.
No.369

Herriot, James,
Oscar, Cat-About-Town.
No.370

Morey, Walt,
Kavik the Wolf Dog.
No.582

Hall, Lynn,
Danza.
No.594

Ness, Evaline,
Sam, Bangs & Moonshine.
No.595

Sewell, Anna; adapted by Robin McKinley,
Black Beauty.
No.698

Thomas, Jane Resh,
The Comeback Dog.
No.760

Viorst, Judith,
The Tenth Good Thing about Barney.
No.781

Whelan, Gloria,
A Week of Raccoons.
No.796

ANIMALS-FISH

Arnold, Caroline,
Watch Out for Sharks!
No.30

Bender, Lionel,
Fish to Reptiles.
No.66

Downer, Ann,
Don't Blink Now!
No.228

Maestro, Betsy,
A Sea Full of Sharks.
No.514

McGovern, Ann,
Sharks.
No.560

McGovern, Anne; Eugenie Clarke,
The Desert Beneath the Sea.
No.561

Sargent, William,
Night Reef: Dusk to Dawn on a Coral Reef.
No.673

Stratton, Barbara,
What Is a Fish.
No.746

Sussman, Susan; Robert James,
Big Friend, Little Friend: A Book about Symbiosis.
No.751

ANIMALS-HABITAT

Baker, Keith,
Who Is the Beast?
No.44

Baker, Lucy,
Life in the Rainforest.
No.45

Bender, Lionel,
Fish to Reptiles.
No.66

Bodsworth, Nan,
A Nice Walk in the Jungle.
No.81

Brown, Ruth,
The World That Jack Built.
No.98

Burningham, John,
Hey! Get Off Our Train.
No.111

Butterworth, Nick,
One Snowy Night.
No.118

Carle, Eric,
The Grouchy Ladybug.
No.126

Simon, Seymour,
The Largest Dinosaurs.
No.709

Walker, Paul Robert,
*Bigfoot & Other Legendary
Creatures.*
No.786

ANIMALS-REAL

Cole, Joanna,
My Puppy Is Born.
No.170

Cowcher, Helen,
Rain Forest.
No.184

Dabcovich, Lydia,
Busy Beavers.
No.191

Dorros, Arthur,
Animal Tracks.
No.225

Dorros, Arthur,
Rain Forest Secrets.
No.226

Downer, Ann,
Don't Blink Now!
No.228

Ehlert, Lois,
Feathers for Lunch.
No.240

Farm Animals.
No.259

Fischer-Nagel, Heiderose;
Andreas Fischer-Nagel,
Life of the Ladybug.
No.263

Gardner, Robert,
The Whale Watchers' Guide.
No.299

George, Jean Craighead,
Julie of the Wolves.
No.301

Gibbons, Gail,
Monarch Butterfly.
No.308

Gibbons, Gail,
Zoo.
No.312

Glimmerveen, Ulco,
A Tale of Antarctica.
No.316

Goldin, Augusta,
Spider Silk.
No.324

Goor, Ron; Nancy Goor,
Insect Metamorphosis.
No.327

Hale, Sarah Josepha,
Mary Had a Little Lamb.
No.342

Hawes, Judy,
Bees and Beelines.
No.356

Heller, Ruth,
*Chickens Aren't the Only
Ones.*
No.360

Hirschi, Ron,
*Who Lives in
the Mountains.*
No.373

Hirschi, Ron,
Winter.
No.374

Horton, Casey,
Insects.
No.387

Howard, Jane R.,
When I Am Sleepy.
No.389

Huntington, Harriet,
Let's Look at Insects.
No.393

Jeunesse, Galimard;
Pascale de Bourgoing,
The Egg.
No.403

Jeunesse, Galimard;
Pascale de Bourgoing,
*The Ladybug and Other
Insects.*
No.405

Kaizuki, Kiyonori,
A Calf Is Born.
No.411

Kalas, Sybille,
The Goose Family Book.
No.413

Lindbergh, Reeve,
The Midnight Farm.
No.482

McCloskey, Robert,
Make Way for Ducklings.
No.549

McGovern, Anne;
Eugenie Clarke,
The Desert Beneath the Sea.
No.561

McNulty, Faith,
*Orphan: The Story of a
Baby Woodchuck.*
No.569

Parker, Nancy Winslow;
Joan Richards Wright,
*Frogs, Toads, Lizards,
and Salamanders.*
No.619

Patent, Dorothy Hinshaw,
Humpback Whales.
No.621

Paulsen, Gary,
Woodsong.
No.630

Pringle, Laurence,
*Twist, Wiggle, and Squirm: A
Book about Earthworms.*
No.647

Rockwell, Anne,
Our Yard Is Full of Birds.
No.657

Ryder, Joanne,
Where Butterflies Grow.
No.662

San Souci, Daniel,
North Country Night.
No.668

Sargent, William,
*Night Reef: Dusk to Dawn
on a Coral Reef.*
No.673

Sattler, Helen Roney,
The Book of Eagles.
No.675

Seddon, Tonny Bailey, Jill,
The Living World.
No.695

Simon, Seymour,
Big Cats.
No.706

Simon, Seymour,
Little Giants.
No.710

Simon, Seymour,
Snakes.
No.712

Stratton, Barbara,
What Is a Fish.
No.746

Sussman, Susan;
Robert James,
*Big Friend, Little Friend: A
Book about Symbiosis.*
No.751

Tsuchiya, Yukio,
*Faithful Elephants: A True
Story of Animals, People
and War.*
No.768

Ward, Leila,
I Am Eyes Ni Macho.
No.788

William, Sue,
I Went Walking.
No.809

Yoshida, Toshi,
Elephant Crossing.
No.830

ANIMALS-WILD

Baker, Keith,
Who Is the Beast?
No.44

Baker, Lucy,
Life in the Rainforest.
No.45

Bender, Lionel,
Fish to Reptiles.
No.66

Bodsworth, Nan,
A Nice Walk in the Jungle.
No.81

Cherry, Lynne,
The Great Kapok Tree.
No.144

Dabcovich, Lydia,
Busy Beavers.
No.191

Dorros, Arthur,
Animal Tracks.
No.225

Dorros, Arthur,
Rain Forest Secrets.
No.226

Eckert, Allan W.,
Incident at Hawk's Hill.
No.236

Ehlert, Lois,
Color Zoo.
No.238

Eichenberg, Fritz,
Ape in a Cape: An Alphabet of Odd Animals.
No.244

Gackenbach, Dick,
Mighty Tree.
No.290

Gibbons, Gail,
Zoo.
No.312

Hirschi, Ron,
Who Lives in the Mountains.
No.373

Hirschi, Ron,
Winter.
No.374

Jeunesse, Galimard;
Pascale de Bourgoing,
The Egg.
No.403

Jonas, Ann,
Aardvarks, Disembark!
No.409

Kalas, Sybille,
The Goose Family Book.
No.413

Lewin, Hugh,
Jafta.
No.479

Lindbergh, Reeve,
The Midnight Farm.
No.482

Milton, Nancy,
The Giraffe That Walked to Paris.
No.577

Parker, Nancy Winslow; Joan
Richards Wright,
Frogs, Toads, Lizards, and Salamanders.
No.619

Patent, Dorothy Hinshaw,
Humpback Whales.
No.621

Paulsen, Gary,
Woodsong.
No.630

Ryder, Joanne,
White Bear, Ice Bear.
No.663

San Souci, Daniel,
North Country Night.
No.668

Seddon, Tonny Bailey, Jill,
The Living World.
No.695

Simon, Seymour,
Big Cats.
No.706

Simon, Seymour,
Snakes.
No.712

Spier, Peter,
Noah's Ark.
No.729

Tsuchiya, Yukio,
Faithful Elephants: A True Story of Animals, People and War.
No.768

Ward, Leila,
I Am Eyes Ni Macho.
No.788

Yoshida, Toshi,
Elephant Crossing.
No.830

ANTARCTICA

Cowcher, Helen,
Antarctica.
No.183

Glimmerveen, Ulco,
A Tale of Antarctica.
No.316

Swan, Robert,
Destination: Antarctica.
No.755

ANTHOLOGY-FOLK LITERATURE

Climo, Shirley,
Someone Saw A Spider: Spider Facts and Folk tales.
No.156

Cohen, Daniel,
Southern Fried Rat and Other Gruesome Tales.
No.163

dePaola, Tomi,
Tomi dePaola's Favorite Nursery Tales.
No.221

Durell, Ann,
The Diane Goode Book of American Folk Tales & Songs.
No.231

Ehrlich, Amy, adapted by,
The Random House Book of Fairy Tales.
No.243

Evslin, Bernard,
The Dolphin Rider and Other Greek Myths.
No.255

Evslin, Bernard; Dorothy
Evslin; Ned Hoopes,
The Greek Gods.
No.256

Evslin, Bernard; Dorothy
Evslin; Ned Hoopes,
Heroes & Monsters of Greek Myth.
No.257

Gág, Wanda,
Tales from Grimm.
No.293

Hamilton, Virginia,
In the Beginning: Creation Stories from Around the World.
No.350

Hamilton, Virginia,
The People Could Fly:
American Black Folk tales.
No.351

Haviland, Virginia,
The Fairy Tale Treasury.
No.355

Jacobs, Joseph,
English Fairy Tales.
No.396

Jaquith, Priscilla (reteller),
Bo Rabbit Smart for True:
Folk tales from the Gullah.
No.399

Leach, Maria,
How the People Sang the
Mountains Up: How and
Why Stories.
No.461

Lester, Julius,
The Knee-High Man and
Other Tales.
No.474

Lester, Julius,
More Tales of Uncle Remus:
Further Adventures of Brer
Rabbit, His Friends,
Enemies, and Others.
No.475

Mayo, Gretchen Will,
Star Tales: North American
Indian Stories about the Stars.
No.547

Osborne, Mary Pope,
American Tall Tales.
No.611

Osborne, Mary Pope,
Favorite Greek Myths.
No.612

Phelps, Ethel Johston,
The Maid of the North:
Feminist Folk Tales from
Around the World.
No.634

Rockwell, Anne,
The Old Woman and Her Pig
and 10 Other Stories.
No.656

Rockwell, Anne,
The Three Bears and 15
Other Stories.
No.658

Schwartz, Alvin, collected by,
Flapdoodle: Pure Nonsense
from American Folklore.
No.685

Schwartz, Alvin, collected by,
Scary Tales to Tell in
the Dark.
No.686

Schwartz, Alvin, collected by,
Tomfoolery: Trickery and
Foolery with Words.
No.687

Schwartz, Alvin, collected by,
A Twister of Twists, A
Tangler of Tongues.
No.688

Stoutenburg, Adrien,
American Tall Tales.
No.745

Tripp, Wallace compiled by,
Granfa' Grig Had a A Pig
and Other Rhymes Without
Reason from Mother Goose.
No.765

Verdy, Violette,
Of Swans, Sugarplums,
and Satin Slippers.
No.779

Wildsmith, Brian,
Brian Wildsmith's Mother
Goose: Nursery Rhymes.
No.803

Yep, Laurence,
The Rainbow People.
No.820

ANTHOLOGY-MIXED

Durell, Ann; Marilyn
Sachs, editors,
The Big Book of Peace.
No.232

Wyndham, Robert,
The Chinese Mother
Goose Rhymes.
No.818

ANTHOLOGY-POETRY

Booth, David,
'Til All the Stars Have
Fallen: A Collection of
Poems for Children.
No.83

Carle, Eric, selected by,
Animals Animals.
No.125

de Regniers, Beatrice Schenk;
Eva Moore; Mary
Michaels White; Jan Carr,
Sing A Song of Popcorn.
No.208

Larrick, Nancy,
Cats Are Cats.
No.448

Larrick, Nancy (selector),
I Heard a Scream in the
Street: Poems by Young
People in the City.
No.449

Provenson, Martin; Alice
Provenson,
The Mother Goose Book.
No.649

Tripp, Wallace compiled by,
Marguerite, Go Wash
Your Feet.
No.766

ANTHOLOGY-PROSE

Babbitt, Natalie,
The Devil's Storybook.
No.37

Babbitt, Natalie,
The Devil's Other Storybook.
No.38

Brooke, William J.,
A Telling of the Tales:
Five Stories.
No.95

Carle, Eric (reteller),
Twelve Tales from Aesop.
No.129

Chase, Richard,
Grandfather Tales: American-
English Folk Tales.
No.141

Chase, Richard,
The Jack Tales.
No.143

Hamilton, Virginia,
The People Could Fly:
American Black Folk tales.
No.351

Haviland, Virginia,
The Fairy Tale Treasury.
No.355

Lionni, Leo,
Fredrick's Fables.
No.484

Miles, Bernard,
Favorite Tales from
Shakespeare.
No.574

Pollarck, Pamela,
The Random House
Book of Humor for Children.
No.640

Sadler, Catherine Edwards
adapted by,
Sir Arthur Conan Doyle's
The Adventures of Sherlock
Holmes: Volume I.
No.666

Levine, Ellen,
Ready, Aim, Fire! The Real Adventures of Annie Oakley.
No.477

McGill, Marci Ridlon,
The Story of Louisa May Alcott: Determined Writer.
No.556

McGovern, Anne,
The Secret Soldier: The Story of Deborah Sampson.
No.559

McKissack, Patricia,
Jesse Jackson.
No.564

Meigs, Cornelia,
Invincible Louisa.
No.571

O'Dell Scott,
Streams to the River, River to the Sea: A Novel of Sacagawea.
No.607

Peck, Ira,
The Life and Words of Denenberg, Barry,
No.631

Sterling, Dorothy,
Freedom Train The Story of Harriet Tubman.
No.743

Weinberg, Larry,
The Story of Abraham Lincoln, President for the People.
No.793

White, Ellen Emerson,
Jim Abbot Against All Odds.
No.799

BIOGRAPHY–PICTURE BOOK

Aliki,
A Weed Is a Flower: The Life of George Washington Carver.
No.19

Blos, Joan,
The Heroine of the Titanic: A Tale Both True and Otherwise of the Life of Molly Brown.
No.79

Fritz, Jean,
George Washington's Breakfast.
No.285

Fritz, Jean,
Where Was Patrick Henry on the 29th of May?
No.287

Fritz, Jean,
Will You Sign Here, John Hancock?
No.288

Griffin, Judith Berry,
Phoebe The Spy.
No.331

Provensen, Alice;
Martin Provensen,
The Glorious Flight Across the Channel with Louis Blériot.
No.648

Stanley, Diane;
Peter Vennema,
Shaka, King of the Zulus.
No.736

Zhensun, Zheng; Alice Low,
A Young Painter.
No.839

BRITISH ISLES– FICTION–CHAPTER BOOK

Aiken, Joan,
The Wolves of Willoughby Chase.
No.7

Banks, Lynne Reid,
The Fairy Rebel.
No.50

Clements, Bruce,
The Treasure of Plunderell Manor.
No.154

Cooper, Susan,
The Dark Is Rising.
No.177

Cooper, Susan,
Dawn of Fear.
No.178

Cooper, Susan,
Over Sea, Under Stone.
No.179

Dahl, Roald,
Danny: Champion of the World.
No.193

Dahl, Roald,
George's Marvelous Medicine.
No.195

Dahl, Roald,
James and the Giant Peach.
No.196

Dahl, Roald,
Matilda.
No.197

de Angeli, Marguerite,
The Door in the Wall.
No.202

Follett, Ken,
The Mystery Hideout.
No.268

McGovern, Ann,
Robin Hood of Sherwood Forest.
No.558

Sadler, Catherine Edwards, adapted by,
Sir Arthur Conan Doyle's The Adventures of Sherlock Holmes: Volume I.
No.666

Sutcliff, Rosemary,
Flame-Colored Taffeta.
No.752

Sutcliff, Rosemary,
Tristan and Iseult.
No.754

Thomas, Dylan,
A Child's Christmas in Wales.
No.759

Westall, Robert,
Ghost Abby.
No.794

Yolen, Jane,
Dragon's Boy.
No.823

BRITISH ISLES– FICTION–PICTURE BOOK

Briggs, Raymond,
Father Christmas.
No.90

Herriot, James,
The Christmas Day Kitten.
No.368

Herriot, James,
Moses the Kitten.
No.369

Herriot, James,
Oscar, Cat-About-Town.
No.370

Hoffman, Mary,
Amazing Grace.
No.380

Yolen, Jane (reteller),
Tam Lin.
No.828

CANADA-FICTION- CHAPTER BOOK

Eckert, Allan W.,
Incident at Hawk's Hill.
No.236

Korman, Gordon,
The Zucchini Warriors.
No.439

Lunn, Janet,
The Root Cellar.
No.507

Mowat, Farley,
Lost in the Barrens.
No.588

Paulsen, Gary,
Hatchet.
No.627

CHINESE

Louie, Ai-Ling (reteller),
Yeh-Shen.
No.505

Wyndham, Robert,
*The Chinese Mother
Goose Rhymes.*
No.818

CHINESE-FOLK TALE

Louie, Ai-Ling (reteller),
Yeh-Shen.
No.505

Martin, Rafe,
*Foolish Rabbit's
Big Mistake.*
No.530

Mosel, Arlene (reteller),
Tikki Tikki Tembo.
No.586

Yep, Laurence,
The Rainbow People.
No.820

Young, Ed,
Lon Po Po.
No.831

CHINESE–INFORMATIONAL

Waters, Kate; Madeline
Slovenz-Low,

*Lion Dancer: Ernie Wan's
Chinese New Year.*
No.791

Zhensun, Zheng; Alice Low,
A Young Painter.
No.839

CINDERELLA

Brooke, William J.,
*A Telling of the Tales:
Five Stories.*
No.95

Chase, Richard,
*Grandfather Tales:
American-English
Folk Tales.*
No.141

Climo, Shirley,
The Egyptian Cinderella.
No.155

Cohlene, Terri,
Little Firefly.
No.164

Ehrlich, Amy adapted by,
*The Random House Book of
Fairy Tales.*
No.243

Gág, Wanda,
Tales from Grimm.
No.293

Haviland, Virginia,
The Fairy Tale Treasury.
No.355

Hooks, William H.,
Moss Gown.
No.381

Huck, Charlotte (reteller),
Princess Furball.
No.392

Jacobs, Joseph,
English Fairy Tales.
No.396

Jacobs, Joseph,
Tattercoats.
No.397

Louie, Ai-Ling (reteller),
Yeh-Shen.
No.505

Winthrop, Elizabeth,
Vasilissa the Beautiful.
No.813

Yorinks, Arthur,
Ugh.
No.829

CIVIL WAR

Alphin, Elaine Marie,
Ghost Cadet.
No.21

Freedman, Russell,
Lincoln: A Photobiography.
No.280

Hayman, Leroy,
*The Death of Lincoln:
A Picture History of
the Assassination*
No.358

Lunn, Janet,
The Root Cellar.
No.507

Murphy, Jim,
The Boys War.
No.591

Sterling, Dorothy,
*Freedom Train The Story
of Harriet Tubman.*
No.743

Weinberg, Larry,
*The Story of Abraham
Lincoln, President for
the People.*
No.793

Winter, Jeanette,
Follow the Drinking Gourd.
No.811

COLONIAL AMERICA

Barth, Edna,
*Turkeys, Pilgrims,
and Indian Corn.*
No.56

Bulla, Clyde Robert,
*Pocahontas and
the Strangers.*
No.105

Clapp, Patricia,
*Constance, The Story of
Early Plymouth.*
No.147

Lester, Julius,
To Be A Slave.
No.476

Locker, Thomas,
The Land of the Gray Wolf.
No.502

McGovern, Ann,
*The Pilgrims' First
Thanksgiving.*
No.557

Speare, Elizabeth George,
The Sign of the Beaver.
No.726

Speare, Elizabeth George,
*The Witch of
Blackbird Pond.*
No.727

Waters, Kate,
Sarah Morton's Day.
No.789

COLORS

Berger, Barbara Helen,
When the Sun Rose.
No.68

Crews, Donald,
Freight Train.
No.186

Ehlert, Lois,
Color Zoo.
No.238

Jeunesse, Galimard;
Pascale de Bourgoing,
Colors.
No.402

McMillan, Bruce,
Growing Colors.
No.568

Spier, Peter,
Oh, Were They Ever Happy!
No.730

COMING OF AGE

Byars, Betsy,
The Midnight Fox.
No.120

Fox, Paula,
One-Eyed Cat.
No.274

George, Jean Craighead,
Julie of the Wolves.
No.301

Guccione, Leslie Davis,
Nobody Listens to Me.
No.338

LeGuin, Ursula K.,
A Wizard of Earthsea.
No.465

O'Dell, Scott,
Island of the Blue Dolphins.
No.604

Paterson, Katherine,
Bridge to Terabithia.
No.622

Paterson, Katherine,
Jacob Have I Loved.
No.623

Paterson, Katherine,
Lyddie.
No.624

Paterson, Katherine,
Park's Quest.
No.625

Paulsen, Gary,
The Island.
No.628

Paulsen, Gary,
Tracker.
No.629

Snyder, Zilpha Keatly,
The Velvet Room.
No.722

Speare, Elizabeth George,
The Sign of the Beaver.
No.726

Speare, Elizabeth George,
*The Witch of
Blackbird Pond.*
No.727

Voigt, Cynthia,
Dicey's Song.
No.782

CONCEPT BOOK

Adams, Barbara Johnson,
The Go-around Dollar.
No.5

Aliki,
Feelings.
No.13

Crews, Donald,
Freight Train.
No.186

Ehlert, Lois,
Color Zoo.
No.238

Emberley, Ed,
The Wing on a Flea.
No.250

Finzel, Julia,
Large As Life.
No.262

Gibbons, Gail,
Flying.
No.306

Gibbons, Gail,
Zoo.
No.312

Heller, Ruth,
A Cache of Jewels.
No.359

Heller, Ruth,
*Kites Sail High: A
Book about Verbs.*
No.361

Heller, Ruth,
Many Luscious Lollipops.
No.362

Heller, Ruth,
*Merry-Go-Round: A Book
about Nouns.*
No.363

Hoberman, Mary Ann,
A House Is a House for Me.
No.376

Jeunesse, Galimard; Pascale
de Bourgoing,
Colors.
No.402

Kitamura, Satoshi,
*When Sheep Cannot Sleep:
The Counting Book.*
No.435

McMillan, Bruce,
Growing Colors.
No.568

Morris, Ann,
Bread Bread Bread.
No.585

Rogers, Paul,
The Shapes Game.
No.659

Simon, Norma,
I Am Not A Crybaby .
No.705

Sorting.
No.724

Spier, Peter,
People.
No.731

William, Sue,
I Went Walking.
No.809

CONTEMPORARY FICTION-CHAPTER BOOK

Alexander, Lloyd,
The Drackenberg Adventure.
No.10

Alphin, Elaine Marie,
Ghost Cadet.
No.21

Avi,
*Something Upstairs:
A Tale of Ghosts.*
No.35

Banks, Lynne Reid,
The Fairy Rebel.
No.50

Bauer, Marion Dane,
On My Honor.
No.61

Budbill, David,
*Bones on Black Spruce
Mountain.*
No.102

Budbill, David,
*Snowshoe Trek to Otter
River.*
No.103

Butler, Beverly,
Ghost Cat.
No.117

Byars, Betsy,
*The Blossoms Meet the
Vulture Lady.*
No.119

CONTEMPORARY FICTION-PICTURE BOOK

Fleischman, Sid,
The Scarebird.
No.266

Fox, Mem,
*Wilfrid Gordon
McDonald Partridge.*
No.273

Gomi, Taro,
Hi, Butterfly!
No.325

Henkes, Kevin,
Jessica.
No.366

Herriot, James,
The Christmas Day Kitten.
No.368

Herriot, James,
Moses the Kitten.
No.369

Herriot, James,
Oscar, Cat-About-Town.
No.370

Hoffman, Mary,
Amazing Grace.
No.380

Hutchins, Pat,
The Doorbell Rang.
No.394

Keats, Ezra Jack,
Maggie and the Pirate.
No.417

Keats, Ezra Jack,
Peter's Chair.
No.419

Keats, Ezra Jack,
The Snowy Day.
No.420

Keats, Ezra Jack,
Whistle for Willie.
No.421

Lasky, Kathryn,
Sea Swan.
No.452

Lewin, Hugh,
Jafta.
No.479

Locker, Thomas,
Family Farm.
No.501

Locker, Thomas,
Sailing with the Wind.
No.503

Locker, Thomas,
Where the River Begins.
No.504

Lovik, Craig,
Andy and the Tire.
No.506

Mahy, Margaret,
A Lion in the Meadow.
No.517

Mathis, Sharon Bell,
The Hundred Penny Box.
No.537

McCloskey, Robert,
Blueberries For Sal.
No.548

McCloskey, Robert,
Make Way for Ducklings.
No.549

McCloskey, Robert,
One Morning in Maine.
No.550

McDonald, Megan,
The Great Pumpkin Switch.
No.555

Ness, Evaline,
Sam, Bangs & Moonshine.
No.595

Polacco, Patricia,
Mrs. Katz and Tush.
No.638

Say, Allen,
Tree of Cranes.
No.682

Spier, Peter,
Oh, Were They Ever Happy!
No.730

Williams, Vera,
A Chair For My Mother.
No.810

Yolen, Jane,
Owl Moon.
No.825

CONTINUING SERIES

Alexander, Lloyd,
The Book of Three.
No.9

Alexander, Lloyd,
The Drackenberg Adventure.
No.10

Burch, Robert,
*Ida Early Comes over the
Mountain.*
No.110

Byars, Betsy,
*The Blossoms Meet
the Vulture Lady.*
No.119

Campbell, Joanna,
A Horse Called Wonder.
No.124

Cole, Joanna,
*The Magic School Bus
Inside the Earth.*
No.167

Cole, Joanna,
*The Magic School Bus
Inside the Human Body.*
No.168

Cole, Joanna,
*The Magic School Bus Lost
in the Solar System.*
No.169

Cooper, Susan,
The Dark Is Rising.
No.177

Cooper, Susan,
Over Sea, Under Stone.
No.179

Corbett, Scott,
The Disappearing Dog Trick.
No.181

Day, Alexandra,
Carl's Christmas.
No.199

Day, Alexandra,
Good Dog, Carl.
No.200

Farley, Walter,
The Black Stallion.
No.258

Howe, James,
*What Eric Knew: A
Sebastian Barth Mystery.*
No.391

Korman, Gordon,
The Zucchini Warriors.
No.439

LeGuin, Ursula K.,
A Wizard of Earthsea.
No.465

L'Engle, Madeleine,
A Wind in the Door.
No.468

Lester, Julius,
*More Tales of Uncle Remus:
Further Adventures of
Brer Rabbit, His Friends,
Enemies, and Others.*
No.475

Lobel, Arnold,
Frog and Toad All Year.
No.496

Lobel, Arnold,
Frog and Toad Are Friends.
No.497

Lobel, Arnold,
Frog and Toad Together.
No.498

McKinley, Robin,
The Hero and the Crown.
No.563

Minarik, Else Holmelund,
Little Bear.
No.578

Minarik, Else Holmelund,
Little Bear's Visit.
No.579

Parish, Peggy,
Amelia Bedelia.
No.617

Peck, Robert Newton,
Soup.
No.632

Rylant, Cynthia,
*Henry and Mudge and
the Long Weekend.*
No.664

Schwartz, Alvin, collected by,
*Scary Tales to Tell
in the Dark.*
No.686

Sharmat, Marjorie Weinman,
Nate the Great.
No.699

COOKING

Carle, Eric,
Pancakes, Pancakes!
No.128

Cobb, Vicki,
*Science Experiments
You Can Eat.*
No.158

dePaola, Tomie (reteller),
Strega Nona.
No.220

Ehlert, Lois,
Growing Vegetable Soup.
No.241

Forest, Heather,
*The Woman Who
Flummoxed the Fairies.*
No.269

Lansky, Vicki,
Microwave Cooking for Kids.
No.447

Lasky, Kathryn,
Sugaring Time.
No.453

McMillan, Bruce,
Eating Fractions.
No.567

Morris, Ann,
Bread Bread Bread.
No.585

Walker, Barbara,
The Little House Cookbook.
No.785

COUNTING

Aker, Suzanne,
*What Comes in 2's, 3's,
& 4's?*
No.8

Bodsworth, Nan,
A Nice Walk in the Jungle.
No.81

Crews, Donald,
Ten Black Dots.
No.187

Feelings, Murial,
*Moja Means One: Swahili
Counting Book.*
No.261

Galdone, Paul,
*Over in the Meadow: An Old
Nursery Counting Rhyme.*
No.295

Giganti, Paul Jr.,
Each Orange Had 8 Slices.
No.314

Hutchins, Pat,
The Doorbell Rang.
No.394

Kitamura, Satoshi,
*When Sheep Cannot Sleep:
The Counting Book.*
No.435

Langstaff, John,
Over in the Meadow.
No.446

Lindbergh, Reeve,
The Midnight Farm.
No.482

Mathews, Louise,
*Bunches and Bunches
of Bunnies.*
No.536

Morozumi, Atsuko,
One Gorilla.
No.584

Rees, Mary,
Ten in a Bed.
No.652

Schwartz, David,
How Much Is a Million?
No.690

Wadsworth, Olive A.,
*Over in the Meadow:
An Old Counting Rhyme.*
No.784

Young, Ed adapted by,
Seven Blind Mice.
No.832

CUMULATIVE

Aardema, Verna,
*Bringing the Rain to
Kapiti Plain.*
No.1

Aardema, Verna,
*Why Mosquitoes Buzz
in People's Ears.*
No.3

Arnold, Tedd,
No Jumping on the Bed!
No.31

Emberley, Barbara,
Drummer Hoff.
No.249

Galdone, Paul,
The Gingerbread Boy.
No.294

Kalan, Robert,
Jump, Frog, Jump!
No.412

Lindbergh, Reeve,
The Midnight Farm.
No.482

Lobel, Anita,
The Pancake.
No.492

Rounds, Glen,
*I Know an Old Lady Who
Swallowed a Fly.*
No.661

Zemach, Harve,
*Mommy, Buy Me a
China Doll.*
No.835

DEATH

Babbitt, Natalie,
Tuck Everlasting.
No.42

Bauer, Marion Dane,
On My Honor.
No.61

Blos, Joan,
A Gathering of Days.
No.78

Budbill, David,
*Bones on Black
Spruce Mountain.*
No.102

Bunting, Eve,
The Wall.
No.108

Cleaver, Vera; Bill Cleaver,
Where the Lilies Bloom.
No.153

Coerr, Eleanor,
*Sadako and the Thousand
Paper Cranes.*
No.161

dePaola, Tomie,
*Nana Upstairs and
Nana Downstairs.*
No.218

Keats, Ezra Jack,
Maggie and the Pirate.
No.417

L'Engle, Madeleine,
Meet the Austins.
No.467

Miles, Miska,
Annie and the Old One.
No.575

Paterson, Katherine,
Bridge to Terabithia.
No.622

Snyder, Zilpha Keatley,
And Condors Danced.
No.720

Steig, William,
*Sylvester and the
Magic Pebble.*
No.740

Tsuchiya, Yukio,
*Faithful Elephants: A True
Story of Animals, People
and War.*
No.768

Viorst, Judith,
*The Tenth Good Thing
about Barney.*
No.781

Voigt, Cynthia,
Dicey's Song.
No.782

White, E. B.,
Charlotte's Web.
No.797

DEPRESSION ERA

Burch, Robert,
*Ida Early Comes over
the Mountain.*
No.110

Gates, Doris,
The Blue Willow.
No.300

Lauber, Patricia,
*Lost Star, The Story
of Amelia Earhart.*
No.456

Snyder, Zilpha Keatly,
The Velvet Room.
No.722

DIARIES

Asch, Frank,
Dear Brother.
No.32

Blos, Joan,
A Gathering of Days.
No.78

Clapp, Patricia,
*Constance, The Story
of Early Plymouth.*
No.147

Cleary, Beverly,
Dear Mr. Henshaw.
No.152

DISABILITY

Blos, Joan,
Brothers of the Heart.
No.77

Clavell, James,
Thrump-O-Moto.
No.150

de Angeli, Marguerite,
The Door in the Wall.
No.202

Duvoisin, Roger,
Petunia.
No.233

Fox, Paula,
One-Eyed Cat.
No.274

Martin Jr., Bill;
Archambault, John,
Knots on a Counting Rope.
No.527

Sullivan, Mary Beth;
Linda Bourke,
A Show of Hands.
No.749

Voigt, Cynthia,
Dicey's Song.
No.782

White, Ellen Emerson,
Jim Abbot Against All Odds.
No.799

EARLY CHAPTER BOOK

Cameron, Ann,
The Stories Julian Tells.
No.123

Cole, Joanna,
Bony-Legs.
No.165

Hoff, Syd,
Julius.
No.379

Kessler, Leonard,
Here Comes the Strikeout
No.429

Kuskin, Karla,
Soap Soup.
No.443

Lobel, Arnold,
Frog and Toad All Year.
No.496

Lobel, Arnold,
Frog and Toad Are Friends.
No.497

Lobel, Arnold,
Frog and Toad Together.
No.498

Lobel, Arnold,
Grasshopper on the Road.
No.498

Lobel, Arnold,
Mouse Tales.
No.499

Minarik, Else Holmelund,
Little Bear.
No.578

Minarik, Else Holmelund,
Little Bear's Visit.
No.579

Parish, Peggy,
Amelia Bedelia.
No.617

Parish, Peggy,
Good Hunting, Blue Sky.
No.618

Prelutsky, Jack,
It's Thanksgiving.
No.643

Rylant, Cynthia,
*Henry and Mudge and
the Long Weekend.*
No.664

Sattler, Helen Roney,
Baby Dinosaurs.
No.674

Sattler, Helen Roney,
*Pterosaurs, the
Flying Reptiles.*
No.678

Sattler, Helen Roney,
*Tyrannosaurus Rex and Its
Kin: The Mesozoic Monsters.*
No.679

Simon, Seymour,
The Largest Dinosaurs.
No.709

Simon, Seymour,
Saturn.
No.711

Simon, Seymour,
Storms.
No.713

Simon, Seymour,
Volcanoes.
No.714

EARTHQUAKES
& VOLCANOES

Barrett, Norman,
Volcanoes.
No.54

Bisel, Sara,
The Secrets of Vesuvius.
No.73

Challand, Helen,
Earthquakes.
No.140

Lauber, Patricia,
*Volcano: The Eruption and
Healing of Mount St. Helens.*
No.460

Lauber, Patricia,
Volcanoes and Earthquakes.
No.461

Simon, Seymour,
Volcanoes.
No.714

EASTERN EUROPEAN

Brett, Jan,
The Mitten.
No.89

Cole, Joanna,
Bony-Legs.
No.165

Freedman, Russell,
Immigrant Kids.
No.278

Kimmel, Eric,
*Hershel and the
Hanukkah Goblins.*
No.431

Lasky, Kathryn,
The Night Journey.
No.451

Lobel, Anita,
The Pancake.
No.492

Manushkin, Fran,
*Latkes and Applesauce:
A Hanukkah Story.*
No.519

Marshak, Samuel,
*The Month-Brothers:
A Slavic Tale.*
No.520

Shulevitz, Uri,
The Magician.
No.703

Tresselt, Alvin,
The Mitten.
No.764

Winthrop, Elizabeth,
Vasilissa the Beautiful.
No.813

Zemach, Harve,
Salt.
No.836

Zemach, Margot,
*It Could Always Be Worse:
A Yiddish Folk Tale.*
No.837

EMOTIONS

Aliki,
Feelings.
No.13

Babbitt, Natalie,
The Something.
No.41

Blos, Joan,
Old Henry.
No.80

Cazet, Denys,
"I'm Not Sleepy."
No.138

Crowe, Robert,
Clyde Monster.
No.188

dePaola, Tomie,
*Nana Upstairs and
Nana Downstairs.*
No.218

dePaola, Tomie,
Oliver Button Is a Sissy .
No.219

Eisenberg, Phyllis Rose,
You're My Nikki.
No.245

Fox, Paula,
One-Eyed Cat.
No.274

Keats, Ezra Jack,
Maggie and the Pirate.
No.417

Kellogg, Steven,
Best Friends.
No.423

Lester, Helen,
A Porcupine Named Fluffy.
No.472

Levitin, Sonia,
*The Man Who Kept His
Heart in a Bucket.*
No.478

Lewis, Rob,
*Friska The Sheep That Was
Too Small.*
No.481

Lovik, Craig,
Andy and the Tire.
No.506

Mahy, Margaret,
A Lion in the Meadow.
No.517

Martin, Bill Jr.;
John Archambault,
The Ghost Eye Tree.
No.525

McCloskey, Robert,
One Morning in Maine.
No.550

Murphy, Joanne Brisson,
Feelings.
No.592

Otey, Mimi,
*Daddy Has a Pair
of Striped Pants.*
No.615

Pfister, Marcus,
Penguin Pete's New Friends.
No.633

Pittman, Hellena Clare,
Once When I Was Scared.
No.636

Porter-Gaylord, Laurel,
I Love My Daddy Because…
No.641

Porter-Gaylord, Laurel,
*I Love My Mommy
Because…*
No.642

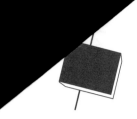

rtner.

Simon, No....
I Am Not A Crybaby.
No.705

Steig, William,
Sylvester and the Magic Pebble.
No.740

Tejima,
Swan Sky.
No.757

Thomas, Jane Resh,
The Comeback Dog.
No.760

Viorst, Judith,
The Good-Bye Book.
No.780

Wild, Margaret,
Mr. Nick's Knitting.
No.801

Williams, Linda,
The Little Old Lady Who Was Not Afraid of Anything.
No.808

Zolotow, Charlotte,
River Winding.
No.841

ENVIRONMENT-FICTION-CHAPTER BOOK

George, Jean Craighead,
On the Far Side of the Mountain.
No.302

George, Jean Craighead,
Who Really Killed Cock Robin?
No.303

Guccione, Leslie Davis,
Nobody Listens to Me.
No.338

Snyder, Zilpha Keatley,
And Condors Danced.
No.720

ENVIRONMENT-FICTION-PICTURE BOOK

Bodsworth, Nan,
A Nice Walk in the Jungle.
No.81

Brown, Ruth,
The World That Jack Built.
No.98

Burningham, John,
Hey! Get Off Our Train.
No.111

Burton, Virginia Lee,
The Little House.
No.115

Cherry, Lynne,
The Great Kapok Tree.
No.144

Cooney, Barbara,
Miss Rumphius.
No.176

Freeman, Don,
The Seal and the Slick.
No.282

Jonas, Ann,
Aardvarks, Disembark!
No.409

Locker, Thomas,
The Land of the Gray Wolf.
No.502

Snape, Juliet; Charles Snape,
Frog Odyssey.
No.717

Turner, Ann,
Heron Street.
No.771

Tyler, Linda Wagner,
The After-Christmas Tree.
No.772

Van Allsburg, Chris,
Just A Dream.
No.774

Vyner, Sue,
The Stolen Egg.
No.783

Yolen, Jane,
Owl Moon.
No.825

ENVIRONMENT-INFORMATIONAL

Baker, Lucy,
Life in the Rainforest.
No.45

Bright, M.,
The Ozone Layer.
No.93

Cherry, Lynne,
A River Ran Wild.
No.145

Cowcher, Helen,
Antarctica.
No.183

Cowcher, Helen,
Rain Forest.
No.184

Dorros, Arthur,
Rain Forest Secrets.
No.226

Earth Works Group,
50 Simple Things Kids Can Do To Save the Earth.
No.235

Elkington, John; Julia Hailes; Douglas Hill; Joel Makower,
Going Green: A Kid's Handbook to Saving the Planet.
No.247

Glimmerveen, Ulco,
A Tale of Antarctica.
No.316

Himmelman, John,
Ibis: A True Whale Story.
No.371

Koral, April,
Our Global Greenhouse.
No.438

Krensky, Stephen,
Four Against the Odds: The Struggle to Save Our Environment.
No.441

Lauber, Patricia,
Seeing Earth From Space.
No.458

Sargent, William,
Night Reef: Dusk to Dawn on a Coral Reef.
No.673

Schwartz, Linda,
Earth Book for Kids.
No.691

Seattle, Chief adapted by Susan Jeffers,
Brother Eagle, Sister Sky.
No.694

EUROPEAN-FICTION-CHAPTER BOOK

Buff, Mary; Conrad Buff,
The Apple and the Arrow.
No.104

Nixon, Lois Lowery,
Number the Stars.
No.597

EUROPEAN-FOLK TALE

Ahlberg, Janet; Allan Ahlberg,
The Jolly Postman; or, Other People's Letters.
No.6

Bell, Anthea adapted by,
Swan Lake.
No.64

Bishop, Gavin (reteller),
The Three Little Pigs.
No.74

Brett, Jan (reteller),
Beauty and the Beast.
No.87

Brett, Jan,
*Goldilocks and the
Three Bears.*
No.88

Cauley, Lorinda Bryan,
Goldilocks and the Three Bears.
No.136

Claverie, Jean (reteller),
The Three Little Pigs.
No.151

Cole, Joanna,
Bony-Legs.
No.165

Cooper, Susan (reteller),
*The Silver Cow:
A Welsh Tale.*
No.180

de Regniers, Beatrice Schenk,
Jack and the Beanstalk.
No.204

de Regniers, Beatrice Schenk,
Red Riding Hood.
No.206

dePaola, Tomie (reteller),
Strega Nona.
No.220

Forest, Heather,
*The Woman Who
Flummoxed the Fairies.*
No.269

Gág, Wanda,
Tales from Grimm.
No.293

Galdone, Paul,
The Gingerbread Boy.
No.294

Galdone, Paul,
The Three Billy Goats Gruff.
No.296

Galdone, Paul,
The Three Little Pigs.
No.297

Goodall, John S.,
Little Red Riding Hood.
No.326

Grimm, Jacob;
Snow White.
No.332

Grimm, Jacob;
Wilhelm Grimm,
*Snow-White and the
Seven Dwarfs.*
No.333

Grimm, Jacob;
Wilhelm Grimm,
Hansel and Gretel.
No.334

Grimm, Jacob;
Wilhelm Grimm,
Little Red Cap.
No.335

Hall, Nancy Christensen,
Macmillan Fairy Tale Book.
No.346

Hort, Lenny (reteller),
*The Boy Who Held Back
the Sea.*
No.386

Jacobs, Joseph,
English Fairy Tales.
No.396

Jacobs, Joseph,
Tattercoats.
No.397

Lesser, Rika,
Hansel and Gretel.
No.471

Littledale, Freyda,
Peter and the North Wind.
No.488

Lobel, Anita,
The Pancake.
No.492

Marshak, Samuel,
*The Month-Brothers:
A Slavic Tale.*
No.520

Marshall, James (reteller),
*Goldilocks and the
Three Bears.*
No.521

Marshall, James,
Red Riding Hood.
No.522

Marshall, James,
Three Little Pigs.
No.523

Mayer, Marianna,
Beauty and the Beast.
No.540

Mayer, Marianna,
The Black Horse.
No.541

Mayer, Marianna,
*The Prince and the Princess:
A Bohemian Fairy Tale.*
No.542

Mayer, Mercer,
*East of the Sun & West
of the Moon.*
No.544

Ormerod, Jan,
The Frog Prince.
No.610

Rockwell, Anne,
*The Old Woman and Her Pig
and 10 Other Stories.*
No.656

Rockwell, Anne,
*The Three Bears and 15
Other Stories.*
No.658

Sutcliff, Rosemary,
Tristan and Iseult.
No.754

Tresselt, Alvin,
The Mitten.
No.764

Verdy, Violette,
*Of Swans, Sugarplums, and
Satin Slippers.*
No.779

Willard, Nancy,
*East of the Sun & West
of the Moon.*
No.805

Winthrop, Elizabeth,
Vasilissa the Beautiful.
No.813

Zelinsky, Paul O.,
Rumplestiltskin.
No.833

Zemach, Harve,
Duffy and the Devil.
No.834

Zemach, Harve,
Salt.
No.836

Zemach, Margot,
*It Could Always Be Worse:
A Yiddish Folk Tale.*
No.837

Zemach, Margot,
The Three Little Pigs.
No.838

EUROPEAN-INFORMATIONAL

Aliki,
*The King's Day: Louis XIV
of France.*
No.16

Munro, Roxie,
*The Inside-Outside
Book of Paris.*
No.589

Oakes, Catherine,
The Middle Ages.
No.602

Provensen, Alice;
Martin Provensen,
*The Glorious Flight
Across the Channel
with Louis Blériot.*
No.648

EXPLORATION & DISCOVERY

Bisel, Sara,
The Secrets of Vesuvius.
No.73

Dyson, John,
*Westward with Christopher
Columbus.*
No.234

Gibbons, Gail,
*Things to Make and Do
on Columbus Day.*
No.310

Lauber, Patricia,
*Lost Star, The Story
of Amelia Earhart.*
No.456

Locker, Thomas,
Where the River Begins.
No.504

Macaulay, David,
The Motel of the Mysteries.
No.511

Marzollo, Jean,
In 1492.
No.533

O'Dell Scott,
*Streams to the River, River
to the Sea: A Novel
of Sacagawea.*
No.607

Sullivan, George,
*The Day We Walked
on the Moon.*
No.748

Swan, Robert,
Destination: Antarctica.
No.755

Walker, Paul Robert,
*Bigfoot & Other
Legendary Creatures.*
No.786

FABLES

Bierhorst, John,
*Doctor Coyote: A Native
American Aesop's Fables.*
No.70

Carle, Eric (reteller),
Twelve Tales From Aesop.
No.129

La Fontaine,
The Lion and the Rat.
No.444

Lionni, Leo,
Frederick.
No.483

Lionni, Leo,
Fredrick's Fables.
No.484

Lobel, Arnold,
Fables.
No.494

Untermeyer, Louis,
adapted by,
Aesop's Fables.
No.773

FAMILY PROBLEMS

Babbitt, Natalie,
The Eyes of the Amaryllis.
No.39

Bauer, Marion Dane,
On My Honor.
No.61

Bond, Nancy,
A String in the Harp.
No.82

Bunting, Eve,
Fly Away Home.
No.106

Byars, Betsy,
The Midnight Fox.
No.120

Byars, Betsy,
*The Winged Colt of
Casa Mia.*
No.121

Cleaver, Vera; Bill Cleaver,
Where the Lilies Bloom.
No.153

Ellis, Carol,
A Cry in the Night.
No.248

Grifalconi, Ann,
Osa's Pride.
No.330

Hahn, Mary Downing,
*The Doll in the Garden:
A Ghost Story.*
No.340

Hahn, Mary Downing,
*Wait Till Helen Comes:
A Ghost Story.*
No.341

Hamilton, Morse,
Little Sister for Sale.
No.348

Hoban, Russell,
A Baby Sister for Frances.
No.375

Kassem, Lou,
A Haunting in Williamsburg.
No.414

Locker, Thomas,
Family Farm.
No.501

Mathis, Sharon Bell,
The Hundred Penny Box.
No.537

Oppenheim, Joanne,
Left & Right.
No.609

Paterson, Katherine,
Jacob Have I Loved.
No.623

Paterson, Katherine,
Park's Quest.
No.625

Reeder, Carolyn,
Shades of Gray.
No.651

Roberts, Willo Davis,
Megan's Island.
No.654

Sorensen, Virginia,
Plain Girl.
No.723

Voigt, Cynthia,
Dicey's Song.
No.782

Wright, Betty Ren,
A Ghost in the Window.
No.817

FAMILY-CHAPTER BOOK

Burch, Robert,
*Ida Early Comes over
the Mountain.*
No.110

Byars, Betsy,
*The Blossoms Meet the
Vulture Lady.*
No.119

Cameron, Ann,
The Stories Julian Tells.
No.123

Cleaver, Vera; Bill Cleaver,
Where the Lilies Bloom.
No.153

Dahl, Roald,
Danny: Champion of the World.
No.193

Gardiner, John Reynolds,
Stone Fox.
No.298

Guccione, Leslie Davis,
Nobody Listens to Me.
No.338

Lasky, Kathryn,
The Night Journey.
No.451

L'Engle, Madeleine,
Meet the Austins.
No.467

McGraw, Eloise Jarvis,
Moccasin Trail.
No.562

Minarik, Else Holmelund,
Little Bear.
No.578

Minarik, Else Holmelund,
Little Bear's Visit.
No.579

Paterson, Katherine,
Jacob Have I Loved.
No.623

Rylant, Cynthia,
Henry and Mudge and the Long Weekend.
No.664

Taylor, Mildred D.,
Roll of Thunder, Hear My Cry.
No.756

Westall, Robert,
Ghost Abby.
No.794

FAMILY-PICTURE BOOK

Ackerman, Karen,
Song and Dance Man.
No.4

Aliki,
Christmas Tree Memories.
No.11

Asch, Frank,
Dear Brother.
No.32

Bryan, Ashley,
Turtle Knows Your Name.
No.101

Bunting, Eve,
Fly Away Home.
No.106

Bunting, Eve,
The Wall.
No.108

Bunting, Eve,
The Wednesday Surprise.
No.109

Calhoun, Mary,
Cross-Country Cat.
No.122

Cazet, Denys,
"I'm Not Sleepy."
No.138

Chall, Marsha Wilson,
Up North at the Cabin.
No.139

Crowe, Robert,
Clyde Monster.
No.188

dePaola, Tomi,
The Family Christmas Tree Book.
No.215

dePaola, Tomie,
Nana Upstairs and Nana Downstairs.
No.218

Eisenberg, Phyllis Rose,
You're My Nikki.
No.245

Flournoy, Valerie,
The Patchwork Quilt.
No.267

Fox, Mem,
Koala Lou.
No.271

Fox, Mem,
Night Noises.
No.272

Gilman, Phoebe,
Jillian Jiggs.
No.315

Hamilton, Morse,
Little Sister for Sale.
No.348

Hoffman, Mary,
Amazing Grace.
No.380

Johnston, Tony,
The Quilt Story.
No.408

Keats, Ezra Jack,
Peter's Chair.
No.419

Keats, Ezra Jack,
The Snowy Day.
No.420

Keats, Ezra Jack,
Whistle for Willie.
No.421

Kendall, Russ,
Eskimo Boy: Life in an Inupiaq Eskimo Village.
No.425

Locker, Thomas,
Family Farm.
No.501

Locker, Thomas,
Sailing with the Wind.
No.503

Locker, Thomas,
Where the River Begins.
No.504

Mahy, Margaret,
A Lion in the Meadow.
No.517

Manushkin, Fran,
Latkes and Applesauce: A Hanukkah Story.
No.519

Martin Bill Jr;
John Archambault,
The Ghost Eye Tree.
No.525

McCloskey, Robert,
Blueberries for Sal.
No.548

McCloskey, Robert,
One Morning in Maine.
No.550

McDonald, Megan,
The Great Pumpkin Switch.
No.555

McLerran, Alice,
I Want to Go Home.
No.566

McPhail, David,
Ed and Me.
No.570

Mendez, Phil,
The Black Snowman.
No.572

Miles, Miska,
Annie and the Old One.
No.575

Mills, Lauren,
The Rag Coat.
No.576

Ness, Evaline,
Sam, Bangs & Moonshine.
No.595

Noble, Trinka Hakes,
Apple Tree Christmas.
No.598

Oppenheim, Joanne,
Left & Right.
No.609

Otey, Mimi,
*Daddy Has a Pair of
Striped Pants.*
No.615

Pittman, Hellena Clare,
Once When I Was Scared.
No.636

Porter-Gaylord, Laurel,
I Love My Daddy Because…
No.641

Porter-Gaylord, Laurel,
*I Love My Mommy
Because…*
No.642

Rylant, Cynthia,
*When I Was Young in
the Mountains.*
No.665

Schwartz, Amy,
*Annabell Swift,
Kindergartner.*
No.689

Spier, Peter,
Oh, Were They Ever Happy!
No.730

Steig, William,
Brave Irene.
No.738

Surat, Michele Maria,
Angel Child, Dragon Child.
No.750

Van Leuwen,
Going West.
No.778

Viorst, Judith,
The Good-Bye Book.
No.780

Waters, Kate; Madeline
Slovenz-Low,
*Lion Dancer: Ernie Wan's
Chinese New Year.*
No.791

Watson, Wendy,
Thanksgiving at Our House.
No.792

Williams, Vera,
A Chair for My Mother.
No.810

Yolen, Jane,
Owl Moon.
No.825

FAMOUS AMERICANS-CHAPTER BOOK

Archer, Jules,
*They Made a
Revolution: 1776.*
No.26

Avi,
The Man Who Was Poe.
No.34

Baker, Rachel,
The First Woman Doctor.
No.47

Bulla, Clyde Robert,
*Pocahontas and
the Strangers.*
No.105

Davidson, Margaret,
*Frederick Douglass
Fights for Freedom.*
No.198

Denenberg, Barry,
*John Fitzgerald Kennedy:
America's 35th President.*
No.211

Denenberg, Barry,
*Stealing Home: The Story
of Jackie Robinson.*
No.213

Freedman, Russell,
Indian Chiefs.
No.279

Freedman, Russell,
Lincoln: A Photobiography.
No.280

Giff, Patricia Reilly,
*Laura Ingalls Wilder:
Growing Up in the
Little House.*
No.313

Hamilton, Virginia,
*Anthony Burns: The Defeat
and Triumph of a
Fugitive Slave.*
No.350

Haskins, Jim,
*The Day Martin Luther
King Jr. Was Shot.*
No.354

Hayman, Leroy,
*The Death of Lincoln: A
Picture History of
the Assassination.*
No.358

Krensky, Stephen,
*Four Against the Odds:
The Struggle to Save
Our Environment.*
No.441

Krensky, Stephen,
*George Washington: The
Man Who Would Not
Be King.*
No.442

Lauber, Patricia,
*Lost Star, The Story
of Amelia Earhart.*
No.456

Levine, Ellen,
*Ready, Aim, Fire!
The Real Adventures
of Annie Oakley.*
No.477

McGill, Marci Ridlon,
*The Story of Louisa May
Alcott: Determined Writer.*
No.556

McKissack, Patricia,
Jesse Jackson.
No.564

Meigs, Cornelia,
Invincible Louisa.
No.571

O'Dell Scott,
*Streams to the River, River
to the Sea: A Novel
of Sacagawea.*
No.607

Peck, Ira,
*The Life and Words of
Martin Luther King, Jr.*
No.631

Sterling, Dorothy,
*Freedom Train: The Story
of Harriet Tubman.*
No.743

Weinberg, Larry,
*The Story of Abraham
Lincoln, President for
the People.*
No.793

FAMOUS AMERICANS-PICTURE BOOK

Aliki,
*A Weed Is a Flower:
The Life of George
Washington Carver.*
No.19

Blos, Joan,
*The Heroine of the Titanic:
A Tale Both True and
Otherwise of the Life
of Molly Brown.*
No.79

Fritz, Jean,
*George Washington's
Breakfast.*
No.285

Fritz, Jean,
*Shh! We're Writing
the Constitution.*
No.286

Fritz, Jean,
*Where Was Patrick Henry
on the 29th of May?*
No.287

Fritz, Jean,
*Will You Sign Here,
John Hancock?*
No.288

Griffin, Judith Berry,
Phoebe The Spy.
No.331

McGovern, Anne,
*The Secret Soldier: The Story
of Deborah Sampson.*
No.559

FANTASY-CHAPTER BOOK

Alexander, Lloyd,
The Book of Three.
No.9

Babbitt, Natalie,
The Devil's Storybook.
No.37

Babbitt, Natalie,
The Devil's Other Storybook.
No.38

Babbitt, Natalie,
The Eyes of the Amaryllis.
No.39

Babbitt, Natalie,
The Search for Delicious.
No.40

Babbitt, Natalie,
Tuck Everlasting.
No.42

Banks, Lynne Reid,
The Fairy Rebel.
No.50

Banks, Lynne Reid,
*The Farthest-Away
Mountain.*
No.51

Bond, Nancy,
A String in the Harp.
No.82

Brooke, William J.,
*A Telling of the Tales:
Five Stories.*
No.95

Byars, Betsy,
*The Winged Colt of
Casa Mia.*
No.121

Clavell, James,
Thrump-O-Moto.
No.150

Cole, Joanna,
Bony-Legs.
No.165

Cooper, Susan,
The Dark Is Rising.
No.177

Cooper, Susan,
Over Sea, Under Stone.
No.179

Coville, Bruce,
*Jeremy Thatcher, Dragon
Hatcher.*
No.182

Dahl, Roald,
*Charlie and the Chocolate
Factory.*
No.192

Dahl, Roald,
Fantastic Mr. Fox.
No.194

Dahl, Roald,
*George's Marvelous
Medicine.*
No.195

Dahl, Roald,
James and the Giant Peach.
No.196

Dahl, Roald,
Matilda.
No.197

Hoff, Syd,
Julius.
No.379

Konigsburg, E. L.,
Up From Jericho Tell.
No.437

LeGuin, Ursula K.,
A Wizard of Earthsea.
No.465

L'Engle, Madeleine,
A Wind in the Door.
No.468

Lobel, Arnold,
Grasshopper on the Road.
No.498

Lobel, Arnold,
Mouse Tales.
No.499

Lunn, Janet,
The Root Cellar.
No.507

Macaulay, David,
The Motel of the Mysteries.
No.511

Mahy, Margaret,
*The Blood-and-Thunder
Adventure on
Hurricane Peak.*
No.516

McKinley, Robin,
The Hero and the Crown.
No.563

Parish, Peggy,
Amelia Bedelia.
No.617

Parish, Peggy,
Good Hunting, Blue Sky.
No.618

Snyder, Zilpha Keatley,
Black and Blue Magic.
No.721

White, E. B.,
Charlotte's Web.
No.797

White, E. B.,
The Trumpet of the Swan.
No.798

Winthrop, Elizabeth,
The Castle in the Attic.
No.812

Woodruff, Elvira,
George Washington's Socks.
No.816

Yolen, Jane,
The Devil's Arithmetic.
No.821

FANTASY-PICTURE BOOK

Ahlberg, Janet;
Ahlberg, Allan,
*The Jolly Postman; or, Other
People's Letters.*
No.6

Allard, Harry,
Miss Nelson is Missing.
No.20

Andersen, Hans Christian,
Thumbeline.
No.23

Andersen, Hans Christian,
The Wild Swans.
No.24

Arnold, Tedd,
No Jumping on the Bed!
No.31

Babbitt, Natalie,
The Something.
No.41

Snape, Juliet; Charles Snape,
Frog Odyssey.
No.717

Steig, William,
Shrek!
No.739

Steig, William,
*Sylvester and the
Magic Pebble.*
No.740

Van Allsburg, Chris,
Just A Dream.
No.774

Van Allsburg, Chris,
*The Mysteries of Harris
Burdick.*
No.775

Van Allsburg, Chris,
Polar Express.
No.776

Wilde, Oscar,
The Selfish Giant.
No.802

Willard, Nancy,
*A Visit to William Blake's
Inn: Poems for the Innocent
& Experienced Travelers.*
No.807

Wood, Audrey,
*King Bidgood's in
the Bathtub.*
No.814

Wood, Audrey,
Little Penguin's Tale.
No.815

Yolen, Jane,
Dove Isabeau.
No.822

Yorinks, Arthur,
Ugh.
No.829

Young, Ed adapted by,
Seven Blind Mice.
No.832

FRIENDSHIP-
CHAPTER BOOK

Aiken, Joan,
*The Wolves of
Willoughby Chase.*
No.7

Banks, Lynne Reid,
The Fairy Rebel.
No.50

Banks, Lynne Reid,
*The Farthest-Away
Mountain.*
No.51

Bauer, Marion Dane,
On My Honor.
No.61

Bellairs, John,
*The Spell of the
Sorcerer's Skull.*
No.65

Blos, Joan,
Brothers of the Heart.
No.77

Blos, Joan,
A Gathering of Days.
No.78

Budbill, David,
*Bones on Black
Spruce Mountain.*
No.102

Budbill, David,
*Snowshoe Trek to
Otter River.*
No.103

Byars, Betsy,
*The Winged Colt of
Casa Mia.*
No.121

Clements, Bruce,
*The Treasure of
Plunderell Manor.*
No.154

Conrad, Pam,
Stonewords.
No.175

Cooper, Susan,
Dawn of Fear.
No.178

Corbett, Scott,
The Disappearing Dog Trick.
No.181

Coville, Bruce,
*Jeremy Thatcher,
Dragon Hatcher.*
No.182

Dahl, Roald,
*Danny: Champion of the
World.*
No.193

Dahl, Roald,
James and the Giant Peach.
No.196

de Angeli, Marguerite,
The Door in the Wall.
No.202

Enright, Elizabeth,
Gone-Away Lake.
No.252

Gardiner, John Reynolds,
Stone Fox.
No.298

Gates, Doris,
The Blue Willow.
No.300

Howe, James,
*What Eric Knew: A
Sebastian Barth Mystery.*
No.391

Kessler, Leonard,
Here Comes the Strikeout.
No.429

Korman, Gordon,
The Zucchini Warriors.
No.439

Lobel, Arnold,
Frog and Toad Together.
No.495

Lobel, Arnold,
Frog and Toad All Year.
No.496

Lobel, Arnold,
Frog and Toad Are Friends.
No.497

MacLachlan, Patricia,
Sarah, Plain and Tall.
No.513

Morey, Walt,
Kavik the Wolf Dog.
No.582

Mowat, Farley,
Lost in the Barrens.
No.588

Nixon, Lois Lowery,
Number the Stars.
No.597

Paterson, Katherine,
Bridge to Terabithia.
No.622

Paulsen, Gary,
The Island.
No.628

Peck, Robert Newton,
Soup.
No.632

Rylant, Cynthia,
*Henry and Mudge and
the Long Weekend.*
No.664

Snyder, Zilpha Keatley,
And Condors Danced.
No.720

Snyder, Zilpha Keatly,
The Velvet Room.
No.722

Speare, Elizabeth George,
The Sign of the Beaver.
No.726

Sutcliff, Rosemary,
Flame-Colored Taffeta.
No.752

Thomas, Jane Resh,
The Comeback Dog.
No.760

Wallace, Bill,
Danger on Panther Peak.
No.787

White, E. B.,
Charlotte's Web.
No.797

Winthrop, Elizabeth,
The Castle in the Attic.
No.812

FRIENDSHIP-PICTURE BOOK

Barracca, Debra and Sal,
The Adventures of Taxi Dog.
No.53

Berger, Barbara Helen,
When the Sun Rose.
No.68

Blocksma, Mary,
Apple Tree! Apple Tree!
No.76

Blos, Joan,
Old Henry.
No.80

Brett, Jan (reteller),
Beauty and the Beast.
No.87

Briggs, Raymond,
The Snowman.
No.92

Brisson, Pat,
Your Best Friend, Kate.
No.94

Bryan, Ashley,
The Cat's Purr.
No.99

Butterworth, Nick,
One Snowy Night.
No.118

Cole, Joanna; Philip Cole,
Big Goof and Little Goof.
No.171

Coleridge, Ann,
*The Friends of
Emily Culpepper.*
No.172

Cutting, Michael,
*The Crooked Little
Christmas Tree.*
No.189

Day, Alexandra,
Carl's Christmas.
No.199

Day, Alexandra,
Good Dog, Carl.
No.200

de Regniers, Beatrice Schenk,
May I Bring a Friend?
No.205

de Regniers, Beatrice Schenk,
*A Week in the Life of Best
Friends and Other Poems
of Friendship.*
No.207

dePaola, Tomie,
Oliver Button Is a Sissy.
No.219

Devlin, Wende; Harry Devlin,
Cranberry Summer.
No.222

Ernst, Lisa Campbell,
*Sam Johnson and the Blue
Ribbon Quilt.*
No.253

Fleischman, Sid,
The Scarebird.
No.266

Flournoy, Valerie,
The Patchwork Quilt.
No.267

Fox, Mem,
*Wilfrid Gordon
McDonald Partridge.*
No.273

Goble, Paul,
*The Girl Who Loved
Wild Horses.*
No.319

Hale, Sarah Josepha,
Mary Had a Little Lamb.
No.342

Henkes, Kevin,
Jessica.
No.366

Hutchins, Pat,
The Doorbell Rang.
No.394

Keats, Ezra Jack,
Maggie and the Pirate.
No.417

Keats, Ezra Jack,
Pet Show.
No.418

Kellogg, Steven,
Best Friends.
No.423

Lester, Helen,
Tacky the Penguin.
No.473

Lovik, Craig,
Andy and the Tire.
No.506

Marzollo, Jean,
Pretend You're A Cat.
No.534

Marzollo, Jean,
The Silver Bear.
No.535

Matsutani, Miyoko; (reteller)
Alvin Tresselt,
The Crane Maiden.
No.538

McLerran, Alice,
I Want To Go Home.
No.566

McPhail, David,
Ed and Me.
No.570

Mills, Lauren,
The Rag Coat.
No.576

Milton, Nancy,
*The Giraffe that Walked
to Paris.*
No.577

Munsch, Robert,
The Paper Bag Princess.
No.590

Numeroff, Laura,
*If You Give a Mouse
a Cookie.*
No.600

Numeroff, Laura Joffe,
*If You Give A Moose
A Muffin.*
No.601

Oppenheim, Joanne,
Left & Right.
No.609

Otey, Mimi,
*Daddy Has a Pair of
Striped Pants.*
No.615

Paterson, Katherine,
The Tale of the

Mandarin Duck.
No.626

Pfister, Marcus,
Penguin Pete's New Friends.
No.633

Polacco, Patricia,
Mrs. Katz and Tush.
No.638

Sadler, Marilyn,
Elizabeth and Larry.
No.667

Steig, William,
Amos & Boris.
No.737

Surat, Michele Maria,
Angel Child, Dragon Child.
No.750

Tejima,
Swan Sky.
No.757

Tyler, Linda Wagner,
The After-Christmas Tree.
No.772

Viorst, Judith,
The Tenth Good Thing about Barney.
No.781

Wild, Margaret,
Mr. Nick's Knitting.
No.801

Wilde, Oscar,
The Selfish Giant.
No.802

Wildsmith, Brian,
The Lazy Bear.
No.804

GHOSTS

Alphin, Elaine Marie,
Ghost Cadet.
No.21

Avi,
Something Upstairs: A Tale of Ghosts.
No.35

Butler, Beverly,
Ghost Cat.
No.117

Conrad, Pam,
Stonewords.
No.175

DeFelice, Cynthia C.,
The Dancing Skeleton.
No.209

Ellis, Carol,
A Cry in the Night.
No.248

Foster, John chosen by,
Never Say Boo To A Ghost and Other Haunting Rhymes.
No.270

Hahn, Mary Downing,
The Doll in the Garden: A Ghost Story.
No.340

Hahn, Mary Downing,
Wait Till Helen Comes: A Ghost Story.
No.341

Kassem, Lou,
A Haunting in Williamsburg.
No.414

Lehr, Norma,
The Shimmering Ghost of Riversend.
No.466

Schwartz, Alvin collected by,
Scary Tales to Tell in the Dark.
No.686

Westall, Robert,
Ghost Abby.
No.794

Wright, Betty Ren,
A Ghost in the Window.
No.817

GREAT PLAINS

Baker, Olaf,
Where the Buffaloes Begin.
No.46

Conrad, Pam,
Prairie Songs.
No.174

Freedman, Russell,
Children of the Wild West.
No.276

Freedman, Russell,
Cowboys of the Wild West.
No.277

Giff, Patricia Reilly,
Laura Ingalls Wilder: Growing Up in the Little House.
No.313

MacLachlan, Patricia,
Sarah, Plain and Tall.
No.513

Turner, Ann,
Dakota Dugout.
No.770

Van Leuwen,
Going West.
No.778

Yolen, Jane,
Sky Dogs.
No.827

HISTORICAL FICTION-CHAPTER BOOK

Avi,
The Man Who was Poe.
No.34

Blos, Joan,
Brothers of the Heart.
No.77

Blos, Joan,
A Gathering of Days.
No.78

Buff, Mary and Conrad Buff,
The Apple and the Arrow.
No.104

Clapp, Patricia,
Constance, The Story of Early Plymouth.
No.147

Clark, Margaret Goff,
Freedom Crossing.
No.148

Clements, Bruce,
The Treasure of Plunderell Manor.
No.154

Conrad, Pam,
Prairie Songs.
No.174

Cooper, Susan,
Dawn of Fear.
No.178

de Angeli, Marguerite,
The Door in the Wall.
No.202

Eckert, Allan W.,
Incident at Hawk's Hill.
No.236

Gates, Doris,
The Blue Willow.
No.300

Haynes, Betsy,
Spies on the Devil's Belt.
No.358

Lasky, Kathryn,
The Bone Wars.
No.450

Lasky, Kathryn,
The Night Journey.
No.451

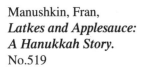

Manushkin, Fran,
*Latkes and Applesauce:
A Hanukkah Story.*
No.519

HOLIDAYS-PASSOVER

Polacco, Patricia,
Mrs. Katz and Tush.
No.638

Shulevitz, Uri,
The Magician.
No.703

HOLIDAYS-THANKSGIVING

Barth, Edna,
*Turkeys, Pilgrims,
and Indian Corn.*
No.56

Dragonwagon, Crescent,
*Alligator Arrived with
Apples: A Potluck
Alphabet Feast.*
No.229

Gibbons, Gail,
Thanksgiving Day.
No.309

Graham-Barber, Lynda,
*Gobble! The Complete Book
of Thanksgiving Words.*
No.328

McGovern, Ann,
*The Pilgrims' First
Thanksgiving.*
No.557

Prelutsky, Jack,
It's Thanksgiving.
No.643

Waters, Kate,
Sarah Morton's Day.
No.789

Watson, Wendy,
Thanksgiving At Our House.
No.792

HOLOCAUST

Bunting, Eve,
Terrible Things.
No.107

Innocenti, Roberto,
Rose Blanche.
No.395

Nixon, Lois Lowery,
Number the Stars.
No.597

Yolen, Jane,
The Devil's Arithmetic.
No.821

HUMAN BODY

Aliki,
I'm Growing.
No.15

Aliki,
My Five Senses.
No.17

Aliki,
My Hands.
No.18

Cole, Joanna,
*Cut, Breaks, Bruises,
and Burns: How Your
Body Heals.*
No.166

Cole, Joanna,
*The Magic School Bus
Inside the Human Body.*
No.168

Martin Jr, Bill;
Archambault, John,
Here Are My Hands.
No.526

Mayle, Peter,
What's Happening to Me?
No.545

Mayle, Peter,
Where Did I Come From?
No.546

Murphy, Joanne Brisson,
Feelings.
No.592

Settel, Joanne; Nancy Baggett,
*Why Does My Nose Run?
(And Other Questions Kids
Ask About Their Bodies).*
No.697

Ward, Leila,
I Am Eyes Ni Macho.
No.788

HUMOR

Barracca, Debra and Sal,
The Adventures of Taxi Dog.
No.53

Bodsworth, Nan,
A Nice Walk in the Jungle.
No.81

Briggs, Raymond,
Father Christmas.
No.90

Burch, Robert,
*Ida Early Comes over
the Mountain.*
No.110

Carle, Eric selected by,
Animals Animals.
No.125

Cohen, Daniel,
*Southern Fried Rat and
Other Gruesome Tales.*
No.163

Cole, Joanna; Philip Cole,
Big Goof and Little Goof.
No.171

Corbett, Scott,
The Disappearing Dog Trick.
No.181

Dahl, Roald,
*Danny: Champion
of the World.*
No.193

Dahl, Roald,
Fantastic Mr. Fox.
No.194

Dahl, Roald,
*George's Marvelous
Medicine.*
No.195

Dahl, Roald,
James and the Giant Peach.
No.196

Dahl, Roald,
Matilda.
No.197

Gilman, Phoebe,
Jillian Jiggs.
No.315

Houghton, Eric,
Walter's Magic Wand.
No.388

Kellogg, Steven,
The Mysterious Tadpole.
No.424

Korman, Gordon,
The Zucchini Warriors.
No.439

Lester, Helen,
Tacky the Penguin.
No.473

Lobel, Arnold,
The Book of Pigericks.
No.493

Macaulay, David,
Black and White.
No.509

Moss, Jeff,
The Butterfly Jar.
No.587

Munsch, Robert,
The Paper Bag Princess.
No.590

Numeroff, Laura,
*If You Give a Mouse
a Cookie.*
No.600

Numeroff, Laura Joffe,
*If You Give A Moose
A Muffin.*
No.601

Peck, Robert Newton,
Soup.
No.632

Pollarck, Pamela,
*The Random House Book
of Humor for Children.*
No.640

Prelutsky, Jack,
Ride A Purple Pelican.
No.644

Prelutsky, Jack,
*Something Big Has
Been Here.*
No.645

Robinson, Barbara,
*The Best Christmas
Pageant Ever.*
No.655

Sadler, Marilyn,
Elizabeth and Larry.
No.667

Schwartz, Alvin collected by,
*Flapdoodle: Pure Nonsense
from American Folklore.*
No.685

Schwartz, Alvin collected by,
*Tomfoolery: Trickery and
Foolery with Words.*
No.687

Schwartz, Alvin collected by,
*A Twister of Twists,
A Tangler of Tongues.*
No.688

Scieszka, Jon,
The Frog Prince Continued.
No.692

Scieszka, Jon,
*The True Story of the
3 Little Pigs.*
No.693

Spinelli, Jerry,
Maniac Magee.
No.735

Terban, Marvin,
*Mad as a Wet Hen!
And Other Funny Idioms.*
No.758

Turkle, Brinton,
Deep in the Forest.
No.769

Van Laan, Nancy,
Possum Come a-Knockin'.
No.777

Willard, Nancy,
*Pish, Posh, Said
Hieronymus Bosch.*
No.806

JACK AND THE BEANSTALK

Briggs, Raymond,
Jim and the Beanstalk.
No.91

Brooke, William J.,
*A Telling of the Tales:
Five Stories.*
No.95

Chase, Richard,
The Jack Tales.
No.143

de Regniers, Beatrice Schenk,
Jack and the Beanstalk.
No.204

Ehrlich, Amy adapted by,
*The Random House Book
of Fairy Tales.*
No.243

Haley, Gail E.,
Jack and the Bean Tree.
No.343

Haviland, Virginia,
The Fairy Tale Treasury.
No.355

Jacobs, Joseph,
English Fairy Tales.
No.396

JAPANESE-FOLK TALE

Lobel, Anita,
The Dwarf Giant.
No.491

Matsutani, Miyoko; (reteller)
Alvin Tresselt,
The Crane Maiden.
No.538

Paterson, Katherine,
*The Tale of the Mandarin
Duck.*
No.626

Tejima,
Swan Sky.
No.757

Yagawa, Sumiko,
The Crane Wife.
No.819

JAPANESE-INFORMATIONAL

Coerr, Eleanor,
*Sadako and the Thousand
Paper Cranes.*
No.161

Maruki, Toshi,
Hiroshima No Pika.
No.532

Morimoto, Junko,
My Hiroshima.
No.583

Tsuchiya, Yukio,
*Faithful Elephants:
A True Story of Animals,
People and War.*
No.768

JAPANESE-PICTURE BOOK

Morimoto, Junko,
My Hiroshima.
No.583

Say, Allen,
Tree of Cranes.
No.682

Tsuchiya, Yukio,
*Faithful Elephants:
A True Story of Animals,
People and War.*
No.768

Yagawa, Sumiko,
The Crane Wife.
No.819

KING ARTHUR

Cooper, Susan,
The Dark is Rising.
No.177

Cooper, Susan,
Over Sea, Under Stone.
No.179

Hodges, Margaret,
*The Kitchen Knight:
A Tale of King Arthur.*
No.377

Lister, Robin (reteller),
The Legend of King Arthur.
No.487

San Souci, Robert D.,
Young Merlin.
No.670

Sutcliff, Rosemary,
*The Light Beyond the Forest:
The Quest for the Holy Grail.*
No.753

Yolen, Jane,
Dragon's Boy.
No.823

LANGUAGE

Babbitt, Natalie,
The Search for Delicious.
No.40

Bryan, Ashley,
Turtle Knows Your Name.
No.101

Carlstrom, Nancy White,
*Jesse Bear, What Will
You Wear?*
No.132

Dahl, Roald,
James and the Giant Peach.
No.196

Ehlers, Laurie Lattig,
Canoeing.
No.237

Gág, Wanda,
The ABC Bunny.
No.291

Graham-Barber, Lynda,
*Gobble! The Complete Book
of Thanksgiving Words.*
No.328

Gross, Ruth Belov,
You Don't Need Words!
No.336

Guarino, Deborah,
Is Your Mama A Llama?
No.337

Gwynne, Fred,
*A Chocolate Moose
for Dinner.*
No.339

Heller, Ruth,
A Cache of Jewels.
No.359

Heller, Ruth,
*Kites Sail High:
A Book About Verbs.*
No.361

Heller, Ruth,
Many Luscious Lollipops.
No.362

Heller, Ruth,
*Merry-Go-Round:
A Book About Nouns.*
No.363

Hepworth, Cathi,
Antics!
No.367

Hoberman, Mary Ann,
A House Is a House for Me.
No.376

Juster, Norman,
As: A Surfeit of Similes.
No.410

Klasky, Charles,
*Rugs Have Naps (But
Never Take Them).*
No.436

Lear, Edward,
An Edward Lear Alphabet.
No.462

Lewin, Hugh,
Jafta.
No.479

Lewis, Claudia,
Long Ago in Oregon.
No.480

Martin Jr., Bill,
*Brown Bear, Brown Bear
What Do You See?*
No.524

Martin Jr., Bill; John
Archambault,
Listen to the Rain.
No.528

Marzollo, Jean,
Pretend You're A Cat.
No.534

Murphy, Joanne Brisson,
Feelings.
No.592

Schwartz, Alvin collected by,
*A Twister of Twists,
A Tangler of Tongues.*
No.688

Shaw, Nancy,
Sheep in a Jeep.
No.700

Shaw, Nancy,
Sheep in a Shop.
No.701

Shaw, Nancy,
Sheep on a Ship.
No.702

Sullivan, Mary Beth,
Linda Bourke,
A Show of Hands.
No.749

Terban, Marvin,
*Mad as a Wet Hen!
And Other Funny Idioms.*
No.758

LEGEND

Bierhorst, John,
The Ring in the Prairie.
No.72

Cohlene, Terri,
Little Firefly.
No.164

Hodges, Margaret,
*The Kitchen Knight:
A Tale of King Arthur.*
No.377

Hodges, Margaret,
Saint George and the Dragon.
No.378

Lister, Robin (reteller),
The Legend of King Arthur.
No.487

Mayo, Gretchen Will,
*Star Tales:
North American Indian
Stories about the Stars.*
No.547

McDermott, Gerald,
Arrow to the Sun.
No.554

McGovern, Ann,
*Robin Hood of
Sherwood Forest.*
No.558

San Souci, Robert D.,
Young Merlin.
No.670

Sloat, Teri,
The Eye of the Needle.
No.715

Sutcliff, Rosemary,
*The Light Beyond the Forest:
The Quest for the Holy Grail.*
No.753

Yolen, Jane,
Dragon's Boy.
No.823

LIFE CYCLE-
CHAPTER BOOK

Micucci, Charles,
*The Life and Times
of the Apple.*
No.573

Seddon, Tony, Jill Bailey,
The Living World.
No.695

LIFE CYCLE-PICTURE BOOK

Aliki,
I'm Growing.
No.15

Borden, Louise,
*Caps, Hats, Socks,
and Mittens.*
No.84

Carle, Eric,
*The Very Hungry
Caterpillar.*
No.131

LIFE SCIENCE-
CHAPTER BOOK

LIFE SCIENCE-
PICTURE BOOK

Carle, Eric,
The Grouchy Ladybug.
No.126

Carle, Eric,
The Very Busy Spider.
No.130

Cole, Joanna,
*Cut, Breaks, Bruises,
and Burns: How Your
Body Heals.*
No.166

Cole, Joanna,
*The Magic School Bus
Inside the Human Body.*
No.168

Cole, Joanna,
My Puppy is Born.
No.170

Dorros, Arthur,
Animal Tracks.
No.225

Dorros, Arthur,
Rain Forest Secrets.
No.226

Downer, Ann,
Don't Blink Now!
No.228

Fischer-Nagel, Heiderose;
Andreas Fischer-Nagel,
Life of the Ladybug.
No.263

Frasier, Debra,
On the Day You Were Born.
No.275

Gackenbach, Dick,
Mighty Tree.
No.290

Gibbons, Gail,
From Seed to Plant.
No.307

Goldin, Augusta,
Spider Silk.
No.324

Goor, Ron; Nancy Goor,
Insect Metamorphosis.
No.327

Hawes, Judy,
Bees and Beelines.
No.356

Heller, Ruth,
*Chickens Aren't
the Only Ones.*
No.360

Heller, Ruth,
*Plants That Never
Ever Bloom.*
No.364

Heller, Ruth,
The Reason for a Flower.
No.365

Hirschi, Ron,
*Who Lives in
the Mountains.*
No.373

Hirschi, Ron,
Winter.
No.374

Horner, John R.;
James Gorman,
Maia: A Dinosaur Grows Up.
No.385

Horton, Casey,
Insects.
No.387

Huntington, Harriet,
Let's Look at Insects.
No.393

Jeunesse, Galimard;
Pascale de Bourgoing,
The Egg.
No.403

Jeunesse, Galimard;
Pascale de Bourgoing,
Fruit.
No.404

Jeunesse, Galimard;
Pascale de Bourgoing,
*The Ladybug and
Other Insects.*
No.405

Jeunesse, Galimard;
Pascale de Bourgoing,
The Tree.
No.406

Kaizuki, Kiyonori,
A Calf Is Born.
No.411

Kent, Jack,
*The Caterpillar
and the Polliwog.*
No.428

Koral, April,
Our Global Greenhouse.
No.438

Lerner, Carol,
*Moonseed and Mistletoe:
A Book of Poisonous
Wild Plants.*
No.469

Leslie, Clare Walker,
Nature All Year Long.
No.470

Martin Jr, Bill;
Archambault, John,
Here Are My Hands.
No.526

Mayle, Peter,
What's Happening to Me?
No.545

Mayle, Peter,
Where Did I Come From?
No.546

Oechsli, Helen; Kelly Oechsli,
*In My Garden:
A Child's Gardening Book.*
No.608

Parker, Nancy Winslow;
Joan Richards Wright,

Fro
and
No.619

Rockwell, Anne,
Our Yard is Full of Birds.
No.657

Ryder, Joanne,
Where Butterflies Grow.
No.662

Sargent, William,
*Night Reef: Dusk to
Dawn on a Coral Reef.*
No.673

Sattler, Helen Roney,
Baby Dinosaurs.
No.674

Sattler, Helen Roney,
*Pterosaurs,
the Flying Reptiles.*
No.678

Sattler, Helen Roney,
*Tyrannosaurus Rex and its
Kin: The Mesozoic Monsters.*
No.679

Simon, Seymour,
Big Cats.
No.706

Simon, Seymour,
Little Giants.
No.710

Simon, Seymour,
Snakes.
No.712

Stratton, Barbara,
What is a Fish.
No.746

Sussman, Susan;
Robert James,
*Big Friend, Little Friend:
A Book about Symbiosis.*
No.751

erington, Jeanne,
ampkin Pumpkin.
No.763

Vyner, Sue,
The Stolen Egg.
No.783

Wexler, Jerome,
Wonderful Pussy Willows.
No.795

LITERARY FAIRY TALE

Andersen, Hans Christian,
The Little Mermaid.
No.22

Andersen, Hans Christian,
Thumbeline.
No.23

Andersen, Hans Christian,
The Wild Swans.
No.24

Briggs, Raymond,
Jim and the Beanstalk.
No.91

French, Fiona,
Snow White in New York.
No.284

Haviland, Virginia,
The Fairy Tale Treasury.
No.355

Huck, Charlotte reteller,
Princess Furball.
No.392

Kaye, Marilyn,
The Real Tooth Fairy.
No.415

Kimmel, Eric,
Hershel and the Hanukkah Goblins.
No.431

Levitin, Sonia,
The Man Who Kept His Heart in a Bucket.
No.478

Scieszka, Jon,
The Frog Prince Continued.
No.692

Scieszka, Jon,
The True Story of the 3 Little Pigs.
No.693

Thurber, James,
Many Moons.
No.761

Thurber, James,
Many Moons.
No.762

Yolen, Jane,
Dove Isabeau.
No.822

Yolen, Jane (reteller),
Tam Lin.
No.828

Yorinks, Arthur,
Ugh.
No.829

MATHEMATICS

Adams, Barbara Johnson,
The Go-around Dollar.
No.5

Aker, Suzanne,
What Comes in 2's, 3's, & 4's?
No.8

Burns, Marilyn,
The I Hate Mathematics! Book.
No.113

Crews, Donald,
Ten Black Dots.
No.187

Giganti Jr., Paul,
Each Orange Had 8 Slices.
No.314

Hutchins, Pat,
The Doorbell Rang.
No.394

Kitamura, Satoshi,
When Sheep Cannot Sleep: The Counting Book.
No.435

Lionni, Leo,
Inch by Inch.
No.485

Mathews, Louise,
Bunches and Bunches of Bunnies.
No.536

McMillan, Bruce,
Eating Fractions.
No.567

Rogers, Paul,
The Shapes Game.
No.659

Schwartz, David,
How Much is a Million?
No.690

Sorting.
No.724

MID-ATLANTIC STATES

Enright, Elizabeth,
Gone-Away Lake.
No.252

George, Jean Craighead,
On the Far Side of the Mountain.
No.302

Hahn, Mary Downing,
Wait Till Helen Comes: A Ghost Story.
No.341

Haynes, Betsy,
Spies on the Devil's Belt.
No.358

Paterson, Katherine,
Bridge to Terabithia.
No.622

Paterson, Katherine,
Jacob Have I Loved.
No.623

Sorensen, Virginia,
Plain Girl.
No.723

MIDDLE AGES

de Angeli, Marguerite,
The Door in the Wall.
No.202

Hodges, Margaret,
The Kitchen Knight: A Tale of King Arthur.
No.377

Hodges, Margaret,
Saint George and the Dragon.
No.378

Lister, Robin (reteller),
The Legend of King Arthur.
No.487

Macaulay, David,
Castle.
No.510

McGovern, Ann,
Robin Hood of Sherwood Forest.
No.558

Miles, Bernard,
Favorite Tales From Shakespeare.
No.574

Oakes, Catherine,
The Middle Ages.
No.602

Sutcliff, Rosemary,
Tristan and Iseult.
No.754

Yolen, Jane,
Dragon's Boy.
No.823

Yolen, Jane (reteller),
Tam Lin.
No.828

MIDWEST STATES

Blos, Joan,
Brothers of the Heart.
No.77

Butler, Beverly,
Ghost Cat.
No.117

Paulsen, Gary,
The Island.
No.628

Paulsen, Gary,
Tracker.
No.629

Polacco, Patricia,
*Boat Ride with Lillian
Two Blossom.*
No.637

Roberts, Willo Davis,
Megan's Island.
No.654

Siebert, Diane,
Heartland.
No.704

Wright, Betty Ren,
A Ghost in the Window.
No.817

MULTICULTURAL-
CHAPTER BOOK

Avi,
*Something Upstairs:
A Tale of Ghosts.*
No.35

Bierhorst, John edited by,
*In the Trail of the Wind:
American Indian Poems
and Ritual Orations.*
No.71

Cameron, Ann,
The Stories Julian Tells.
No.123

Clark, Margaret Goff,
Freedom Crossing.
No.148

Davidson, Margaret,
*Frederick Douglass
Fights for Freedom.*
No.198

Denenberg, Barry,
*Nelson Mandela "No Easy
Walk to Freedom".*
No.212

Denenberg, Barry,
*Stealing Home: The Story
of Jackie Robinson.*
No.213

George, Jean Craighead,
Julie of the Wolves.
No.301

Hall, Lynn,
Danza.
No.594

Hamilton, Virginia,
*Anthony Burns:
The Defeat and Triumph
of a Fugitive Slave.*
No.349

Hamilton, Virginia,
*In the Beginning:
Creation Stories from
Around the World.*
No.350

Haskins, Jim,
*The Day Martin Luther
King Jr. Was Shot.*
No.353

Haviland, Virginia,
The Fairy Tale Treasury.
No.355

Leach, Maria,
How the People Sang the

*Mountains Up: How and
Why Stories.*
No.461

Lester, Julius,
*More Tales of Uncle Remus:
Further Adventures of
Brer Rabbit, His Friends,
Enemies, and Others.*
No.475

Mayo, Gretchen Will,
*Star Tales:
North American Indian
Stories about the Stars.*
No.547

McKissack, Patricia,
Jesse Jackson.
No.564

Mendez, Phil,
The Black Snowman.
No.572

O'Dell, Scott,
Island of the Blue Dolphins.
No.604

O'Dell, Scott; Elizabeth Hall,
*Thunder Rolling in
the Mountains.*
No.606

Paterson, Katherine,
Park's Quest.
No.625

Peck, Ira,
*The Life and Words of
Martin Luther King, Jr.*
No.631

Phelps, Ethel Johston,
*The Maid of the North:
Feminist Folk Tales from
Around the World.*
No.634

Sorensen, Virginia,
Plain Girl.
No.723

Speare, Elizabeth George,
The Sign of the Beaver.
No.726

Spinelli, Jerry,
Maniac Magee.
No.735

Sterling, Dorothy,
*Freedom Train The Story
of Harriet Tubman.*
No.743

Taylor, Mildred D.,
*Roll of Thunder,
Hear My Cry.*
No.756

Thomas, Dylan,
*A Child's
Christmas in Wales.*
No.759

MULTICULTURAL-
INFORMATIONAL

Aliki,
*A Weed is a Flower:
The Life of George
Washington Carver.*
No.19

Baer, Edith,
*This Is the Way
We Go To School.*
No.43

Freedman, Russell,
Immigrant Kids.
No.278

Freedman, Russell,
Indian Chiefs.
No.279

MULTICULTURAL-
PICTURE BOOK

Aardema, Verna,
*Bringing the Rain to
Kapiti Plain.*
No.1

Louie, Ai-Ling (reteller),
Yeh-Shen.
No.505

Manushkin, Fran,
Latkes and Applesauce:
A Hanukkah Story.
No.519

Martin Jr., Bill;
Archambault, John,
Knots on a Counting Rope.
No.527

Martin, Rafe,
Foolish Rabbit's
Big Mistake.
No.530

Marzollo, Jean,
Pretend You're a Cat.
No.534

Mathis, Sharon Bell,
The Hundred Penny Box.
No.537

Matsutani, Miyoko; (reteller)
Alvin Tresselt,
The Crane Maiden.
No.538

McDermott, Gerald,
Anansi the Spider.
No.553

McDermott, Gerald,
Arrow to the Sun.
No.554

McKissack, Patricia,
Mirandy and Brother Wind.
No.565

Miles, Miska,
Annie and the Old One.
No.575

Mills, Lauren,
The Rag Coat.
No.576

Morimoto, Junko,
My Hiroshima.
No.583

Mosel, Arlene (reteller),
Tikki Tikki Tembo.
No.586

Musgrove, Margaret,
Ashanti to Zulu:
African Traditions.
No.593

Paterson, Katherine,
The Tale of the
Mandarin Duck.
No.626

Polacco, Paticia,
Boat Ride with Lillian
Two Blossom.
No.637

Polacco, Patricia,
Mrs. Katz and Tush.
No.638

San Souci, Robert,
The Talking Eggs.
No.669

Say, Allen,
Tree of Cranes.
No.682

Seeger, Pete,
Abiyoyo: A South African
Lullaby and Folk Story.
No.696

Shulevitz, Uri,
The Magician.
No.703

Sneve, Virginia
Driving Hawk,
Dancing Teepees:
Poems From American
Indian Youth.
No.718

Spier, Peter,
People.
No.731

Stanley, Diane;
Peter Vennema,
Shaka, King of the Zulus.
No.736

Steptoe, John,
Mufaro's Beautiful
Daughters: An African Tale.
No.741

Steptoe, John (reteller),
The Story of Jumping Mouse.
No.742

Stevenson, Robert Louis,
My Shadow.
No.744

Surat, Michele Maria,
Angel Child, Dragon Child.
No.750

Tejima,
Swan Sky.
No.757

Tsuchiya, Yukio,
Faithful Elephants:
A True Story of Animals,
People and War.
No.768

Ward, Leila,
I Am Eyes Ni Macho.
No.788

Waters, Kate;
Madeline Slovenz-Low,
Lion Dancer: Ernie Wan's
Chinese New Year.
No.791

Winter, Jeanette,
Follow the Drinking Gourd.
No.811

Wyndham, Robert,
The Chinese Mother
Goose Rhymes.
No.818

Yagawa, Sumiko,
The Crane Wife.
No.819

Yep, Laurence,
The Rainbow People.
No.820

Yolen, Jane,
Sky Dogs.
No.827

Young, Ed,
Lon Po Po.
No.831

Zhensun, Zheng; Alice Low,
A Young Painter.
No.839

MYSTERY

Alphin, Elaine Marie,
Ghost Cadet.
No.21

Avi,
The Man Who was Poe.
No.34

Avi,
Something Upstairs: A Tale
of Ghosts. No.35

Base, Graeme,
The Eleventh Hour.
No.59

Bellairs, John,
The Spell of the
Sorcerer's Skull.
No.65

Butler, Beverly,
Ghost Cat.
No.117

Conrad, Pam,
Stonewords.
No.175

Ellis, Carol,
A Cry in the Night.
No.248

Follett, Ken,
The Mystery Hideout.
No.268

George, Jean Craighead,
*Who Really Killed
Cock Robin?*
No.303

Hahn, Mary Downing,
*The Doll in the Garden:
A Ghost Story.*
No.340

Hahn, Mary Downing,
*Wait Till Helen Comes:
A Ghost Story.*
No.341

Howe, James,
*What Eric Knew:
A Sebastian Barth Mystery.*
No.391

Kassem, Lou,
A Haunting in Williamsburg.
No.414

Konigsburg, E. L.,
Up From Jericho Tell.
No.437

Lehr, Norma,
*The Shimmering Ghost
of Riversend.*
No.466

Roberts, Willo Davis,
Megan's Island.
No.654

Sadler, Catherine Edwards
adapted by,
*Sir Arthur Conan Doyle's
The Adventures of Sherlock
Holmes: Volume I.*
No.666

Sharmat, Marjorie Weinman,
Nate the Great.
No.699

Van Allsburg, Chris,
*The Mysteries of
Harris Burdick.*
No.775

Westall, Robert,
Ghost Abby.
No.794

Wright, Betty Ren,
A Ghost in the Window.
No.817

MYTHOLOGY

Evslin, Bernard,
*The Dolphin Rider and
Other Greek Myths.*
No.255

Evslin, Bernard; Dorothy
Evslin; Ned Hoopes,
The Greek Gods.
No.256

Evslin, Bernard; Dorothy
Evslin; Ned Hoopes,
*Hereos & Monsters of
Greek Myth.*
No.257

Hamilton, Virginia,
*In the Beginning:
Creation Stories from
Around the World.*
No.350

Osborne, Mary Pope,
Favorite Greek Myths.
No.612

Osborne, Will;
Mary Pope Osborne,
The Deadly Power of Medusa.
No.613

Osborne, Will;
Mary Pope Osborne,
Jason and the Argonauts.
No.614

Spier, Peter,
Noah's Ark.
No.729

NATIVE AMERICAN-
FICTION-CHAPTER BOOK

George, Jean Craighead,

Julie of the Wolves.
No.301

McGraw, Eloise Jarvis,
Moccasin Trail.
No.562

Mowat, Farley,
Lost in the Barrens.
No.588

O'Dell, Scott,
Bright Star, Bright Dawn.
No.603

O'Dell, Scott,
Island of the Blue Dolphins.
No.604

O'Dell, Scott; Elizabeth Hall,
*Thunder Rolling in the
Mountains.*
No.606

Parish, Peggy,
Good Hunting, Blue Sky.
No.618

Speare, Elizabeth George,
The Sign of the Beaver.
No.726

NATIVE AMERICAN-
FICTION-PICTURE BOOK

Locker, Thomas,
The Land of the Gray Wolf.
No.502

Martin Jr., Bill;
Archambault, John,
Knots on a Counting Rope.
No.527

Miles, Miska,
Annie and the Old One.
No.575

Polacco, Paticia,
Boat Ride with Lillian

Two Blossom.
No.637

NATIVE AMERICAN-
FOLK TALE

Baker, Olaf,
Where the Buffaloes Begin.
No.46

Bierhorst, John,
*Doctor Coyote: A Native
American Aesop's Fables.*
No.70

Bierhorst, John,
The Ring in the Prairie.
No.72

Cohen, Caron Lee,
*The Mud Pony: A Traditional
Skidi Pawnee Tale.*
No.162

Cohlene, Terri,
Little Firefly.
No.164

dePaola, Tomie,
The Legend of Bluebonnet.
No.216

dePaola, Tomie,
*The Legend of the
Indian Paintbrush.*
No.217

Esbensen, Barbara Juster,
*The Star Maiden:
An Ojibeway Tale.*
No.254

Goble, Paul,
Crow Chief.
No.317

Goble, Paul,
The Gift of the Sacred Dog.
No.318

Goble, Paul,
*The Girl Who Loved
Wild Horses.*
No.319

Goble, Paul,
Iktomi and the Boulder.
No.320

Goble, Paul,
Iktomi and the Berries.
No.321

Goble, Paul,
Iktomi and the Ducks.
No.322

Goble, Paul,
Star Boy.
No.323

Mayo, Gretchen Will,
Star Tales:
North American Indian
Stories about the Stars.
No.547

McDermott, Gerald,
Arrow to the Sun.
No.554

Sloat, Teri,
The Eye of the Needle.
No.715

Steptoe, John (reteller),
The Story of Jumping Mouse.
No.742

Yolen, Jane,
Sky Dogs.
No.827

NATIVE AMERICAN-
INFORMATIONAL

Bierhorst, John edited by,
In the Trail of the Wind:
American Indian Poems
and Ritual Orations.
No.71

Bulla, Clyde Robert,
Pocahontas and
the Strangers.
No.105

Cohlene, Terri,
Little Firefly.
No.164

Ekoomiak, Normee,
Arctic Memories.
No.246

Freedman, Russell,
Indian Chiefs.
No.279

Hirschfelder, Arlene,
Happily May I Walk:
American Indians and
Alaska Natives Today.
No.372

Kendall, Russ,
Eskimo Boy: Life in an
Inupiaq Eskimo Village.
No.425

McGovern, Ann,
The Pilgrims'
First Thanksgiving.
No.557

O'Dell Scott,
Streams to the River, River
to the Sea: A Novel of
Sacagawea.
No.607

Seattle, Chief adapted by
Susan Jeffers,
Brother Eagle, Sister Sky.
No.694

NEW ENGLAND

Babbitt, Natalie,
The Eyes of the Amaryllis.
No.39

Bellairs, John,
The Spell of the
Sorcerer's Skull.
No.65

Blos, Joan,
A Gathering of Days.
No.78

Budbill, David,
Bones on Black
Spruce Mountain.
No.102

Budbill, David,
Snowshoe Trek to
Otter River.
No.103

Clapp, Patricia,
Constance, The Story
of Early Plymouth.
No.147

Conrad, Pam,
Stonewords.
No.175

Ellis, Carol,
A Cry in the Night.
No.248

Guccione, Leslie Davis,
Nobody Listens to Me.
No.338

Howe, James,
What Eric Knew: A
Sebastian Barth Mystery.
No.391

Lasky, Kathryn,
Sugaring Time. No.453

Locker, Thomas,
The Land of the Gray Wolf.
No.502

McCloskey, Robert,
Time of Wonder.
No.551

McGovern, Ann,
The Pilgrims'
First Thanksgiving.
No.557

Paterson, Katherine,
Lyddie.
No.624

Speare, Elizabeth George,
The Sign of the Beaver.
No.726

Speare, Elizabeth George,
The Witch of
Blackbird Pond.
No.727

NURSERY RHYMES

Cawthorne, W. A.,
Who Killed Cockatoo?
No.137

dePaola, Tomi,
Tomi dePaola's Favorite
Nursery Tales.
No.221

Galdone, Paul,
Over in the Meadow: An Old
Nursery Counting Rhyme.
No.295

Hopkins, Lee Bennnett,
Animals from Mother Goose.
No.383

Hopkins, Lee Bennett,
People from Mother Goose.
No.384

Jeffers, Susan adapted by,
The Three Jovial Huntsmen.
No.401

Langstaff, John,
Frog Went A-Courtin'.
No.445

Langstaff, John,
Over in the Meadow.
No.446

Lobel, Arnold,
The Random House Book of
Mother Goose.
No.500

Provenson, Martin;
Provenson, Alice,
The Mother Goose Book.
No.649

Spier, Peter,
To Market! To Market!
No.733

Tripp, Wallace compiled by,
Granfa' Grig Had A Pig and
other Rhymes Without
Reason from Mother Goose.
No.765

What Do You See?
No.524

Martin Jr, Bill;
Archambault, John,
Here Are My Hands.
No.526

Martin Jr., Bill;
John Archambault,
Listen to the Rain.
No.528

Marzollo, Jean,
Pretend You're A Cat.
No.534

Numeroff, Laura,
*If You Give a Mouse
a Cookie.*
No.600

Numeroff, Laura Joffe,
*If You Give A Moose
A Muffin.*
No.601

Rees, Mary,
Ten in a Bed.
No.652

Rosen, Michael,
We're Going on a Bear Hunt.
No.660

Rounds, Glen,
*I Know an Old Lady
Who Swallowed a Fly.*
No.661

Shaw, Nancy,
Sheep in a Jeep.
No.700

Shaw, Nancy,
Sheep in a Shop.
No.701

Shaw, Nancy,
Sheep on a Ship.
No.702

Whelan, Gloria,
A Week of Raccoons.
No.796

Williams, Linda,
*The Little Old Lady Who
Was Not Afraid of Anything.*
No.808

William, Sue,
I Went Walking.
No.809

Young, Ed adapted by,
Seven Blind Mice.
No.832

PEER PRESSURE

Bauer, Marion Dane,
On My Honor.
No.61

Blos, Joan,
Old Henry.
No.80

Burch, Robert,
*Ida Early Comes
over the Mountain.*
No.110

dePaola, Tomie,
*Oliver Button Is a
Sissy.*
No.219

Kessler, Leonard,
Here Comes the Strikeout.
No.429

Lester, Helen,
Tacky the Penguin.
No.473

Lewis, Rob,
*Friska the Sheep that
Was Too Small.*
No.481

Lovik, Craig,
Andy and the Tire.
No.506

Mills, Lauren,
The Rag Coat.
No.576

Reeder, Carolyn,
Shades of Gray.
No.651

Simon, Norma,
I Am Not A Crybaby .
No.705

Sorensen, Virginia,
Plain Girl.
No.723

Speare, Elizabeth George,
*The Witch of
Blackbird Pond.*
No.727

Surat, Michele Maria,
Angel Child, Dragon Child.
No.750

PENGUINS

Glimmerveen, Ulco,
A Tale of Antarctica.
No.316

Lester, Helen,
Tacky the Penguin.
No.473

Pfister, Marcus,
Penguin Pete's New Friends.
No.633

Wood, Audrey,
Little Penguin's Tale.
No.815

PHOTOJOURNALISM

Apfel, Necia,
Voyager to the Planets.
No.25

Arnold, Caroline,
Watch Out for Sharks!
No.30

Bisel, Sara,
The Secrets of Vesuvius.
No.73

Conley, Andrea,
Window on the Deep:The

*Adventures of Underwater
Explorer Sylvia Earle.*
No.173

Downer, Ann,
Don't Blink Now!
No.228

Dyson, John,
*Westward With
Christopher Columbus.*
No.234

Freedman, Russell,
Children of the Wild West.
No.276

Freedman, Russell,
Cowboys of the Wild West.
No.277

Freedman, Russell,
Immigrant Kids.
No.278

Freedman, Russell,
Indian Chiefs.
No.279

Haskins, Jim,
*The Day Martin Luther
King Jr. Was Shot.*
No.353

Hayman, Leroy,
*The Death of Lincoln:
A Picture History of
the Assassination.*
No.357

Kendall, Russ,
*Eskimo Boy: Life in an
Inupiaq Eskimo Village.*
No.425

King, Elizabeth,
The Pumpkin Patch.
No.432

Lasky, Kathryn,
Sugaring Time.
No.453

PHYSICAL SCIENCE-CHAPTER BOOK

PHYSICAL SCIENCE-PICTURE BOOK

PICTURE BOOK-CONCEPT BOOK

Jonas, Ann,
Aardvarks, Disembark!
No.409

Kellog, Steven,
*Aster Aardvark's
Alphabet Adventures.*
No.422

Kitamura, Satoshi,
*From Acorn to Zoo and
Everything in Between in
Alphabetical Order.*
No.433

Kitamura, Satoshi,
*What's Inside:
The Alphabet Book.*
No.434

Kitamura, Satoshi,
*When Sheep Cannot Sleep:
The Counting Book.*
No.435

Lear, Edward,
An Edward Lear Alphabet.
No.462

Lewin, Hugh,
Jafta.
No.479

Maass, Robert,
When Autumn Comes.
No.508

Martin Jr., Bill;
John Archambault,
Listen to the Rain.
No.528

Marzollo, Jean,
Pretend You're A Cat.
No.534

Mathews, Louise,
*Bunches and Bunches
of Bunnies.*
No.536

McMillan, Bruce,
Eating Fractions.
No.567

Morozumi, Atsuko,
One Gorilla.
No.584

Murphy, Joanne Brisson,
Feelings.
No.592

Musgrove, Margaret,
*Ashanti to Zulu:
African Traditions.*
No.593

Polette, Nancy,
The Hole by the Apple Tree.
No.639

Porter-Gaylord, Laurel,
I Love My Daddy Because…
No.641

Porter-Gaylord, Laurel,
*I Love My Mommy
Because…*
No.642

Rees, Mary,
Ten in a Bed.
No.652

Rogers, Paul,
The Shapes Game.
No.659

Schwartz, David,
How Much is a Million?
No.690

Simon, Norma,
I Am Not A Crybaby .
No.705

Snow, Nicholas,
*The Monster Book
of ABC Sounds.*
No.719

Sorting.
No.724

Spier, Peter,
People.
No.731

Spier, Peter,
Rain.
No.732

Viorst, Judith,
*The Tenth Good Thing
about Barney.*
No.781

Watson, Wendy,
Thanksgiving At Our House.
No.792

Williams, Linda,
*The Little Old Lady Who
Was Not Afraid of Anything.*
No.808

William, Sue,
I Went Walking.
No.809

PICTURE BOOK-FANTASY

Allard, Harry,
Miss Nelson is Missing.
No.20

Andersen, Hans Christian,
The Little Mermaid.
No.22

Andersen, Hans Christian,
Thumbeline.
No.23

Andersen, Hans Christian,
The Wild Swans.
No.24

Arnold, Tedd,
No Jumping on the Bed!
No.31

Babbitt, Natalie,
The Something.
No.41

Bang, Molly,
The Paper Crane.
No.48

Barracca, Debra and Sal,
The Adventures of Taxi Dog.
No.53

Base, Graeme,
The Eleventh Hour.
No.59

Berger, Barbara Helen,
When the Sun Rose.
No.68

Blocksma, Mary,
Apple Tree! Apple Tree!
No.76

Bodsworth, Nan,
A Nice Walk in the Jungle.
No.81

Briggs, Raymond,
Father Christmas.
No.90

Briggs, Raymond,
Jim and the Beanstalk.
No.91

Briggs, Raymond,
The Snowman.
No.92

Brown, Jeff,
Flat Stanley.
No.96

Brown, Marc,
*Arthur's Tooth: An
Arthur Adventure.*
No.97

Bunting, Eve,
Terrible Things.
No.107

Burningham, John,
Hey! Get Off Our Train.
No.111

Burningham, John,
Mr. Gumpy's Outing.
No.112

Burton, Virginia Lee,
Katy and the Big Snow.
No.114

Marzollo, Jean,
The Silver Bear.
No.535

Mayer, Marianna,
The Unicorn and the Lake.
No.543

Mendez, Phil,
The Black Snowman.
No.572

Moore, Clement C.,
The Night Before Christmas.
No.581

Munsch, Robert,
The Paper Bag Princess.
No.590

Noble, Trinka Hakes,
Apple Tree Christmas.
No.598

Noble, Trinka Hakes,
*The Day Jimmy's Boa
Ate the Wash.*
No.599

Numeroff, Laura,
*If You Give a Mouse
a Cookie.*
No.600

Numeroff, Laura Joffe,
*If You Give A Moose
A Muffin.*
No.601

Pfister, Marcus,
Penguin Pete's New Friends.
No.633

Polacco, Paticia,
*Boat Ride with
Lillian Two Blossom.*
No.637

Ryder, Joanne,
White Bear, Ice Bear.
No.663

Sadler, Marilyn,
Elizabeth and Larry.
No.667

Scieszka, Jon,
The Frog Prince Continued.
No.692

Scieszka, Jon,
*The True Story of
the 3 Little Pigs.*
 No.693

Shaw, Nancy,
Sheep in a Jeep.
No.700

Shaw, Nancy,
Sheep in a Shop.
 No.701

Shaw, Nancy,
Sheep on a Ship.
No.702

Small, David,
Imogene's Antlers.
No.716

Snape, Juliet; Charles Snape,
Frog Odyssey.
No.717

Steig, William,
Amos & Boris.
No.737

Steig, William,
Shrek!
No.739

Steig, William,
*Sylvester and the
Magic Pebble.*
 No.740

Thurber, James,
Many Moons.
No.761

Thurber, James,
Many Moons.
No.762

Turkle, Brinton,
Deep in the Forest.
No.769

Van Allsburg, Chris,
Just A Dream.
No.774

Van Allsburg, Chris,
Polar Express.
No.776

Wilde, Oscar,
The Selfish Giant.
No.802

Wildsmith, Brian,
The Lazy Bear.
No.804

Wood, Audrey,
*King Bidgood's in
the Bathtub.*
No.814

Wood, Audrey,
Little Penguin's Tale.
No.815

Yolen, Jane,
Dove Isabeau.
No.822

Yorinks, Arthur,
Ugh.
No.829

Zolotow, Charlotte,
*The Bunny Who
Found Easter.*
No.840

PICTURE BOOK-FICTION

Aliki,
Christmas Tree Memories.
No.11

Asch, Frank,
Dear Brother.
No.32

Blos, Joan,
*The Heroine of the Titanic:
A Tale Both True and
Otherwise of the Life
of Molly Brown.*
No.79

Blos, Joan,
Old Henry.
No.80

Brisson, Pat,
Your Best Friend, Kate.
No.94

Bunting, Eve,
Fly Away Home.
No.106

Bunting, Eve,
The Wall. No.108

Bunting, Eve,
The Wednesday Surprise.
No.109

Carle, Eric, *Pancakes,
Pancakes!*
No.128

Cazet, Denys,
"I'm Not Sleepy".
No.138

Chall, Marsha Wilson,
Up North at the Cabin.
No.139

Cole, Joanna; Philip Cole,
Big Goof and Little Goof.
No.171

Cooney, Barbara,
Miss Rumphius.
No.176

Cuyler, Margery,
That's Good! That's Bad!
No.190

dePaola, Tomi,
*The Family Christmas
Tree Book.*
No.215

dePaola, Tomie,
*Nana Upstairs and
Nana Downstairs.*
No.218

4Rosen, Michael,
We're Going on a Bear Hunt.
No.660

Rylant, Cynthia,
*When I Was Young in
the Mountains.*
No.665

Say, Allen,
Tree of Cranes.
No.682

Schwartz, Amy,
*Annabell Swift,
Kindergartner.*
No.689

Sewell, Anna; adapted by
Robin McKinley,
Black Beauty.
No.698

Shulevitz, Uri,
The Magician.
No.703

Spier, Peter,
Oh, Were They Ever Happy!
No.730

Steig, William,
Brave Irene.
No.738

Surat, Michele Maria,
Angel Child, Dragon Child.
No.750

Tyler, Linda Wagner,
The After-Christmas Tree.
No.772

Van Leuwen,
Going West.
No.778

Viorst, Judith,
The Good-Bye Book.
No.780

Whelan, Gloria,
A Week of Raccoons.
No.796

Wild, Margaret,
Mr. Nick's Knitting.
No.801

Williams, Vera,
A Chair For My Mother.
No.810

Yolen, Jane,
Owl Moon.
No.825

PICTURE BOOK-
FOLK LITERATURE

Aardema, Verna,
*Bringing the Rain to Kapiti
Plain.*
No.1

Aardema, Verna (reteller),
*Rabbit Makes a Monkey
of the Lion.*
No.2

Aardema, Verna,
*Why Mosquitoes Buzz
in People's Ears.*
No.3

Ahlberg, Janet;
Ahlberg, Allan,
*The Jolly Postman; or,
Other People's Letters.*
No.6

Baker, Olaf,
Where the Buffaloes Begin.
No.46

Bang, Molly,
Wiley and the Hairy Man.
No.49

Bell, Anthea adapted by,
Swan Lake.
No.64

Bierhorst, John,
The Ring in the Prairie.
No.72

Bishop, Gavin (reteller),
The Three Little Pigs.
No.74

Brett, Jan (reteller),
Beauty and the Beast.
No.87

Brett, Jan,
*Goldilocks and the
Three Bears.*
No.88

Brett, Jan,
The Mitten.
No.89

Bryan, Ashley,
The Cat's Purr.
No.99

Bryan, Ashley,
Turtle Knows Your Name.
No.101

Carle, Eric (reteller),
Twelve Tales From Aesop.
No.129

Cauley, Lorinda Bryan,
*Goldilocks and the
Three Bears.*
No.136

Chase, Richard,
Jack and the Three Sillies.
No.142

Claverie, Jean (reteller),
The Three Little Pigs.
No.151

Climo, Shirley,
The Egyptian Cinderella.
No.155

Cohen, Caron Lee,
*The Mud Pony: A Traditional
Skidi Pawnee Tale.*
No.162

Cohlene, Terri,
Little Firefly.
No.164

Cooper, Susan (reteller),
*The Silver Cow:
A Welsh Tale.*
No.180

Dayrell, Elphinstone,
*Why the Sun and the
Moon Live in the Sky.*
No.201

de Regniers, Beatrice Schenk,
Jack and the Beanstalk.
No.204

de Regniers, Beatrice Schenk,
Red Riding Hood.
No.206

DeFelice, Cynthia C.,
The Dancing Skeleton.
No.209

Delaney, A.,
The Gunnywolf.
No.210

dePaola, Tomie,
The Legend of Bluebonnet.
No.216

dePaola, Tomie,
*The Legend of the
Indian Paintbrush.*
No.217

dePaola, Tomie (reteller),
Strega Nona.
No.220

dePaola, Tomi,
*Tomi dePaola's
Favorite Nursery Tales.*
No.221

Durell, Ann,
*The Diane Goode Book of
American Folk Tales
& Songs.*
No.231

Emberley, Barbara,
Drummer Hoff.
No.249

Esbensen, Barbara Juster,
*The Star Maiden:
An Ojibeway Tale.*
No.254

Mayer, Marianna,
The Black Horse.
No.541

Mayer, Marianna,
The Prince and the Princess:
A Bohemian Fairy Tale.
No.542

Mayer, Mercer,
East of the Sun & West
of the Moon.
No.544

McDermott, Gerald,
Anansi the Spider.
No.553

Mosel, Arlene (reteller),
Tikki Tikki Tembo.
No.586

Ormerod, Jan,
The Frog Prince.
No.610

Osborne, Mary Pope,
American Tall Tales.
No.611

Paterson, Katherine,
The Tale of the
Mandarin Duck.
No.626

Provenson, Martin; Alice
Provenson,
The Mother Goose Book.
No.649

Rockwell, Anne,
The Old Woman and Her
Pig and 10 Other Stories.
No.656

Rounds, Glen,
I Know an Old Lady
Who Swallowed a Fly.
No.661

San Souci, Robert,
The Talking Eggs.
No.669

San Souci, Robert D.,
Young Merlin.
No.670

Sawyer, Ruth,
Journey Cake, Ho!
No.681

Seeger, Pete,
Abiyoyo: A South African
Lullaby and Folk Story.
No.696

Sloat, Teri,
The Eye of the Needle.
No.715

Spier, Peter,
Noah's Ark.
No.729

Spier, Peter,
To Market! To Market!
No.733

Steptoe, John,
Mufaro's Beautiful
Daughters: An African Tale.
No.741

Steptoe, John (reteller),
The Story of Jumping Mouse.
No.742

Tejima,
Swan Sky.
No.757

Tresselt, Alvin,
The Mitten.
No.764

Tripp, Wallace compiled by,
Granfa' Grig Had A Pig and
other Rhymes Without
Reason from Mother Goose.
No.765

Untermeyer, Louis
adapted by,
Aesop's Fables.
No.773

Van Laan, Nancy,
Possum Come a-Knockin'.
No.777

Wadsworth, Olive A.,
Over in the Meadow:
An old Counting Rhyme.
No.784

Wildsmith, Brian,
Brian Wildsmith's Mother
Goose: Nursery Rhymes.
No.803

Willard, Nancy,
East of the Sun & West
of the Moon.
No.805

Winter, Jeanette,
Follow the Drinking Gourd.
No.811

Winthrop, Elizabeth,
Vasilissa the Beautiful.
No.813

Wyndham, Robert,
The Chinese Mother
Goose Rhymes.
No.818

Yagawa, Sumiko,
The Crane Wife.
No.819

Yolen, Jane,
Sky Dogs.
No.827

Yolen, Jane (reteller),
Tam Lin.
No.828

Young, Ed,
Lon Po Po.
No.831

Young, Ed adapted by,
Seven Blind Mice.
No.832

Zelinsky, Paul O.,
Rumplestiltskin.
No.833

Zemach, Harve,
Duffy and the Devil.
No.834

Zemach, Harve,
Mommy, Buy Me a
China Doll.
No.835

Zemach, Harve,
Salt.
No.836

Zemach, Margot,
It Could Always Be Worse:
A Yiddish Folk Tale.
No.837

Zemach, Margot,
The Three Little Pigs.
No.838

PICTURE BOOK-
INFORMATIONAL

Adams, Barbara Johnson,
The Go-around Dollar.
No.5

Aliki,
Digging Up Dinosaurs.
No.12

Aliki,
How A Book is Made.
No.14

Aliki,
I'm Growing.
No.15

Aliki,
The King's Day: Louis
XIV of France.
No.16

Aliki,
My Five Senses.
No.17

Aliki,
My Hands.
No.18

Gross, Ruth Belov,
You Don't Need Words!
No.336

Hamanaka, Sheila,
The Journey.
No.347

Hatchett, Clint,
*The Glow-in-the-Dark
Night Sky Book.*
No.354

Hawes, Judy, *Bees and
Beelines.*
No.356

Heller, Ruth,
*Chickens Aren't
the Only Ones.*
No.360

Heller, Ruth,
*Plants That Never
Ever Bloom.*
No.364

Heller, Ruth,
The Reason for a Flower.
No.365

Himmelman, John,
Ibis: A True Whale Story.
No.371

Hirschi, Ron,
*Who Lives in
the Mountains.*
No.373

Hirschi, Ron,
Winter.
No.374

Horton, Casey,
Insects.
No.387

Huntington, Harriet,
Let's Look at Insects.
No.393

Jeunesse, Galimard;
Pascale de Bourgoing,

The Egg.
No.403

Jeunesse, Galimard;
Pascale de Bourgoing,
Fruit.
No.404

Jeunesse, Galimard;
Pascale de Bourgoing,
*The Ladybug and
Other Insects.*
No.405

Jeunesse, Galimard;
Pascale de Bourgoing,
The Tree.
No.406

Jeunesse, Galimard;
Pascale de Bourgoing,
Weather.
No.407

Kaizuki, Kiyonori,
A Calf Is Born.
No.411

Kalas, Sybille,
The Goose Family Book.
No.413

Kendall, Russ,
*Eskimo Boy: Life in an
Inupiaq Eskimo Village.*
No.425

King, Elizabeth,
The Pumpkin Patch.
No.432

Koral, April,
Our Global Greenhouse.
No.438

Lasky, Kathryn,
Sugaring Time.
No.453

Lauber, Patricia,
*Dinosaurs Walked Here &
Other Stories Fossils Tell.*
No.454

Lauber, Patricia,
Living with Dinosaurs.
No.455

Lauber, Patricia,
The News About Dinosaurs.
No.457

Lauber, Patricia,
Seeing Earth From Space.
No.458

Leedy, Loreen,
*Messages in the Mailbox:
How to Write a Letter.*
No.464

Leslie, Clare Walker,
Nature All Year Long.
No.470

Macaulay, David,
Castle.
No.510

Macauley, David,
The Way Things Work.
No.512

Maestro, Betsy,
A Sea Full of Sharks.
No.514

Maestro, Betsy;
Giulio Maestro,
*A More Perfect Union: The
Story of Our Constitution.*
No.515

Martin Jr, Bill;
Archambault, John,
Here Are My Hands.
No.526

Martin, Rodney,
*The Making of a
Picture Book.*
No.531

Maruki, Toshi,
Hiroshima No Pika.
No.532

Marzollo, Jean,
In 1492.
No.533

Matthews, Rupert,
The Dinosaur Age.
No.539

Mayle, Peter,
What's Happening to Me?
No.545

Mayle, Peter,
Where Did I Come From?
No.546

McGovern, Ann,
*The Pilgrims'
First Thanksgiving.*
No.557

McGovern, Ann,
Sharks.
No.560

McGovern, Anne;
Eugenie Clarke,
The Desert Beneath the Sea.
No.561

McMillan, Bruce,
Growing Colors.
No.568

Micucci, Charles,
*The Life and Times
of the Apple.*
No.573

Milton, Nancy,
*The Giraffe that Walked
to Paris.*
No.577

Morimoto, Junko,
My Hiroshima.
No.583

Morris, Ann,
Bread Bread Bread.
No.585

Munro, Roxie,
*The Inside-Outside Book
of Paris.*
No.589

Lear, Edward,
The Owl and the Pussycat.
No.463

Lindbergh, Reeve,
The Midnight Farm.
No.482

Livingston, Myra Cohn,
A Circle of Seasons.
No.489

Livingston, Myra Cohn,
Earth Songs.
No.490

Lobel, Arnold,
The Book of Pigericks.
No.493

Martin Jr., Bill;
John Archambault,
The Ghost Eye Tree.
No.525

Prelutsky, Jack,
Tyrannosaurus Was A Beast.
No.646

Sandburg, Carl,
Lee Bennett Hopkins,
selector*Rainbows are Made.*
No.671

Siebert, Diane,
Heartland.
No.704

Sneve, Virginia
Driveing Hawk,
*Dancing Teepees:
Poems From American
Indian Youth.*
No.718

Stevenson, Robert Louis,
My Shadow.
No.744

Tripp, Wallace, compiled by,
*Marguerite, Go Wash
Your Feet.*
No.766

Willard, Nancy,
*Pish, Posh, Said
Hieronymus Bosch.*
No.806

Willard, Nancy,
*A Visit to William Blake's
Inn: Poems for the Innocent
& Experienced Travelers.*
No.807

Yolen, Jane, edited by,
*The Lap-Time Song
and Play Book.*
No.824

Yolen, Jane,
Ring of Earth.
No.826

Zolotow, Charlotte,
River Winding.
No.841

PLANTS

Aliki,
*A Weed is a Flower:
The Life of George
Washington Carver.*
No.19

Bjork, Christina
Anderson , Lena,
Linnea's Windowsill Garden.
No.75

Blocksma, Mary,
Apple Tree! Apple Tree!
No.76

Cooney, Barbara,
Miss Rumphius.
No.176

Dorros, Arthur,
Rain Forest Secrets.
No.226

Ehlert, Lois,
*Eating the Alphabet: Fruits
and Vegetables From A to Z.*
No.239

Ehlert, Lois,
Growing Vegetable Soup.
No.241

Ehlert, Lois,
Planting a Rainbow.
No.242

Gackenbach, Dick,
Mighty Tree.
No.290

Gibbons, Gail,
From Seed to Plant.
No.307

Heller, Ruth,
*Plants That Never
Ever Bloom.*
No.364

Heller, Ruth,
The Reason for a Flower.
No.365

Jeunesse, Galimard;
Pascale de Bourgoing,
Fruit.
No.404

Jeunesse, Galimard;
Pascale de Bourgoing,
The Tree.
No.406

King, Elizabeth,
The Pumpkin Patch.
No.432

Lasky, Kathryn,
Sugaring Time.
No.453

Lerner, Carol,
*Moonseed and Mistletoe:
A Book of Poisonous
Wild Plants.*
No.469

McGovern, Anne;
Eugenie Clarke,
The Desert Beneath the Sea.
No.561

McMillan, Bruce,
Growing Colors.
No.568

Micucci, Charles,
*The Life and Times of
the Apple.*
No.573

Oechsli, Helen; Kelly Oechsli,
*In My Garden: A Child's
Gardening Book.*
No.608

Patent, Dorothy Hinshaw,
*An Apple A Day:
From Orchard to You.*
No.620

Titherington, Jeanne,
Pumpkin Pumpkin.
No.763

Wexler, Jerome,
Wonderful Pussy Willows.
No.795

POETRY

Baer, Edith,
*This Is the Way We
Go To School.*
No.43

Barnstone, Aliki,
The Real Tin Flower.
No.52

Baylor, Byrd,
*If You Are a Hunter
of Fossils.*
No.63

Bierhorst, John edited by,
*In the Trail of the Wind:
American Indian Poems
and Ritual Orations.*
No.71

Blos, Joan,
*The Heroine of the Titanic:
A Tale Both True and
Otherwise of the Life
of Molly Brown.*
No.79

Blos, Joan,
Old Henry.
No.80

Booth, David,
*'Til All the Stars Have
Fallen: A Collection of
Poems for Children.*
No.83

Carle, Eric, selected by,
Animals Animals.
No.125

de Regniers, Beatrice Schenk,
*A Week in the Life of Best
Friends and Other Poems
of Friendship.*
No.207

Duncan, Beverly (collector),
Christmas in the Stable.
No.230

Durell, Ann;
Marilyn Sachs; editors,
The Big Book of Peace.
No.232

Ehlers, Laurie Lattig,
Canoeing.
No.237

Emberley, Ed,
The Wing on a Flea.
No.250

Fleischman, Paul,
*I Am Phoenix: Poems
for Two Voices.*
No.264

Fleischman, Paul,
*Joyful Noise: Poems
for Two Voices.*
No.265

Foster, John chosen by,
*Never Say Boo To A Ghost
and Other Haunting Rhymes.*
No.270

Frasier, Debra,
On the Day You Were Born.
No.275

Frost, Robert,
*Stopping By Woods
on a Snowy Evening .*
No.289

Greenfield, Eloise,
*Night on Neighborhood
Street.*
No.329

Jarrell, Randall,
The Bat Poet.
No.400

Kennedy, X. J. ;
Dorothy M. Kennedy,
*Knock At A Star: A Child's
Introduction to Poetry.*
No.427

Kuskin, Karla,
Soap Soup.
No.443

Larrick, Nancy,
Cats Are Cats.
No.448

Larrick, Nancy (selector),
*I Heard a Scream in the
Street: Poems by Young
People in the City.*
No.449

Lear, Edward,
An Edward Lear Alphabet.
No.462

Lear, Edward,
The Owl and the Pussycat.
No.463

Lewis, Claudia,
Long Ago in Oregon.
No.480

Livingston, Myra Cohn,
A Circle of Seasons.
No.489

Livingston, Myra Cohn,
Earth Songs.
No.490

Lobel, Arnold,
The Book of Pigericks.
No.493

Lobel, Arnold,
*The Random House
Book of Mother Goose.*
No.500

Martin Bill Jr.;
John Archambault,
The Ghost Eye Tree.
No.525

McCord, David,
All Small.
No.552

Moore, Clement C.,
The Night Before Christmas.
No.581

Moss, Jeff,
The Butterfly Jar.
No.587

Prelutsky, Jack,
It's Thanksgiving.
No.643

Prelutsky, Jack,
Ride A Purple Pelican.
No.644

Prelutsky, Jack,
*Something Big Has
Been Here.*
No.645

Prelutsky, Jack,
Tyrannosaurus Was A Beast.
No.646

Ryder, Joanne,
Where Butterflies Grow.
No.662

Sandburg, Carl,
Lee Bennett Hopkins, selector
Rainbows are Made.
No.671

Siebert, Diane,
Heartland.
No.704

Sneve, Virginia
Driveing Hawk,
*Dancing Teepees:
Poems From American
Indian Youth.*
No.718

Soto, Gary,
*A Fire In My Hands: A
Book of Poems.*
No.725

Stevenson, Robert Louis,
My Shadow.
No.744

Tripp, Wallace, compiled by,
*Marguerite, Go Wash
Your Feet.*
No.766

Willard, Nancy,
*East of the Sun & West
of the Moon.*
No.805

Willard, Nancy,
*Pish, Posh, Said
Hieronymus Bosch.*
No.806

Willard, Nancy,
*A Visit to William Blake's
Inn: Poems for the Innocent
& Experienced Travelers.*
No.807

Yolen, Jane,
Ring of Earth.
No.826

Zolotow, Charlotte,
River Winding.
No.841

POST–CIVIL WAR

Baker, Rachel,
The First Woman Doctor.
No.47

Conrad, Pam,
Prairie Songs.
No.174

Eckert, Allan W.,
Incident at Hawk's Hill.
No.236

Freedman, Russell,
Children of the Wild West.
No.276

Freedman, Russell,
Cowboys of the Wild West.
No.277

Freedman, Russell,
Immigrant Kids.
No.278

Giff, Patricia Reilly,
*Laura Ingalls Wilder:
Growing Up in
the Little House.*
No.313

Lasky, Kathryn,
The Bone Wars.
No.450

McGill, Marci Ridlon,
*The Story of Louisa May
Alcott: Determined Writer.*
No.556

Reeder, Carolyn,
Shades of Gray.
No.651

Van Leuwen,
Going West.
No.778

POST–REVOLUTIONARY WAR

Fritz, Jean,
*Shh! We're Writing
the Constitution.*
No.286

Maestro, Betsy;
Giulio Maestro,
*A More Perfect Union: The
Story of Our Constitution.*
No.515

Spier, Peter,
*We the People:
The Constitution of the
United States of America.*
No.734

Turner, Ann,
Dakota Dugout.
No.770

PRE-CIVIL WAR

Clark, Margaret Goff,
Freedom Crossing.
No.148

Hamilton, Virginia,
*Anthony Burns:
The Defeat and Triumph
of a Fugitive Slave.*
No.349

Lester, Julius,
To Be A Slave.
No.476

Paterson, Katherine,
Lyddie.
No.624

Sterling, Dorothy,
*Freedom Train: The Story of
Harriet Tubman.*
No.743

PRESIDENTS

Archer, Jules,
*They Made a
Revolution: 1776.*
No.26

Denenberg, Barry,
*John Fitzgerald Kennedy:
America's 35th President.*
No.211

Freedman, Russell,
Lincoln: A Photobiography.
No.280

Fritz, Jean,
*George Washington's
Breakfast.*
No.285

Hayman, Leroy,
*The Death of Lincoln:
A Picture History of the
Assassination.*
No.357

Krensky, Stephen,
*George Washington:
The Man Who Would
Not Be King.*
No.442

Waters, Kate,
*The Story of the
White House.*
No.790

Weinberg, Larry,
*The Story of Abraham
Lincoln, President
for the People.*
No.793

Woodruff, Elvira,
George Washington's Socks.
No.816

PRINCESS & THE FROG

Mayer, Mercer,
*East of the Sun & West
of the Moon.*
No.544

Ormerod, Jan,
The Frog Prince.
No.610

Scieszka, Jon,
The Frog Prince Continued.
No.692

RAIN FORESTS

Baker, Lucy,
Life in the Rainforest.
No.45

Cherry, Lynne,
The Great Kapok Tree.
No.144

Cowcher, Helen,
Rain Forest.
No.184

Dorros, Arthur,
Rain Forest Secrets.
No.226

RED RIDING HOOD

de Regniers, Beatrice Schenk,
Red Riding Hood.
No.206

Ehrlich, Amy, adapted by,
*The Random House
Book of Fairy Tales.*
No.243

Emberley, Michael,
Ruby.
No.251

Grimm, Jacob;
Wilhelm Grimm,
Little Red Cap.
No.335

Haviland, Virginia,
The Fairy Tale Treasury.
No.355

Marshall, James,
Red Riding Hood.
No.522

Rockwell, Anne,
*The Three Bears
and 15 Other Stories.*
No.658

Young, Ed,
Lon Po Po.
No.831

REPRODUCTION

Cole, Joanna,
My Puppy Is Born.
No.170

Heller, Ruth,
*Chickens Aren't
the Only Ones.*
No.360

Kaizuki, Kiyonori,
A Calf Is Born.
No.411

Mayle, Peter,
What's Happening to Me?
No.545

Mayle, Peter,
Where Did I Come From?
No.546

SCHOOL

Allard, Harry,
Miss Nelson is Missing.
No.20

Baer, Edith,
*This Is the Way We
Go To School.*
No.43

Brown, Jeff,
Flat Stanley.
No.96

dePaola, Tomie,
The Art Lesson.
No.214

Henkes, Kevin,
Jessica.
No.366

Howe, James,
*The Day the Teacher
Went Bananas.*
No.390

Mahy, Margaret,
*The Blood-and-Thunder
Adventure on
Hurricane Peak.*
No.516

Mills, Lauren,
The Rag Coat.
No.576

Noble, Trinka Hakes,
*The Day Jimmy's Boa
Ate the Wash.*
No.599

Schwartz, Amy,
*Annabell Swift,
Kindergartner.*
No.689

SEASONS-FICTION

Chall, Marsha Wilson,
Up North at the Cabin.
No.139

Martin, Bill Jr.;
John Archambault,
The Magic Pumpkin.
No.529

McPhail, David, *Ed and Me.*
No.570

SEASONS-INFORMATIONAL

Berger, Melvin,
Seasons.
No.69

Branley, Franklyn M.,
Sunshine Makes the Seasons.
No.86

Leslie, Clare Walker,
Nature All Year Long.
No.470

Maass, Robert,
When Autumn Comes.
No.508

Patent, Dorothy Hinshaw,
*An Apple A Day:
From Orchard to You.*
No.620

Whitfield, Dr. Philip;
Joyce Pope,
*Why Do the Seasons
Change? Questions on
Nature's Rythms and Cycles.*
No.800

SEASONS-PICTURE BOOK

Berger, Melvin,
Seasons.
No.69

Blocksma, Mary,
Apple Tree! Apple Tree!
No.76

Borden, Louise,
*Caps, Hats, Socks,
and Mittens.*
No.84

Branley, Franklyn M.,
Sunshine Makes the Seasons.
No.86

Butterworth, Nick,
One Snowy Night.
No.118

Chall, Marsha Wilson,
Up North at the Cabin.
No.139

Frost, Robert,
*Stopping By Woods on a
Snowy Evening.*
No.289

Jeunesse, Galimard;
Pascale de Bourgoing,
The Tree.
No.406

Jeunesse, Galimard;
Pascale de Bourgoing,
Weather.
No.407

Keats, Ezra Jack,
The Snowy Day.
No.420

Livingston, Myra Cohn,
A Circle of Seasons.
No.489

Maass, Robert,
When Autumn Comes.
No.508

Martin, Bill Jr.;
John Archambault,
The Ghost Eye Tree.
No.525

McPhail, David,
Ed and Me.
No.570

San Souci, Daniel,
North Country Night.
No.668

Williams, Linda,
*The Little Old Lady Who
Was Not Afraid of Anything.*
No.808

Yolen, Jane,
Ring of Earth.
No.826

SNOW WHITE

Ehrlich, Amy adapted by,
*The Random House
Book of Fairy Tales.*
No.243

French, Fiona,
Snow White in New York.
No.284

Grimm, Jacob;
Wilhelm Grimm,
Snow White.
No.332

Grimm, Jacob;
Wilhelm Grimm,
*Snow-White and the
Seven Dwarfs.*
No.333

SOCIAL ISSUES

Blos, Joan,
A Gathering of Days.
No.78

Bunting, Eve,
Fly Away Home.
No.106

Bunting, Eve,
Terrible Things.
No.107

Bunting, Eve,
The Wednesday Surprise.
No.109

Byars, Betsy,
*The Blossoms Meet the
Vulture Lady.*
No.119

Clark, Margaret Goff,
Freedom Crossing.
No.148

Cleary, Beverly,
Dear Mr. Henshaw.
No.152

Coerr, Eleanor,
*Sadako and the Thousand
Paper Cranes.*
No.161

dePaola, Tomie,
Oliver Button Is a Sissy.
No.219

Durell, Ann; Marilyn
Sachs; editors,
The Big Book of Peace.
No.232

Ernst, Lisa Campbell,
*Sam Johnson and the Blue
Ribbon Quilt.*
No.253

Freedman, Russell,
Immigrant Kids.
No.278

Glimmerveen, Ulco,
A Tale of Antarctica.
No.316

Greenfield, Eloise,
*Night on Neighborhood
Street.*
No.329

Hamanaka, Sheila,
The Journey.
No.347

Hamilton, Virginia,
*Anthony Burns:
The Defeat and Triumph of a
Fugitive Slave.*
No.349

Hirschfelder, Arlene,
*Happily May I Walk:
American Indians and
Alaska Natives Today.*
No.372

Hoffman, Mary,
Amazing Grace.
No.380

Larrick, Nancy (selector),
*I Heard a Scream in the
Street: Poems by Young
People in the City.*
No.449

Lasky, Kathryn,
The Night Journey.
No.451

Maruki, Toshi,
Hiroshima No Pika.
No.532

Mathis, Sharon Bell,
The Hundred Penny Box.
No.537

Morimoto, Junko,
My Hiroshima.
No.583

Speare, Elizabeth George,
The Witch of Blackbird Pond.
No.727

Spinelli, Jerry,
Maniac Magee.
No.735

Sterling, Dorothy,
*Freedom Train: The Story of
Harriet Tubman.*
No.743

Tsuchiya, Yukio,
*Faithful Elephants:
A True Story of Animals,
People and War.*
No.768

SOUTHERN STATES

Bulla, Clyde Robert,
*Pocahontas and
the Strangers.*
No.105

Byars, Betsy,
*The Winged Colt of
Casa Mia.*
No.121

Hooks, William H.,
Moss Gown.
No.381

Kassem, Lou,
A Haunting in Williamsburg.
No.414

Reeder, Carolyn,
Shades of Gray.
No.651

San Souci, Robert,
The Talking Eggs.
No.669

SOUTHWESTERN STATES

Baylor, Byrd,
*If You Are a Hunter
of Fossils.*
No.63

dePaola, Tomie,
The Legend of Bluebonnet.
No.216

dePaola, Tomie,
*The Legend of the
Indian Paintbrush.*
No.217

Freedman, Russell,
Children of the Wild West.
No.276

Freedman, Russell,
Cowboys of the Wild West.
No.277

SPACE

Apfel, Necia,
Voyager to the Planets.
No.25

Ardley, Neil,
The Inner Planets.
No.27

Ardley, Neil,
The Other Planets.
No.28

Bates, Robin; Cheryl Simon,
*The Dinosaurs and
the Dark Star.*
No.60

Branley, Franklyn M.,
Sunshine Makes the Seasons.
No.86

Cole, Joanna,
*The Magic School Bus Lost
in the Solar System.*
No.169

Goble, Paul,
Star Boy.
No.323

Hatchett, Clint,
*The Glow-in-the-Dark
Night Sky Book.*
No.354

Lauber, Patricia,
Seeing Earth From Space.
No.458

Livingston, Myra Cohn,
Earth Songs.
No.490

Mayo, Gretchen Will,
*Star Tales:
North American Indian
Stories about the Stars.*
No.547

Cooper, Susan,
Dawn of Fear.
No.178

Hamanaka, Sheila,
The Journey.
No.347

Innocenti, Roberto,
Rose Blanche.
No.395

Maruki, Toshi,
Hiroshima No Pika.
No.532

Morimoto, Junko,
My Hiroshima.
No.583

Nixon, Lois Lowery,
Number the Stars.
No.597

Sullivan, George,
*The Day Pearl Harbor
Was Bombed.*
No.747

Tsuchiya, Yukio,
*Faithful Elephants:
A True Story of Animals,
People and War.*
No.768

Yolen, Jane,
The Devil's Arithmetic.
No.821

WRITING-FICTION-
CHAPTER BOOK

Blos, Joan,
A Gathering of Days.
No.78

Clapp, Patricia,
*Constance, The Story of
Early Plymouth.*
No.147

Cleary, Beverly,
Dear Mr. Henshaw.
No.152

WRITING-FICTION-
PICTURE BOOK

Asch, Frank,
Dear Brother.
No.32

Brisson, Pat,
Your Best Friend, Kate.
No.94

James, Simon,
Dear Mr. Blueberry.
No.398

Jarrell, Randall,
The Bat Poet.
No.400

WRITING-INFORMATIONAL

Asher, Sandy,
*Where Do You Get
Your Ideas?*
No.33

Benjamin, Carol Lea,
Writing for Kids.
No.67

Kennedy, X. J. ;
Dorothy M. Kennedy,
*Knock At A Star: A Child's
Introduction to Poetry.*
No.427

Leedy, Loreen,
*Messages in the Mailbox:
How to Write a Letter.*
No.464

Nixon, Joan Lowery,
If You Were A Writer.
No.596

Paulsen, Gary,
Woodsong.
No.630

Spector, Marjorie,
*Pencil to Press:
How This Book Came To Be.*
No.728

Brett, Jan (reteller),
Beauty and the Beast.
No.87

Briggs, Raymond,
Father Christmas.
No.90

Briggs, Raymond,
Jim and the Beanstalk.
No.91

Briggs, Raymond,
The Snowman.
No.92

Bright, M.,
The Ozone Layer.
No.93

Brisson, Pat,
Your Best Friend, Kate.
No.94

Brooke, William J.,
A Telling of the Tales:
Five Stories.
No.95

Brown, Jeff,
Flat Stanley.
No.96

Brown, Marc,
Arthur's Tooth:
An Arthur Adventure.
No.97

Brown, Ruth,
The World That Jack Built.
No.98

Bryan, Ashley,
The Cat's Purr.
No.99

Bryan, Ashley,
Lion and the Ostrich Chicks
& Other African Folk Tales.
No.100

Bryan, Ashley,
Turtle Knows Your Name.
No.101

Budbill, David, *Bones on*
Black Spruce Mountain.
No.102

Budbill, David,
Snowshoe Trek to
Otter River.
No.103

Buff, Conrad; Mary Buff,
The Apple and the Arrow.
No.104

Buff, Mary; Conrad Buff,
The Apple and the Arrow.
No.104

Bulla, Robert Clyde,
Pocahontas and the
Strangers.
No.105

Bunting, Eve,
Fly Away Home.
No.106

Bunting, Eve,
Terrible Things.
No.107

Bunting, Eve,
The Wall.
No.108

Bunting, Eve,
The Wednesday Surprise.
No.109

Burch, Robert,
Ida Early Comes over
the Mountain.
No.110

Burningham, John,
Hey! Get Off Our Train.
No.111

Burningham, John,
Mr. Gumpy's Outing.
No.112

Burns, Marilyn,
The I Hate Mathematics! Book.
No.113

Burton, Virginia Lee,
Katy and the Big Snow.
No.114

Burton, Virginia Lee,
The Little House.
No.115

Burton, Virginia Lee,
Mike Mulligan and His
Steam Shovel.
No.116

Butler, Beverly,
Ghost Cat.
No.117

Butterworth, Nick,
One Snowy Night.
No.118

Byars, Betsy,
The Blossoms Meet the
Vulture Lady.
No.119

Byars, Betsy,
The Midnight Fox.
No.120

Byars, Betsy,
The Winged Colt of
Casa Mia.
No.121

C

Calhoun, Mary,
Cross-Country Cat.
No.122

Cameron, Ann,
The Stories Julian Tells.
No.123

Campbell, Joanna,
A Horse Called Wonder.
No.124

Carle, Eric,
The Grouchy Ladybug.
No.126

Carle, Eric,
Have You Seen My Cat?
No.127

Carle, Eric,
Pancakes, Pancakes!
No.128

Carle, Eric,
The Very Busy Spider.
No.130

Carle, Eric,
The Very Hungry
Caterpillar.
No.131

Carle, Eric (reteller),
Twelve Tales From Aesop.
No.129

Carle, Eric (selector),
Animals Animals.
No.125

Carlstrom, Nancy White,
Jesse Bear, What Will
You Wear?
No.132

Carrick, Carol,
Patrick's Dinosaurs.
No.133

Carrick, Carol,
What Happened to Patrick's
Dinosaurs?
No.134

Cauley, Lorinda Bryan,
Goldilocks and the
Three Bears.
No.136

Cawthorne, W. A.,
Who Killed Cockatoo?
No.137

Cazet, Denys,
"I'm Not Sleepy".
No.138

Chall, Marsha Wilson,
Up North at the Cabin.
No.139

Follett, Ken,
The Mystery Hideout.
No.268

Forest, Heather,
*The Woman Who
Flummoxed the Fairies.*
No.269

Foster, John (selector),
*Never Say Boo To A Ghost
and Other Haunting Rhymes.*
No.270

Fox, Mem,
Koala Lou.
No.271

Fox, Mem,
Night Noises.
No.272

Fox, Mem,
*Wilfrid Gordon
McDonald Partridge.*
No.273

Fox, Paula,
One-Eyed Cat.
No.274

Frasier, Debra,
On the Day You Were Born.
No.275

Freedman, Russell,
Children of the Wild West.
No.276

Freedman, Russell,
Cowboys of the Wild West.
No.277

Freedman, Russell,
Immigrant Kids.
No.278

Freedman, Russell,
Indian Chiefs.
No.279

Freedman, Russell,
Lincoln: A Photobiography.
No.280

Freeman, Don,
Corduroy.
No.281

Freeman, Don,
The Seal and the Slick.
No.282

Freeman, Mae,
The Real Magnet Book.
No.283

French, Fiona,
Snow White in New York.
No.284

Fritz, Jean,
*George Washington's
Breakfast.*
No.285

Fritz, Jean,
*Shh! We're Writing the
Constitution.*
No.286

Fritz, Jean,
*Where was Patrick Henry
On the 29th of May?*
No.287

Fritz, Jean,
*Will You Sign Here,
John Hancock?*
No.288

Frost, Robert,
*Stopping by Woods
on a Snowy Evening .*
No.289

G

Gackenbach, Dick,
Mighty Tree.
No.290

Gág, Wanda,
The ABC Bunny.
No.291

Gág, Wanda,
Millions of Cats.
No.292

Gág, Wanda,
Tales from Grimm.
 No.293

Galdone, Paul,
The Gingerbread Boy.
No.294

Galdone, Paul,
*Over in the Meadow: An Old
Nursery Counting Rhyme.*
No.295

Galdone, Paul,
The Three Billy Goats Gruff.
No.296

Galdone, Paul,
The Three Little Pigs.
No.297

Gardiner, John Reynolds,
Stone Fox.
No.298

Gardner, Robert,
The Whale Watchers' Guide.
No.299

Gates, Doris,
The Blue Willow.
No.300

George, Jean Craighead,
Julie of the Wolves.
No.301

George, Jean Craighead,
*On the Far Side
of the Mountain.*
No.302

George, Jean Craighead,
*Who Really Killed
Cock Robin?*
No.303

Gibbons, Gail,
*Check It Out!
The Book About Libraries.*
No.304

Gibbons, Gail,
Dinosaurs.
No.305

Gibbons, Gail,
Flying.
No.306

Gibbons, Gail,
From Seed to Plant.
No.307

Gibbons, Gail,
Monarch Butterfly.
No.308

Gibbons, Gail,
Thanksgiving Day.
No.309

Gibbons, Gail,
*Things To Make and
Do On Columbus Day.*
No.310

Gibbons, Gail,
*Weather Words and
What They Mean.*
No.311

Gibbons, Gail,
Zoo.
No.312

Giff, Patricia Reilly,
*Laura Ingalls Wilder:
Growing Up in the
Little House.*
No.313

Giganti, Paul Jr.,
Each Orange Had 8 Slices.
No.314

Gilman, Phoebe,
Jillian Jiggs.
No.315

Glimmerveen, Ulco,
A Tale of Antarctica.
No.316

Goble, Paul,
Crow Chief.
No.317

Goble, Paul,
The Gift of the Sacred Dog.
No.318

Hayman, Leroy,
The Death of Lincoln:
A Picture History of
the Assassination.
No.358

Haynes, Betsy,
Spies on the Devil's Belt.
No.359

Heller, Ruth,
A Cache of Jewels.
No.360

Heller, Ruth,
Chickens Aren't the
Only Ones.
No.361

Heller, Ruth,
Kites Sail High:
A Book About Verbs.
No.362

Heller, Ruth,
Many Luscious Lollipops.
No.363

Heller, Ruth,
Merry-Go-Round:
A Book About Nouns.
No.364

Heller, Ruth,
Plants That Never
Ever Bloom.
No.365

Heller, Ruth,
The Reason for a Flower.
No.366

Henkes, Kevin,
Jessica.
No.367

Hepworth, Cathi,
Antics!
No.368

Herriot, James,
The Christmas Day Kitten.
No.369

Herriot, James,
Moses the Kitten.
No.370

Herriot, James,
Oscar, Cat-About-Town.
No.371

Hill, Douglas; John Elkington;
Julia Hailes; Joel Makower,
Going Green:
A Kid's Handbook to
Saving the Planet.
No.247

Himmelman, John,
Ibis: A True Whale Story.
No.372

Hirschfelder, Arlene,
Happily May I Walk:
American Indians and
Alaska Natives Today.
No.373

Hirschi, Ron,
Who Lives in...
the Mountains.
No.374

Hirschi, Ron,
Winter.
No.375

Hoban, Russell,
A Baby Sister for Frances.
No.376

Hoberman, Mary Ann,
A House Is a House for Me.
No.377

Hodges, Margaret,
The Kitchen Knight:
A Tale of King Arthur.
No.378

Hodges, Margaret,
Saint George and
the Dragon.
No.379

Hoff, Syd,
Julius.
No.380

Hoffman, Mary,
Amazing Grace.
No.381

Hooks, William H.,
Moss Gown.
No.382

Hooks, William H.,
The Three Little Pigs
and the Fox.
No.383

Hopkins, Lee Bennett,
Animals from Mother Goose.
No.384

Hopkins, Lee Bennett,
People from Mother Goose.
No.385

Hopkins, Lee Bennett
(selector); Carl Sandburg,
Rainbows are Made.
No.671

Hoopes, Ned; Bernard Evslin;
Dorothy Evslin,
The Greek Gods.
No.256

Hoopes, Ned; Bernard Evslin;
Dorothy Evslin,
Heroes & Monsters
of Greek Myth.
No.257

Horner, John R.;
James Gorman,
Maia: A Dinosaur Grows Up.
No.386

Hort, Lenny (reteller),
The Boy Who
Held Back the Sea.
No.387

Horton, Casey,
Insects.
No.388

Houghton, Eric,
Walter's Magic Wand.
No.389

Howard, Jane R.,
When I Am Sleepy.
No.390

Howe, James,
The Day the Teacher
Went Bananas.
No.391

Howe, James,
What Eric Knew:
A Sebastian Barth Mystery.
No.392

Huck, Charlotte (reteller),
Princess Furball.
No.393

Huntington, Harriet,
Let's Look at Insects.
No.394

Hutchins, Pat,
The Doorbell Rang.
No.395

I

Innocenti, Roberto,
Rose Blanche.
No.396

J

Jacobs, Joseph,
English Fairy Tales.
No.397

Jacobs, Joseph,
Tattercoats.
No.398

James, Robert;
Susan Sussman,
Big Friend, Little Friend:
A Book about Symbiosis.
No.751

James, Simon,
Dear Mr. Blueberry.
No.399

Jaquith, Priscilla (reteller),
Bo Rabbit Smart for True:

L

La Fontaine,
The Lion and the Rat.
No.445

Langstaff, John,
Frog Went A-Courtin'.
No.446

Langstaff, John,
Over in the Meadow.
No.447

Lansky, Vicki,
Microwave Cooking for Kids.
No.448

Larrick, Nancy,
Cats Are Cats.
No.449

Larrick, Nancy (selector),
I Heard a Scream in the Street: Poems by Young People in the City.
No.450

Lasky, Kathryn,
The Bone Wars.
No.451

Lasky, Kathryn,
The Night Journey.
No.452

Lasky, Kathryn,
Sea Swan.
No.453

Lasky, Kathryn,
Sugaring Time.
No.454

Lauber, Patricia,
Dinosaurs Walked Here & Other Stories Fossils Tell.
No.455

Lauber, Patricia,
Living with Dinosaurs.
No.456

Lauber, Patricia,
Lost Star, The Story of Amelia Earhart.
No.457

Lauber, Patricia,
The News About Dinosaurs.
No.458

Lauber, Patricia,
Seeing Earth From Space.
No.460

Lauber, Patricia,
Volcano: The Eruption and Healing of Mount St. Helens.
No.459

Lauber, Patricia,
Volcanoes and Earthquakes.
No.461

Leach, Maria,
How the People Sang the Mountains Up: How and Why Stories.
No.462

Lear, Edward,
An Edward Lear Alphabet.
No.463

Lear, Edward,
The Owl and the Pussycat.
No.464

Leedy, Loreen,
Messages in the Mailbox: How to Write a Letter.
No.465

LeGuin, Ursula K.,
A Wizard of Earthsea.
No.466

Lehr, Norma,
The Shimmering Ghost of Riversend.
No.467

L'Engle, Madeleine,
Meet the Austins.
No.468

L'Engle, Madeleine,
A Wind in the Door.
No.469

Lerner, Carol,
Moonseed and Mistletoe: A Book of Poisonous Wild Plants.
No.470

Leslie, Clare Walker,
Nature All Year Long.
No.471

Lesser, Rika,
Hansel and Gretel.
No.472

Lester, Helen,
A Porcupine Named Fluffy.
No.473

Lester, Helen,
Tacky the Penguin.
No.474

Lester, Julius,
The Knee-High Man and Other Tales.
No.475

Lester, Julius,
More Tales of Uncle Remus: Further Adventures of Brer Rabbit, His Friends, Enemies, and Others.
No.476

Lester, Julius,
To Be A Slave.
No.477

Levine, Ellen,
Ready, Aim, Fire! The Real Adventures of Annie Oakley.
No.478

Levine, Joseph; Tillie S. Pine,
Magnets and How to Use Them.
No.635

Levitin, Sonia,
The Man Who Kept His Heart in a Bucket.
No.479

Lewin, Hugh,
Jafta.
No.480

Lewis, Claudia,
Long Ago in Oregon.
No.481

Lewis, Rob,
Friska The Sheep That Was Too Small.
No.482

Lindbergh, Reeve,
The Midnight Farm.
No.483

Lionni, Leo,
Frederick.
No.484

Lionni, Leo,
Fredrick's Fables.
No.485

Lionni, Leo,
Inch by Inch.
No.486

Lionni, Leo,
Mathew's Dream.
No.487

Lister, Robin (reteller),
The Legend of King Arthur.
No.488

Littledale, Freyda,
Peter and the North Wind.
No.489

Livingston, Myra Cohn,
A Circle of Seasons.
No.490

Livingston, Myra Cohn,
Earth Songs.
No.491

Lobel, Anita,
The Dwarf Giant.
No.492

Mathews, Louise,
*Bunches and Bunches
of Bunnies.*
No.537

Mathis, Sharon Bell,
The Hundred Penny Box.
No.538

Matsutani, Miyoko; Alvin
Tresselt (reteller),
The Crane Maiden.
No.539

Matthews, Rupert,
The Dinosaur Age.
No.540

Mayer, Marianna,
Beauty and the Beast.
No.541

Mayer, Marianna,
The Black Horse.
No.542

Mayer, Marianna,
*The Prince and the Princess:
A Bohemian Fairy Tale.*
No.543

Mayer, Marianna,
The Unicorn and the Lake.
No.544

Mayer, Mercer,
*East of the Sun &
West of the Moon.*
No.545

Mayle, Peter,
What's Happening to Me?
No.546

Mayle, Peter,
Where Did I Come From?
No.547

Mayo, Gretchen Will,
*Star Tales:
North American Indian
Stories about the Stars.*
No.548

McCloskey, Robert,
Blueberries for Sal.
No.549

McCloskey, Robert,
Make Way for Ducklings.
No.550

McCloskey, Robert,
One Morning in Maine.
No.551

McCloskey, Robert,
Time of Wonder.
No.552

McCord, David,
All Small.
No.553

McDermott, Gerald,
Anansi the Spider.
No.554

McDermott, Gerald,
Arrow to the Sun.
No.555

McDonald, Megan,
The Great Pumpkin Switch.
No.556

McGill, Marci Ridlon,
*The Story of Louisa May
Alcott: Determined Writer.*
No.557

McGovern, Ann,
*The Pilgrims' First
Thanksgiving.*
No.558

McGovern, Ann,
*Robin Hood of
Sherwood Forest.*
No.560

McGovern, Ann,
Sharks.
No.559

McGovern, Ann,
*The Secret Soldier: The
Story of Deborah Sampson.*
No.561

McGovern, Ann;
Eugenie Clarke,
The Desert Beneath the Sea.
No.562

McGraw, Eloise Jarvis,
Moccasin Trail.
No.563

McKinley, Robin,
The Hero and the Crown.
No.564

McKinley, Robin
(adaptor); Anna Sewell,
Black Beauty.
No.698

McKissack, Patricia,
Jesse Jackson.
No.565

McKissack, Patricia,
Mirandy and Brother Wind.
No.566

McLerran, Alice,
I Want To Go Home.
No.567

McMillan, Bruce,
Eating Fractions.
No.568

McMillan, Bruce,
Growing Colors.
No.569

McNulty, Faith,
*Orphan: The Story of
a Baby Woodchuck.*
No.570

McPhail, David,
Ed and Me.
No.571

Meigs, Cornelia,
Invincible Louisa.
No.572

Mendez, Phil,
The Black Snowman.
No.573

Micucci, Charles,
*The Life and Times
of the Apple.*
No.574

Miles, Bernard,
*Favorite Tales From
Shakespeare.*
No.575

Miles, Miska,
Annie and the Old One.
No.576

Mills, Lauren,
The Rag Coat.
No.577

Milton, Nancy,
*The Giraffe that Walked
to Paris.*
No.578

Minarik, Else Holmelund,
Little Bear.
No.579

Minarik, Else Holmelund,
Little Bear's Visit.
No.580

Moche, Dinah,
What's Up There?
No.581

Moore, Clement C.,
The Night Before Christmas.
No.582

Moore, Eva; Beatrice Schenk
de Regniers; Mary
MichaelsWhite; Jan Carr ,
Sing A Song of Popcorn.
No.208

Paulsen, Gary,
The Island.
No.628

Paulsen, Gary,
Tracker.
No.629

Paulsen, Gary,
Woodsong.
No.630

Peck, Ira,
The Life and Words of
Martin Luther King,
Jr.
No.631

Peck, Robert Newton,
Soup.
No.632

Pfister, Marcus,
Penguin Pete's New
Friends.
No.633

Phelps, Ethel Johnston,
The Maid of the North:
Feminist Folk Tales
from Around the
World.
No.634

Pine, Tillie S.; Levine, Joseph,
Magnets and How
to Use Them.
No.635

Pittman, Hellena Clare,
Once When I Was Scared.
No.636

Polacco, Patricia,
Boat Ride with Lillian
Two Blossom.
No.637

Polacco, Patricia,
Mrs. Katz and Tush.
No.638

Polette, Nancy,
The Hole by the Apple Tree.
No.639

Pollarck, Pamela,
The Random House
Book of Humor for Children.
No.640

Pope, Joyce;
Dr. Phillip Whitfield,
Why Do the Seasons
Change? Questions
on Nature's Rythms
and Cycles.
No.800

Porter-Gaylord, Laurel,
I Love My Daddy Because…
No.641

Porter-Gaylord, Laurel,
I Love My Mommy
Because…
No.642

Prelutsky, Jack,
It's Thanksgiving.
No.643

Prelutsky, Jack,
Ride a Purple Pelican.
No.644

Prelutsky, Jack,
Something Big Has
Been Here.
No.645

Prelutsky, Jack,
Tyrannosaurus Was a Beast.
No.646

Pringle, Laurence,
Twist, Wiggle, and Squirm:
A Book about Earthworms.
No.647

Provensen, Alice;
Martin Provensen,
The Glorious Flight
Across the Channel
with Louis Blériot.
No.648

Provensen, Alice;
Martin Provensen,

The Mother Goose Book.
No.649

Provenson, Martin;
Alice Provensen,
The Glorious Flight
Across the Channel
with Louis Blériot.
No.648

Provenson, Martin;
Alice Provensen,
The Mother Goose Book.
No.649

R

Rathburn, Elizabeth,
Exploring Your
Solar System.
No.650

Reeder, Carolyn,
Shades of Gray.
No.651

Rees, Mary,
Ten in a Bed.
No.652

Reigot, Betty Polisar,
A Book About Planets
and Stars.
No.653

Roberts, Willo Davis,
Megan's Island.
No.654

Robinson, Barbara,
The Best Christmas
Pageant Ever.
No.655

Rockwell, Anne,
The Old Woman and Her Pig
and 10 Other Stories.
No.656

Rockwell, Anne,
Our Yard is Full of Birds.
No.657

Rockwell, Anne,
The Three Bears and
15 Other Stories.
No.658

Rogers, Paul,
The Shapes Game.
No.659

Rosen, Michael,
We're Going on a Bear Hunt.
No.660

Rounds, Glen,
I Know an Old Lady
Who Swallowed a Fly.
No.661

Ryder, Joanne,
Where Butterflies Grow.
No.662

Ryder, Joanne,
White Bear, Ice Bear.
No.663

Rylant, Cynthia,
Henry and Mudge
and the Long Weekend.
No.664

Rylant, Cynthia,
When I Was Young
in the Mountains.
No.665

S

Sachs, Marilyn;
Ann Durell (editors),
The Big Book of Peace.
No.232

Sadler, Catherine
Edwards (adaptor),
Sir Arthur Conan Doyle's
The Adventures of Sherlock
Holmes: Volume I.
No.666

Sadler, Marilyn,
Elizabeth and Larry.
No.667

Sloat, Teri,
The Eye of the Needle.
No.715

Slovenz-Low, Madeline;
Kate Waters,
*Lion Dancer: Ernie Wan's
Chinese New Year.*
No.791

Small, David,
Imogene's Antlers.
No.716

Snape, Charles; Juliet Snape,
Frog Odyssey.
No.717

Snape, Juliet; Charles Snape,
Frog Odyssey.
No.717

Sneve, Virginia
Driving Hawk,
*Dancing Teepees:
Poems From American
Indian Youth.*
No.718

Snow, Nicholas,
*The Monster Book
of ABC Sounds.*
No.719

Snyder, Zilpha Keatley,
And Condors Danced.
No.720

Snyder, Zilpha Keatley,
Black and Blue Magic.
No.721

Snyder, Zilpha Keatley,
The Velvet Room.
No.722

Sorensen, Virginia,
Plain Girl.
No.723

Soto, Gary,
*A Fire In My Hands:
A Book of Poems.*
No.725

Speare, Elizabeth George,
The Sign of the Beaver.
No.726

Speare, Elizabeth George,
*The Witch of
Blackbird Pond.*
No.727

Spector, Marjorie,
*Pencil to Press:
How This Book Came To Be.*
No.728

Spier, Peter,
Noah's Ark.
No.729

Spier, Peter,
Oh, Were They Ever Happy!
No.730

Spier, Peter,
People.
No.731

Spier, Peter,
Rain.
No.732

Spier, Peter,
To Market! To Market!
No.733

Spier, Peter,
*We the People:
The Constitution of the
United States of America.*
No.734

Spinelli, Jerry,
Maniac Magee.
No.735

Stanley, Diane;
Peter Vennema,
Shaka, King of the Zulus.
No.736

Steig, William,
Amos & Boris.
No.737

Steig, William,
Brave Irene.
No.738

Steig, William,
Shrek!
No.739

Steig, William,
*Sylvester and the
Magic Pebble.*
No.740

Steptoe, John,
*Mufaro's Beautiful
Daughters: An African Tale.*
No.741

Steptoe, John (reteller),
The Story of Jumping Mouse.
No.742

Sterling, Dorothy,
*Freedom Train: The Story
of Harriet Tubman.*
No.743

Stevenson, Robert Louis,
My Shadow.
No.744

Stoutenburg, Adrien,
American Tall Tales.
No.745

Stratton, Barbara,
What Is a Fish.
No.746

Sullivan, George,
*The Day Pearl Harbor
Was Bombed.*
No.747

Sullivan, George,
*The Day We Walked
on the Moon.*
No.748

Sullivan, Mary Beth;
Linda Bourke,
A Show of Hands.
No.749

Surat, Michele Maria,
Angel Child, Dragon Child.
No.750

Sussman, Susan;
Robert James,
*Big Friend, Little Friend:
A Book about Symbiosis.*
No.751

Sutcliff, Rosemary,
Flame-Colored Taffeta.
No.752

Sutcliff, Rosemary,
*The Light Beyond the Forest:
The Quest for the Holy Grail.*
No.753

Sutcliff, Rosemary,
Tristan and Iseult.
No.754

Swan, Robert,
Destination: Antarctica.
No.755

T

Taylor, Mildred D.,
*Roll of Thunder,
Hear My Cry.*
No.756

Tejima,
Swan Sky.
No.757

Terban, Marvin,
*Mad as a Wet Hen!
And Other Funny Idioms.*
No.758

Thomas, Dylan,
*A Child's Christmas
in Wales.*
No.759

Thomas, Jane Resh,
The Comeback Dog.
No.760

Thurber, James,
Many Moons.
No.761

Willard, Nancy,
A Visit to William Blake's Inn: Poems for the Innocent & Experienced Travelers.
No.807

William, Sue,
I Went Walking.
No.809

Williams, Linda,
The Little Old Lady Who Was Not Afraid of Anything.
No.808

Williams, Vera,
A Chair For My Mother.
No.810

Winter, Jeanette,
Follow the Drinking Gourd.
No.811

Winthrop, Elizabeth,
The Castle in the Attic.
No.812

Winthrop, Elizabeth,
Vasilissa the Beautiful.
No.813

Wood, Audrey,
King Bidgood's in the Bathtub.
No.814

Wood, Audrey,
Little Penguin's Tale.
No.815

Woodruff, Elvira,
George Washington's Socks.
No.816

Wright, Betty Ren,
A Ghost in the Window.
No.817

Wyndham, Robert,
The Chinese Mother Goose Rhymes.
No.818

Y

Yagawa, Sumiko,
The Crane Wife.
No.819

Yep, Laurence,
The Rainbow People.
No.820

Yolen, Jane,
The Devil's Arithmetic.
No.821

Yolen, Jane,
Dove Isabeau.
No.822

Yolen, Jane,
Dragon's Boy.
No.823

Yolen, Jane,
Owl Moon.
No.825

Yolen, Jane,
Ring of Earth.
No.826

Yolen, Jane,
Sky Dogs.
No.827

Yolen, Jane (editor),
The Lap-Time Song and Play Book.
No.824

Yolen, Jane (reteller),
Tam Lin.
No.828

Yorinks, Arthur,
Ugh.
No.829

Yoshida, Toshi,
Elephant Crossing.
No.830

Young, Ed,
Lon Po Po.
No.831

Young, Ed (adaptor),
Seven Blind Mice.
No.832

Z

Zelinsky, Paul O.,
Rumplestiltskin.
No.833

Zemach, Harve,
Duffy and the Devil.
No.834

Zemach, Harve,
Mommy, Buy Me a China Doll.
No.835

Zemach, Harve,
Salt.
No.836

Zemach, Margot,
It Could Always Be Worse: A Yiddish Folk Tale.
No.837

Zemach, Margot,
The Three Little Pigs.
No.838

Zhensun, Zheng; Alice Low,
A Young Painter.
No.839

Zolotow, Charlotte,
The Bunny Who Found Easter.
No.840

Zolotow, Charlotte,
River Winding.
No.841

The Index of TITLES

*Eskimo Boy: Life in an
Inupiaq Eskimo Village,*
Kendall, Russ.
No.425

The Evolution Book,
Sara Stein.
No.672

*Exploring Your
Solar System,*
Rathburn, Elizabeth.
No.650

The Eye of the Needle,
Sloat, Teri.
No.715

The Eyes of the Amaryllis,
Babbitt, Natalie.
No.39

F

Fables,
Lobel, Arnold.
No.494

The Fairy Rebel,
Banks, Lynne Reid.
No.50

The Fairy Tale Treasury,
Haviland, Virginia.
No.355

*Faithful Elephants:
A True Story of Animals,
People and War,*
Tsuchiya, Yukio.
No.768

*The Family
Christmas Tree Book,*
dePaola, Tomi.
No.215

Family Farm,
Locker, Thomas.
No.501

Fantastic Mr. Fox,
Dahl, Roald.
No.194

Farm Animals,
No.259

*The Farthest-Away
Mountain,*
Banks, Lynne Reid.
No.51

Father Christmas,
Briggs, Raymond.
No.90

Favorite Greek Myths,
Osborne, Mary Pope.
No.612

*Favorite Tales from
Shakespeare,*
Miles, Bernard.
No.574

Feathers for Lunch,
Ehlert, Lois.
No.240

Feelings,
Aliki.
No.13

Feelings,
Murphy, Joanne Brisson.
No.592

*A Fire In My Hands:
A Book of Poems,*
Soto, Gary.
No.725

The First Women Doctor,
Baker, Rachel.
No.47

Fish to Reptiles,
Bender, Lionel.
No.66

*Five Little Monkeys
Jumping on the Bed,*
Christelow, Eileen.
No.146

Flame-Colored Taffeta,
Sutcliff, Rosemary.
No.752

*Flapdoodle: Pure Nonsense
from American Folklore,*
Schwartz, Alvin, collected by.
No.685

Flat Stanley,
Brown, Jeff.
No.96

Fly Away Home,
Bunting, Eve.
No.106

Flying,
Gibbons, Gail.
No.306

Follow the Drinking Gourd,
Winter, Jeanette.
No.811

*Foolish Rabbit's
Big Mistake,*
Martin, Rafe.
No.530

*Four Against the Odds:
The Struggle to Save
Our Environment,*
Krensky, Stephen.
No.441

Frederick,
Lionni, Leo.
No.483

*Frederick Douglass
Fights for Freedom,*
Davidson, Margaret.
No.198

Fredrick's Fables,
Lionni, Leo.
No.484

Freedom Crossing,
Clark, Margaret Goff.
No.148

*Freedom Train The Story
of Harriet Tubman,*
Sterling, Dorothy.
No.743

Freight Train,
Crews, Donald.
No.186

*The Friends of
Emily Culpepper,*
Coleridge, Ann.
No.172

*Friska the Sheep That
Was Too Small,*
Lewis, Rob.
No.481

Frog and Toad All Year,
Lobel, Arnold.
No.496

Frog and Toad Are Friends,
Lobel, Arnold.
No.497

Frog and Toad Together,
Lobel, Arnold.
No.495

Frog Odyssey,
Snape, Juliet; Charles Snape.
No.717

The Frog Prince,
Ormerod, Jan.
No.610

The Frog Prince Continued,
Scieszka, Jon.
No.692

Frog Went A-Courtin',
Langstaff, John.
No.445

*Frogs, Toads, Lizards,
and Salamanders,*
Parker, Nancy Winslow;
Joan Richards Wright.
No.619

*From Acorn to Zoo and
Everything in Between
in Alphabetical Order,*
Kitamura, Satoshi.
No.433

The Knee-High Man and Other Tales,
Lester, Julius.
No.474

Knock At A Star: A Child's Introduction to Poetry,
Kennedy, X. J. ;
Dorothy M. Kennedy.
No.427

Knots on a Counting Rope,
Martin, Bill Jr.;
John Archambault.
No.527

Koala Lou,
Fox, Mem.
No.271

L

The Ladybug and Other Insects,
Jeunesse, Galimard;
Pascale de Bourgoing.
No.405

The Land of the Gray Wolf,
Locker, Thomas.
No.502

The Lap-Time Song and Play Book,
Yolen, Jane, edited by.
No.824

Large As Life,
Finzel, Julia.
No.262

The Largest Dinosaurs,
Simon, Seymour.
No.709

Latkes and Applesauce: A Hanukkah Story,
Manushkin, Fran.
No.519

Laura Ingalls Wilder: Growing Up in the Little House,

Giff, Patricia Reilly.
No.313

The Lazy Bear,
Wildsmith, Brian.
No.804

Left & Right,
Oppenheim, Joanne.
No.609

The Legend of the Bluebonnet,
dePaola, Tomie.
No.216

The Legend of King Arthur,
Lister, Robin (reteller).
No.487

The Legend of the Indian Paintbrush,
dePaola, Tomie.
No.217

Let's Look at Insects,
Huntington, Harriet.
No.393

The Life and Times of the Apple,
Micucci, Charles.
No.573

The Life and Words of Martin Luther King, Jr.,
Peck, Ira.
No.631

Life in the Rainforest,
Baker, Lucy.
No.45

Life of the Ladybug,
Fischer-Nagel, Heiderose;
Andreas Fischer-Nagel.
No.263

The Light Beyond the Forest: The Quest for the Holy Grail,
Sutcliff, Rosemary.
No.753

Lillies, Rabbits, and Painted Eggs,
Barth, Edna.
No.55

Lincoln: A Photobiography,
Freedman, Russell.
No.280

Linnea's Windowsill Garden,
Bjork, Christina
Anderson Lena.
No.75

Lion and the Ostrich Chicks & Other African Folk Tales,
Bryan, Ashley.
No.100

The Lion and the Rat,
La Fontaine.
No.444

Lion Dancer: Ernie Wan's Chinese New Year,
Waters, Kate; Madeline
Slovenz-Low.
No.791

A Lion in the Meadow,
Mahy, Margaret.
No.517

Listen to the Rain,
Martin, Bill Jr.;
John Archambault.
No.528

Little Bear,
Minarik, Else Holmelund.
No.578

Little Bear's Visit,
Minarik, Else Holmelund.
No.579

Little Firefly,
Cohlene, Terri.
No.164

Little Giants,
Simon, Seymour.
No.710

The Little House,
Burton, Virginia Lee.
No.115

The Little House Cookbook,
Walker, Barbara.
No.785

The Little Mermaid,
Andersen, Hans Christian.
No.22

The Little Old Lady Who Was Not Afraid of Anything,
Williams, Linda.
No.808

Little Penguin's Tale,
Wood, Audrey.
No.815

Little Polar Bear,
de Beer, Hans.
No.203

Little Red Cap,
Grimm, Jacob;
Wilhelm Grimm.
No.335

Little Red Riding Hood,
Goodall, John S.
No.326

Little Sister for Sale,
Hamilton, Morse.
No.348

Living with Dinosaurs,
Lauber, Patricia.
No.455

The Living World,
Seddon, Tony; Jill.Bailey
No.695

Lon Po Po,
Young, Ed.
No.831

Long Ago in Oregon,
Lewis, Claudia.
No.480

The Pumpkin Patch,
King, Elizabeth.
No.432

Pumpkin Pumpkin,
Titherington, Jeanne.
No.763

Q

The Quilt Story,
Johnston, Tony.
No.408

R

*Rabbit Makes a Monkey
of the Lion,*
Aardema, Verna (reteller).
No.2

The Rag Coat,
Mills, Lauren.
No.576

Rain,
Spier, Peter.
No.732

Rain Forest,
Cowcher, Helen.
No.184

Rain Forest Secrets,
Dorros, Arthur.
No.226

Rain Makes Applesauce,
Scheer, Julian.
No.683

The Rainbow People,
Yep, Laurence.
No.820

Rainbows Are Made,
Sandburg, Carl Hopkins,
selector; Lee Bennett.
No.671

*The Random House
Book of Fairy Tales,*
Ehrlich, Amy adapted by.
No.243

*The Random House
Book of Humor for Children,*
Pollarck, Pamela.
No.640

*The Random House
Book of Mother Goose,*
Lobel, Arnold.
No.500

*Ready, Aim, Fire! The Real
Adventures of Annie Oakley,*
Levine, Ellen.
No.477

The Real Magnet Book,
Freeman, Mae.
No.283

The Real Tin Flower,
Barnstone, Aliki.
No.52

The Real Tooth Fairy,
Kaye, Marilyn.
No.415

The Reason for a Flower,
Heller, Ruth.
No.365

Red Riding Hood,
de Regniers, Beatrice Schenk.
No.206

Red Riding Hood,
Marshall, James.
No.522

Ride a Purple Pelican,
Prelutsky, Jack.
No.644

The Ring in the Prairie,
Bierhorst, John.
No.72

Ring of Earth,
Yolen, Jane.
No.826

A River Ran Wild,
Cherry, Lynne.
No.145

River Winding,
Zolotow, Charlotte.
No.841

*Robin Hood of
Sherwood Forest,*
McGovern, Ann.
No.558

*Roll of Thunder,
Hear My Cry,*
Taylor, Mildred D.
No.756

The Root Cellar,
Lunn, Janet.
No.507

Rose Blanche,
Innocenti, Roberto.
No.395

Ruby,
Emberley, Michael.
No.251

*Rugs Have Naps
(But Never Take Them),*
Klasky, Charles.
No.436

Rumplestiltskin,
Zelinsky, Paul O.
No.833

S

*Sadako and the
Thousand Paper Cranes,*
Coerr, Eleanor.
No.161

Sailing with the Wind,
Locker, Thomas.
No.503

*Saint George
and the Dragon,*
Hodges, Margaret.
No.378

Salt,
Zemach, Harve.
No.836

Sam, Bangs & Moonshine,
Ness, Evaline.
No.595

*Sam Johnson and
the Blue Ribbon Quilt,*
Ernst, Lisa Campbell.
No.253

Sarah Bishop,
O'Dell, Scott.
No.605

Sarah Morton's Day,
Waters, Kate.
No.789

Sarah, Plain and Tall,
MacLachlan, Patricia.
No.513

Saturn,
Simon, Seymour.
No.711

The Scarebird,
Fleischman, Sid.
No.266

*Scary Tales to Tell
in the Dark,*
Schwartz, Alvin, collected by.
No.686

*Science Experiments
You Can Eat,*
Cobb, Vicki.
No.158

A Sea Full of Sharks,
Maestro, Betsy.
No.514

Sea Swan,
Lasky, Kathryn.
No.452

The Seal and the Slick,
Freeman, Don.
No.282

The Search for Delicious,
Babbitt, Natalie.
No.40

A Week of Raccoons,
Whelan, Gloria.
No.796

We're Going on a Bear Hunt,
Rosen, Michael.
No.660

*Westward With
Christopher Columbus,*
Dyson, John.
No.234

The Whale Watchers' Guide,
Gardner, Robert.
No.299

*Whales, the Nomads
of the Sea,*
Sattler, Helen R.
No.680

*What Comes in 2's,
3's, & 4's?,*
Aker, Suzanne.
No.8

*What Eric Knew:
A Sebastian Barth Mystery,*
Howe, James.
No.391

*What Happened to
Patrick's Dinosaurs?,*
Carrick, Carol.
No.134

What Is a Fish,
Stratton, Barbara.
No.746

What the Mailman Brought,
Craven, Carolyn.
No.185

What's Happening to Me?,
Mayle, Peter.
No.545

*What's Inside:
The Alphabet Book,*
Kitamura, Satoshi.
No.434

What's Up There?,
Moche, Dinah.
No.580

When Autumn Comes,
Maass, Robert.
No.508

When I Am Sleepy,
Howard, Jane R.
No.389

*When I Was Young
in the Mountains,*
Rylant, Cynthia.
No.665

*When Sheep Cannot Sleep:
The Counting Book,*
Kitamura, Satoshi.
No.435

When the Sun Rose,
Berger, Barbara Helen.
No.68

Where Butterflies Grow,
Ryder, Joanne.
No.662

Where Did I Come From?,
Mayle, Peter.
No.546

*Where Do You Get
Your Ideas?,*
Asher, Sandy.
No.33

Where the Buffaloes Begin,
Baker, Olaf.
No.46

Where the Lilies Bloom,
Cleaver, Vera; Bill Cleaver.
No.153

Where the River Begins,
Locker, Thomas.
No.504

*Where Was Patrick Henry
On the 29th of May?,*

Fritz, Jean.
No.287

Whistle for Willie,
Keats, Ezra Jack.
No.421

White Bear, Ice Bear,
Ryder, Joanne.
No.663

Who Is the Beast?,
Baker, Keith.
No.44

Who Killed Cockatoo?,
Cawthorne, W. A.
No.137

*Who Lives in
the Mountains,*
Hirschi, Ron.
No.373

*Who Really Killed
Cock Robin?,*
George, Jean Craighead.
No.303

Whose Mouse Are You?,
Kraus, Robert.
No.440

*Why Do the Seasons
Change? Questions on
Nature's Rythms and Cycles,*
Whitfield, Dr. Philip;
Joyce Pope.
No.800

*Why Does My Nose Run?
(And Other Questions Kids
Ask About Their Bodies),*
Settel, Joanne; Nancy Baggett.
No.697

*Why Doesn't the Earth
Fall Up? And Other Not
Such Dumb Questions
about Motion,*
Cobb, Vickie.
No.159

*Why Mosquitoes Buzz
in People's Ears,*
Aardema, Verna.
No.3

*Why the Sun and the Moon
Live in the Sky,*
Dayrell, Elphinstone.
No.201

The Wild Swans,
Andersen, Hans Christian.
No.24

Wiley and the Hairy Man,
Bang, Molly.
No.49

*Wilfrid Gordon
McDonald Partridge,*
Fox, Mem.
No.273

*Will You Sign Here,
John Hancock?,*
Fritz, Jean.
No.288

A Wind in the Door,
L'Engle, Madeleine.
No.468

*Window on the Deep: The
Adventures of Underwater
Explorer Sylvia Earle,*
Conley, Andrea.
No.173

The Wing on a Flea,
Emberley, Ed.
No.250

*The Winged Colt
of Casa Mia,*
Byars, Betsy.
No.121

Winter,
Hirschi, Ron.
No.374

*The Witch of
Blackbird Pond,*
Speare, Elizabeth George.
No.727

The Index
of
BOOK
ABSTRACTS

A

1. Aardema, Verna.
*Bringing the Rain
to Kapiti Plain.*
Beatriz Vidal, Illustrator. New York: Scholastic, 1989. unpaged ISBN 0-590-42870-5. An East African folk tale adapted to the cadence of the classic English folk rhyme, "This is the House that Jack Built."

2. Aardema, Verna (reteller).
*Rabbit Makes a Monkey
of the Lion.*
Jerry Pinkney, Illustrator. New York: Dial, 1989. unpaged ISBN 0-8037-0298-1. Rabbit and his friends bush rat and turtle continually make a monkey of the lion as they eat the honey from his calabash tree.

3. Aardema, Verna.
*Why Mosquitoes
Buzz in People's Ears.*
Leo and Diane Dillon, Illustrators. New York: Dial, 1975. unpaged ISBN 0-8037-6088-4. A cumulative tale of a series of misunderstandings that ultimately explains why people hate mosquitoes. The illustrations show the point of view of each animal narrator.

4. Ackerman, Karen.
Song and Dance Man.
Steven Gammel, Illustrator. New York: Knopf, 1988. unpaged ISBN 0-394-99330-6. Grandpa dusts off his dusty, brown leather trunk and enraptures his grandchildren with an impromptu song and dance show in the attic.

5. Adams, Barbara Johnson.
The Go-around Dollar.
Joyce Audy Zarins, Illustrator. New York: Four Winds, 1992.
unpaged ISBN 0-02-700031-1. The story of a dollar bill and how it changes hands.

6. Ahlberg, Janet;
Allan Ahlberg.
*The Jolly Postman; or,
Other People's Letters.*
Boston: Little, Brown, 1986. unpaged ISBN 0-316-02036-2. A postman delivers letters to fairy-tale characters. Book contains facsimile letters, postcards, and envelopes.

7. Aiken, Joan.
*The Wolves of
Willoughby Chase.*
New York: Dell, 1987. 168 pages. ISBN 0-440-49603-9. Young Bonnie and cousin Sylvia mistakenly left in the care of Miss Slighcarp must overcome her and her evil accomplice to save Willoughby Chase.

8. Aker, Suzanne.
*What Comes in 2's,
3's, & 4's?*
Bernie Karlin, Illustrator. New York: Simon & Schuster, 1990. unpaged ISBN 0-671-67173-1. A delightful counting book.

9. Alexander, Lloyd.
The Book of Three.
New York: Dell, 1964. 224 pages. ISBN 0-440-40702-8. Taran longs to be a hero. By accident, he becomes caught up in a deadly chase to find an important pig before the evil Arwen does.

10. Alexander, Lloyd.
The Drackenberg Adventure.
New York: Dutton, 1988. 160 pages. ISBN 0-525-44389-4. Holly Vesper is at her best in a robust adventure set in the Drackenberg mountains.

11. Aliki.
Christmas Tree Memories.
New York: HarperCollins, 1991. unpaged ISBN 0-06-020007-3. A family sits around their Christmas tree on Christmas Eve and shares remembrances that are triggered by the ornaments and decorations.

12. Aliki.
Digging Up Dinosaurs.
New York: Crowell, 1981. 34 pages. ISBN 0-690-04714-2-9. A fascinating book that illustrates how dinosaur bones are collected and put back together for display.

13. Aliki.
Feelings.
New York: Greenwillow, 1984. unpaged ISBN 0-688-03831-X. One- and two-page vignettes of incidents that provoke feelings of every sort.

14. Aliki.
How A Book Is Made.
New York: Crowell, 1986. 32 pages. ISBN 0-690-04496-8. Text and drawings describe the various stages of making a book including all of the technical aspects that lead to its being published.

15. Aliki.
I'm Growing.
New York: HarperCollins, 1992. unpaged ISBN 0-06-020244-0. An informative look for young children at human growth and development.

16. Aliki.
*The King's Day:
Louis XIV of France.*
New York: Crowell, 1989. unpaged ISBN 0-690-04588-3. Aliki follows the king through a typical day at Versaille.

17. Aliki.
My Five Senses.
New York: Crowell, 1989. 32 pages. ISBN 0-690-56763-4. An elegantly simple presentation of the five senses and how they are used.

18. Aliki.
My Hands.
New York: HarperCollins, 1962, 1990. unpaged ISBN 0-690-04878-5. A "Let's Read and Find Out" Book that describes hands and what they can do.

19. Aliki.
*A Weed Is a Flower: The Life
of George Washington
Carver.*
New York: Simon & Schuster, 1988. unpaged ISBN 0-671-66490-5. The moving story of an inquisitive young boy, born into slavery, who grows up to be one of the greatest scientists in America.

20. Allard, Harry.
Miss Nelson is Missing.
James Marshall, Illustrator. Boston: Houghton Mifflin, 1977. 32 pages. ISBN 0-395-25296-2. The kind and sensitive Miss Nelson is absent from class one day and is replaced by the mean and cruel Miss Viola Swamp, with disastrous results to the students.

21. Alphin, Elaine Marie.
Ghost Cadet.
New York: Scholastic, 1991. 177 pages. ISBN 0-590-45244-4. Benjy Stark helps a confederate ghost regain a lost family heirloom so that the ghost can finally rest in peace.

22. Andersen, Hans Christian.
The Little Mermaid.
Katie Thamer Treherne, Illustrator. San Diego:

Harcourt Brace Jovanovich, 1989. unpaged ISBN 0-15-246320-8. Arresting watercolors illustrate and interpret a classic fairy-tale.

23. Andersen, Hans Christian. *Thumbeline.*
Lizbeth Zwerger, Illustrator. New York: Morrow, 1980. unpaged ISBN 0-688-22235-8. The classic story of a tiny girl who is born in a tulip, captured in turn by a toad, June bug, and mole, and then rescued by a swallow. In this Andersen tale there is a happy ending.

24. Andersen, Hans Christian. *The Wild Swans.*
Susan Jeffers, Illustrator. New York: Dial, 1981. unpaged ISBN 0-8037-9381-2. A young princess is sent away by her cruel stepmother and is comforted by seven mysterious swans. The princess soon finds out that the swans are really her brothers and attempts to save them from certain death.

25. Apfel, Necia. *Voyager to the Planets.*
New York: Clarion, 1991. 48 pages. ISBN 0-395-55209-5. The story of the space probes Voyager I and II and the stunning information that they have sent back to earth.

26. Archer, Jules. *They Made a Revolution: 1776.*
New York: Scholastic, 1973. 171 pages. ISBN 0-590-44763-7. Interesting biographical data on the men and women who played important roles during the revolutionary war.

27. Ardley, Neil. *The Inner Planets.*

Lexington: Schoolhouse Press, 1988. 48 pages. ISBN 0-8086-1127-5. A look at the four planets closest to the sun with interesting life-like illustrations.

28. Ardley, Neil. *The Other Planets.*
Lexington: Schoolhouse Press, 1988. 48 pages. ISBN 0-8086-1128-3. An interesting look at the five planets that are the farthest from the sun.

29. Arnold, Caroline. *Dinosaurs Down Under and Other Fossils From Australia.*
Photographs by Richard Hewett. New York: Clarion, 1990. 48 pages. ISBN 0-89919-814-7. A unique look at dinosaurs from the Australian perspective as told through an exhibit held in Los Angeles.

30. Arnold, Caroline. *Watch Out for Sharks!*
Photographs by Richard Hewett. New York: Clarion, 1991. 48 pages. ISBN 0-395-57560-5. A pictorial visit to a shark exhibit at the Natural History Museum of Los Angeles County serves as a springboard to an excellent discussion of sharks and speculation about their future.

31. Arnold, Tedd. *No Jumping on the Bed!*
New York: Dial, 1987. unpaged ISBN 0-8037-0039-3. A pattern story with a strong meter about monkeys who are not supposed to be jumping on the bed.

32. Asch, Frank. *Dear Brother.*
Vladimir Vagin, Illustrator. New York: Scholastic, 1992. unpaged ISBN 0-590-43107-2. Two brothers stay up to

read some old letters that they find in the attic and become engrossed in the lives of their great-great-grand uncle and great-great-grandfather.

33. Asher, Sandy. *Where Do You Get Your Ideas?*
Susan Hellard, Illustrator. New York: Walker, 1987. 96 pages. ISBN 0-8027-6690-0. Asher shares her own ideas about writing through small vignettes of famous writers applying their craft.

34. Avi. *The Man Who Was Poe.*
New York: Franklin Watts, 1989. 213 pages. ISBN 0-531-05833-6. Young Edmund must turn to a mysterious stranger, who goes by the name Dupin, for help in locating his missing mother and sister.

35. Avi. *Something Upstairs: A Tale of Ghosts.*
New York: Orchard, 1988. 116 pages. ISBN 0-531-05782-8. Kenny makes a mysterious discovery in the attic of his new home that leads to a trip back in time to solve a murder.

36. Aylesworth, Jim. *Old Black Fly.*
Stephen Gammell, Illustrator. New York: Henry Holt, 1992. unpaged ISBN 0-8050-1401-2. Gammell at his best in a rhythmic romp through the alphabet by an old black fly that won't stop buzzing around.

B

37. Babbitt, Natalie. *The Devil's Other Storybook.*
New York: Farrar, Straus and

Giroux, 1987. 112 pages. ISBN 0-374-31767-4. A sequel to *The Devil's Story Book.*

38. Babbitt, Natalie. *The Devil's Storybook.*
New York: Farrar, Straus and Giroux, 1974. 102 pages. ISBN 0-374-31770-4. Short stories in which the devil takes the role of trickster.

39. Babbitt, Natalie. *The Eyes of the Amaryllis.*
New York: Farrar, Straus and Giroux, 1977. 128 pages. ISBN 0-374-32241-4. A young girl helps her grandmother search the shoreline for a sign from her grandfather. There is a dramatic confrontation between the sea and the grandmother. Great example of personification.

40. Babbitt, Natalie. *The Search for Delicious.*
New York: Farrar, Straus and Giroux, 1969. 176 pages. ISBN 0-374-46536-3. The search is for the perfect description of delicious. A wonderful exploration of simile.

41. Babbitt, Natalie. *The Something.*
New York: Farrar, Straus and Giroux, 1970. 40 pages. ISBN 0-374-37137-7. A little monster is frightened by the boy in his dreams. Compare to *There's a Nightmare in My Closet.*

42. Babbitt, Natalie. *Tuck Everlasting.*
New York: Farrar, Straus and Giroux, 1975. 160 pages ISBN 0-374-48009-5. A young girl is forced to deal with the issues of immortality and greed when she learns of a

spring at the center of the world with the power to make one live forever.

43. Baer, Edith.
This Is the Way We Go to School.
Steve Bjorkman, Illustrator. New York: Scholastic, 1990. unpaged ISBN 0-590-43161-7. A look at the variety of methods that students around the world use to get to school.

44. Baker, Keith.
Who Is the Beast?
San Diego: Harcourt Brace Jovanovich, 1980. unpaged ISBN 0-15296057-0. The tiger, amazed that all the animals are fleeing from him, shows them how similar he and they really are.

45. Baker, Lucy.
Life in the Rainforest.
New York: Franklin Watts, 1990. 32 pages. ISBN 0-531-10983-6. A user-friendly look at the animals, people, and plants that inhabit a tropical rainforest. Excellent illustrations and photos accompany the text, and a glossary is included.

46. Baker, Olaf.
Where the Buffaloes Begin.
Stephen Gammell, Illustrator. New York: Warne, 1981. unpaged ISBN 0-7232-6195-4. Little Wolf, drawn by the irresistible desire to discover the lake that gives birth to the buffalo, becomes part of a stampede that saves his village from their enemies.

47. Baker, Rachel.
The First Woman Doctor.
New York: Scholastic, 1987. 188 pages. ISBN 0-590-40933-6. The absorbing story of Elizabeth Blackwell and her fight to become a doctor.

48. Bang, Molly.
The Paper Crane.
New York: Greenwillow, 1985. unpaged ISBN 0-688-04109-4. Paper crane brings good luck to its owner.

49. Bang, Molly.
Wiley and the Hairy Man.
New York: Macmillan, 1976. unpaged ISBN 0-02-708370-5. Wiley and his mother must trick Hairy Man three times to keep him from getting Wiley. "Ready to Read" book; adapted from a folk tale originally recorded as part of the Federal Writers' Project.

50. Banks, Lynne Reid.
The Fairy Rebel.
New York: Doubleday, 1985. 118 pages. ISBN 0-385-24483-5. A fairy tale set in modern times about a woman's wish to have a baby; the wish is granted by a fairy who offends the powerful fairy queen.

51. Banks, Lynne Reid.
The Farthest-Away Mountain.
New York: Avon, 1976. 130 pages. ISBN 0-380-71303-9. Dakin is called by the mountain to undertake a dangerous journey that might save the world as she knows it.

52. Barnstone, Aliki.
The Real Tin Flower.
Paul Giovanopoulos, Illustrator. New York: Crowell, 1968. 54 pages. ISBN TK. The striking verse of a teenage poet accompanied by pen and ink illustrations.

53. Barracca, Debra and Sal.
The Adventures of Taxi Dog.
Mark Buehner, Illustrator. New York: Dial, 1990. unpaged ISBN 0-8037-0671-

5. A tale of a dog adopted by a taxi driver told in strong verse form.

54. Barrett, Norman.
Volcanoes.
New York: Franklin Watts, 1989. 32 pages. ISBN 0-531-10841-4. Many photos and diagrams that explain why and where volcanoes occur

55. Barth, Edna.
Lilies, Rabbits, and Painted Eggs.
Ursula Arndt, Illustrator. New York: Houghton Mifflin, 1970. 64 pages. ISBN 0-395-28844-4. A thorough explanation of the Easter holiday.

56. Barth, Edna.
Turkeys, Pilgrims, and Indian Corn.
Ursula Arndt, Illustrator. New York: Houghton Mifflin, 1975. 96 pages. ISBN 0-395-28846-0. A thorough explanation of our Thanksgiving holiday.

57. Barth, Edna.
Witches, Pumpkins, and Grinning Ghosts.
Ursula Arndt, Illustrator. New York: Houghton Mifflin, 1972. 96 pages. ISBN 0-395-28847-9. A thorough explanation of the Halloween holiday.

58. Base, Graeme.
Animalia.
New York: Harry N. Abrams, 1986. unpaged ISBN 0-8109-1868-4. A wild collection of illustrations depicting strange, alliterative happenings in this version of an alphabet book.

59. Base, Graeme.
The Eleventh Hour.
New York: Scholastic, 1989. unpaged ISBN 0-590-44789-

0. Horace the Elephant turns eleven and decides to have a party for eleven people who will play eleven games before the banquet at the eleventh hour. Something goes wrong, the food disappears and the reader is invited to solve the mystery.

60. Bates, Robin; Cheryl Simon.
The Dinosaurs and the Dark Star.
Jennifer Dewey, Illustrator. New York: Macmillan, 1985. 48 pages. ISBN 0-02-708340-3. An overview of dinosaur paleontology that leads up to a theory of dinosaur extinction, linking it to periodic bombardment of the earth by comets dislodged by an unseen companion star.

61. Bauer, Marion Dane.
On My Honor.
New York: Dell, 1987. 90 pages. ISBN 0-440-46633-4. Joel goes along with his friend Tony's wild idea and learns the responsibility that results from his behavior.

62. Bayer, Jane.
A, My Name Is Alice.
Steven Kellogg, Illustrator. New York: Dial, 1984. unpaged ISBN 0-8037-0124-1. An alphabet book based on a playground chant where names and occupations are based on alphabet letters.

63. Baylor, Byrd.
If You Are a Hunter of Fossils.
Peter Parnall, Illustrator. New York: Scribner, 1980. unpaged ISBN 0-684-16419-1. A fossil hunter imagines what Texas was like during the times of the fossils he hunts.

64. Bell, Anthea adapted by.
Swan Lake.
Natlick, MA: Picture Book Studio, 1986. unpaged ISBN 0-88708-028-6. A pictorial version of Swan Lake.

65. Bellairs, John.
The Spell of the Sorcerer's Skull.
New York: Dial, 1985. 170 pages. ISBN 0-8037-0122-5. Young Johnny Dixon and his pal Fergie hook up with Father Higgins to help Professor Childermass overcome a century-old curse.

66. Bender, Lionel.
Fish to Reptiles.
New York: Franklin Watts, 1988. 36 pages. ISBN 0-531-17093-4. An informative look at fish, amphibians, and reptiles that is well illustrated.

67. Benjamin, Carol Lea.
Writing for Kids.
New York: Harper, 1985. 96 pages. ISBN 0-690-04490-9. Benjamin provides insights into writing for people who want to write for children, as well as children who want to write.

68. Berger, Barbara Helen.
When the Sun Rose.
New York: Putnam, 1986. unpaged ISBN 0-399-21360-0. A young girl, visited by an imaginary friend and her lion, spends the day playing with them.

69. Berger, Melvin.
Seasons.
Ron Jones, Illustrator. New York: Doubleday, 1990. 45 pages. ISBN 0-385-24877-6. A comprehensive look at the facts and ancient myths surrounding the seasons and their effect on man.

70. Bierhorst, John.
Doctor Coyote: A Native American Aesop's Fables.
Wendy Watson, Illustrator. New York: Macmillan, 1987. unpaged. ISBN 0-02-709780-3. Retellings of Aesop's Fables as they had been interpreted by the Aztecs. The major characters become the typical Native American tricksters such as Coyote and Puma.

71. Bierhorst, John, edited by.
In the Trail of the Wind: American Indian Poems and Ritual Orations.
New York: Farrar, Straus and Giroux, 1971. 224 pages. ISBN 0-374-33640-7. A collection of chants, songs, and prayers from a variety of North and South American Natives.

72. Bierhorst, John.
The Ring in the Prairie. Leo and Diane Dillon, Illustrators. New York: Dial, 1970. unpaged ISBN 0-8037-7455-9. This Shawnee legend, first collected by Schoolcraft, explains how a hunter captures a star maiden who becomes his wife. The legend also tells how the star people became animals and birds.

73. Bisel, Sara.
The Secrets of Vesuvius.
New York: Scholastic, 1990. 64 pages. ISBN 0-59043851-4. A noted anthropologist reconstructs life in the town of Herculaneum, which was destroyed in A.D. 79 by the eruption of Mount Vesuvius.

74. Bishop, Gavin (reteller).
The Three Little Pigs.
Illustrator. New York: Scholastic, 1989. unpaged ISBN 0-590-43358-X. A traditional three pigs tale that

is well illustrated with a more contemporary look and feel.

75. Bjork, Christina Anderson , Lena.
Linnea's Windowsill Garden.
Stockholm, Sweden: Farrar, Straus and Giroux, 1988. 60 pages. ISBN 9-12-959064-7. A tour of an indoor garden that is stuffed full of information and projects for students to do.

76. Blocksma, Mary.
Apple Tree! Apple Tree!
Sandra Cox Kalthoff, Illustrator. Chicago: Children's Press, 1983. 24 pages. ISBN 0-516-01584-2. An apple tree that is a friend to all would like its own true friend and is helped by a friendly worm.

77. Blos, Joan.
Brothers of the Heart.
New York: Macmillan, 1985. 158 pages. ISBN 0-684-18452-4. Shem, crippled from birth, believes that he will not survive the cold Michigan winter until a mysterious Mary Goodhue teaches him about himself and survival.

78. Blos, Joan.
A Gathering of Days.
New York: Scribner, 1979. 144 pages. ISBN 0-684-16340-3. A young girl's journal entries of her life in pre-Civil War New England.

79. Blos, Joan.
The Heroine of the Titanic: A Tale Both True and Otherwise of the Life of Molly Brown.
Tennessee Dixon, Illustrator. New York: Morrow, 1991. unpaged. ISBN 0-688-07546-0. A poetic account of a remarkable American woman,

Molly Brown, who survived the Titanic.

80. Blos, Joan.
Old Henry.
Stephen Gammell, Illustrator. New York: Morrow, 1987. unpaged ISBN 0-688-06400-0. Henry's neighbors, angry that he will not fix up his old beat-up house, drive him out only to find that they really miss him.

81. Bodsworth, Nan.
A Nice Walk in the Jungle.
Victoria, Australia: Viking Kestrel, 1989. unpaged ISBN 0-670-82476-3. A class nature study walk comes to a surprising ending as a hungry, pink boa constrictor eats each member one by one.

82. Bond, Nancy.
A String in the Harp.
New York: Atheneum, 1976. 384 pages. ISBN 0-689-50036-8. A young boy, trying to adjust to living with his father in Wales, finds a harp key that belonged to the legendary bard, Talesin. When he wears the key he is transported back in time to the time of Talesin.

83. Booth, David.
'Til All the Stars Have Fallen: A Collection of Poems for Children.
Dady MacDonald Denton, Illustrator. New York: Viking, 1989. 93 pages. ISBN 0-670-83272-3. This collection contains a wide range of poems, many by Canadian poets. Don't skip the introduction—it's great information for readers, both students and teachers.

84. Borden, Louise.
Caps, Hats, Socks, and Mittens. Lillian Hoban,

Illustrator. New York: Scholastic, 1989. unpaged ISBN 0-590-41257-4. A celebration of sights, smells, and sensations of the seasons.

85. Branley, Franklyn M. *Dinosaurs, Asteroids, and Superstars: Why the Dinosaurs Disappeared.* Jean Zallinger, Illustrator. New York: Crowell, 1982. 84 pages. ISBN 0-690-04482-8. A look at several theories as to why dinosaurs became extinct. Includes hypotheses involving continental drift, encounters with an asteroid, a nearby supernova, and a ring of space debris.

86. Branley, Franklyn M. *Sunshine Makes the Seasons.* Shelly Freshman, Illustrator. New York: Crowell, 1974. 34 pages. ISBN 0-690-00437-0. An interesting scientific explanation of the seasons and their effect on us.

87. Brett, Jan (reteller). *Beauty and the Beast.* New York: Clarion, 1989. unpaged ISBN 0-395-55702-X. A cleverly illustrated version of an old classic.

88. Brett, Jan. *Goldilocks and the Three Bears.* New York: Putnam, 1987. unpaged ISBN 0-396-08925-9. This retelling is accompanied by wonderful Slavic bears and picture borders that predict the next scene.

89. Brett, Jan. *The Mitten.* New York: Putnam, 1989. unpaged ISBN 0-399-21920-X. A retelling of the Ukrainian folk tale that is accompanied by wonderfully costumed

characters and picture borders that anticipate the next animal character.

90. Briggs, Raymond. *Father Christmas.* New York: Coward, 1973. unpaged ISBN 0-698-20272-4. A unique look at Christmas Eve through the eyes of Santa himself that is told in comic-strip style illustrations

91. Briggs, Raymond. *Jim and the Beanstalk.* New York: Putnam, 1970. unpaged ISBN 0-698-20641-X. Jim visits the son of Jack's giant in a wonderful sequel.

92. Briggs, Raymond. *The Snowman.* New York: Random, 1978. unpaged ISBN 0-394-88466-3. Late in the night a snowman that a young boy created comes alive and they spend the rest of the night on a fantastic adventure.

93. Bright, M. *The Ozone Layer.* James Macdonald, Illustrator. New York: Gloucester Press, 1991. 32 pages. ISBN 0-531-17302-X. A politically balanced explanation of the ozone layer and its effect on the earth's environment.

94. Brisson, Pat. *Your Best Friend, Kate.* Rick Brown, Illustrator. Scarsdale: Bradbury Press, 1989. unpaged ISBN 0-02-714350-3. Kate leaves to go on a trip with her family and faithfully mails letters to her best friend Lucy describing her adventures.

95. Brooke, William J. *A Telling of the Tales: Five Stories.* Richard Egielski, Illustrator.

New York: Harper & Row, 1990. 132 pages. ISBN 0-06-020688-8. Brooke twists familiar tales (Sleeping Beauty, Cinderella, Paul Bunyan and Johnny Appleseed, John Henry and Jack and the Beanstalk) giving them contemporary themes. The results are a bit overwritten, but serve as examples of what can happen when setting or point of view is changed.

96. Brown, Jeff. *Flat Stanley.* Tomi Ungerer, Illustrator. New York: Harper, 1964. unpaged ISBN 0-06-020681-0. Adventures of a one-half inch boy, flattened by a bulletin board.

97. Brown, Marc. *Arthur's Tooth: An Arthur Adventure.* Boston: Atlantic Monthly, 1985. unpaged ISBN 0-87113-006-8. Arthur hasn't lost a tooth while everyone else in his class has.

98. Brown, Ruth. *The World That Jack Built.* New York: Dutton, 1991. unpaged ISBN 0-525-44635-4. A play on "This is the House That Jack Built" with an ecological twist.

99. Bryan, Ashley. *The Cat's Purr.* New York: Atheneum, 1985. 44 pages. ISBN 0-689-31086-2. A pourquoi tale from the West Indies that tells how cats got their purr and why they eat rats. This retelling captures the rhythm and the sounds of the storyteller.

100. Bryan, Ashley. *Lion and the Ostrich Chicks & Other African Folk Tales.*

New York: Atheneum, 1986. 87 pages. ISBN 0-689-31311-X. Four African folk tales retold by Bryan in a strong, rhythmic style.

101. Bryan, Ashley. *Turtle Knows Your Name.* New York: Atheneum, 1989. unpaged ISBN 0-689-31578-3. A wonderful, rhythmic telling of an African folk tale involving names and a warm, loving relationship.

102. Budbill, David. *Bones on Black Spruce Mountain.* New York: Bantam, 1978. 126 pages. ISBN 0-553-15596-2. Seth and Daniel hike through the wilderness on a four- or five-day camp-out and discover the grisly cause of the screams from Black Spruce Mountain.

103. Budbill, David. *Snowshoe Trek to Otter River.* New York: Bantam, 1984. 83 pages. ISBN 0-553-15469-9. Three separate short stories about two boys and their adventures camping outdoors.

104. Buff, Mary; Conrad Buff. *The Apple and the Arrow.* New York: Scholastic, 1951. 80 pages. ISBN 0-590-43328-8. A retelling of the history and events surrounding the aborted jailing of Swiss hero William Tell.

105. Bulla, Clyde Robert. *Pocahontas and the Strangers.* New York: Scholastic, 1971. 176 pages. ISBN 0-590-41711-8. The story of a brave young woman and her life during colonial times.

106. Bunting, Eve.
Fly Away Home.
Ronald Himler, Illustrator.
New York: Clarion, 1992.
unpaged ISBN 0-395-55962-6. A young boy who lives with his father in an airport trying to survive unnoticed hopes that he too will be able to fly away home one day like a little bird.

107. Bunting, Eve.
Terrible Things.
Stephen Gammell, Illustrator.
Philadelphia: The Jewish Publication Society, 1989, 1980. unpaged ISBN 0-8276-0325-8. An allegorical treatment of what happens if everyone lets others suffer persecution.

108. Bunting, Eve.
The Wall.
New York: Clarion, 1990.
ISBN 0-395-51588-2. A boy and his father visit the Vietnam Memorial to find his grandfather's name.

109. Bunting, Eve.
The Wednesday Surprise.
Donald Carrick, Illustrator.
New York: Clarion, 1989.
unpaged ISBN 0-395-54776-8. The story of a young girl helping her grandmother learn to read

110. Burch, Robert.
Ida Early Comes over the Mountain. New York: Penguin, 1980. 152 pages.
ISBN 0-670-39169-7. Ida Early is a woman who can do anything, but what she does best is make a motherless family feel whole and warm.

111. Burningham, John.
Hey! Get Off Our Train.
New York: Crown, 1989.
unpaged ISBN 0-517-57638-4. A young boy dreams of a

magical train ride rescuing endangered animals. Several of Burningham's illustrations use crayon resist.

112. Burningham, John.
Mr. Gumpy's Outing.
New York: Henry Holt, 1971.
unpaged ISBN 0-8050-0708-3. Mr. Gumpy takes all his animal friends for a ride.

113. Burns, Marilyn.
The I Hate Mathematics! Book.
Martha Weston, Illustrator.
Boston: Little, Brown, 1975.
127 pages. ISBN 0-316-11745-5. A series of gags, games, and experiments that will excite even the most math-phobic student.

114. Burton, Virginia Lee.
Katy and the Big Snow.
New York: Houghton Mifflin, 1973. unpaged ISBN 0-395-18155-0. Katy is a snow plow that clears the way through a snow storm.

115. Burton, Virginia Lee.
The Little House.
Boston: Houghton Mifflin, 1978. unpaged ISBN 0-395-18156-9. This is a great social studies lesson in how communities grow and change.

116. Burton, Virginia Lee.
Mike Mulligan and His Steam Shovel.
Boston: Houghton Mifflin, 1939. unpaged ISBN 0-395-06681-6. Mike and his steam shovel, Mary Anne, dig out the basement for the town hall. It's so deep that folks decide to turn Mary Anne into the furnace for the new building.

117. Butler, Beverly.
Ghost Cat.

New York: Scholastic, 1984.
189 pages. ISBN 0-590-41837-8. While Annabel is spending the summer with her strange cousins, she is haunted by a cat that appears and disappears.

118. Butterworth, Nick.
One Snowy Night.
Boston: Little, Brown, 1989.
unpaged ISBN 0-316-11918-0. Percy the park keeper opens his warm house to the park animals on a cold winter night with heartwarming results.

119. Byars, Betsy.
The Blossoms Meet the Vulture Lady.
New York: Delacourt, 1987.
134 pages. ISBN 0-385-29485-9. A humorous story of a young boy and his determination to solve an important mystery concerning a homeless old lady.

120. Byars, Betsy.
The Midnight Fox.
New York: Penguin, 1968.
159 pages. ISBN 0-670-47473-8. A black fox becomes very important to Tom during his two-month visit to his aunt and uncle's farm.

121. Byars, Betsy.
The Winged Colt of Casa Mia.
Richard Cuffari, Illustrator.
New York: Penguin, 1973.
128 pages. ISBN 0-670-77318-2. A magical colt that can fly helps a lonely young boy and an angry uncle become friends and come to terms with their emotions.

C

122. Calhoun, Mary.
Cross-Country Cat. Erick Ingraham, Illustrator. New York: Morrow, 1979. unpaged

ISBN 0-688-22186-6. Told from the Siamese cat's point of view, Henry is mistakenly left behind at the ski lodge and must improvise to get back home.

123. Cameron, Ann.
The Stories Julian Tells.
Ann Strugnell, Illustrator.
New York: Pantheon, 1981.
96 pages. ISBN 0-394-94301-5. Family stories about Julian and his brother.

124. Campbell, Joanna.
A Horse Called Wonder.
New York: Harper, 1991. 184 pages. ISBN 0-06-106102-4. Ashleigh fights to save the life of a young filly whom others have given up for dead.

125. Carle, Eric selected by.
Animals Animals.
Eric Carle, Illustrator. New York: Scholastic, 1991. 93 pages. ISBN 0-590-43640-6. An eclectic collection of poetry that will stir student imaginations.

126. Carle, Eric.
The Grouchy Ladybug.
New York: Harper & Row, 1977. unpaged ISBN 0-690-01392-2. A day in the life of a make-believe ladybug.

127. Carle, Eric.
Have You Seen My Cat?
New York: Picture Book Studio, 1987. unpaged ISBN 0-88708-054-5. A predictable story with great illustrations.

128. Carle, Eric.
Pancakes, Pancakes!
New York: Picture Book Studio, 1990. unpaged ISBN 0-88708-120-7. Jack wants a pancake for breakfast and must assemble all of the ingredients before his mother will make it. An excellent

look at how to make real pancakes from scratch.

129. Carle, Eric (reteller). *Twelve Tales from Aesop.* New York: Philomel, 1980. 30 pages. ISBN 0-399-61163-0. Twelve fables that include "The Fox and the Crane" and "The Lion and the Mouse."

130. Carle, Eric. *The Very Busy Spider.* New York: Philomel, 1984. unpaged ISBN 0-399-21166-7. A spider spins a web that you can feel as well as see.

131. Carle, Eric. *The Very Hungry Caterpillar.* New York: Putnam, 1981. ISBN 0-399-21933-1. Unique illustrations and text describe the life cycle of a caterpillar.

132. Carlstrom, Nancy White. *Jesse Bear, What Will You Wear?* Bruce Degen, Illustrator. New York: Macmillan, 1986. unpaged ISBN 0-02-717350-X. Exuberant illustrations complement a fun-filled day with Jesse.

133. Carrick, Carol. *Patrick's Dinosaurs.* Donald Carrick, Illustrator. New York: Clarion, 1983. unpaged ISBN 0-89919-189-4. On a trip to the zoo, Patrick imagines that all the dinosaurs his older brother talks about are real and all around him.

134. Carrick, Carol. *What Happened to Patrick's Dinosaurs?* Donald Carrick, Illustrator. New York: Clarion, 1986. unpaged ISBN 0-89919-406-0. Rejecting his brother's scientific explanations, young Patrick weaves his own, more

imaginative theory of where and why dinosaurs disappeared from the earth.

135. *Cars.* New York: Aladdin, 1991. 21 pages. ISBN 0-689-71517-X. A look at all kind of cars for young readers.

136. Cauley, Lorinda Bryan. *Goldilocks and the Three Bears.* New York: Putnam, 1981. unpaged ISBN 0-399-20795. An interesting retelling of a familiar story.

137. Cawthorne, W. A. *Who Killed Cockatoo?* Rodney McRae, Illustrator. New York: Farrar, Straus and Giroux, 1989. ISBN 0-374-38395-2. The Australian version of a classic English nursery rhyme.

138. Cazet, Denys. *"I'm Not Sleepy."* New York: Orchard, 1992. unpaged ISBN 0-531-05898-0. A father's fantastic bedtime story helps his young son to fall into a happy sleep.

139. Chall, Marsha Wilson. *Up North at the Cabin.* Steve Johnson, Illustrator. New York: Lothrop, 1992. unpaged ISBN 0-688-09732-4. The magic and spirit of a special summer vacation cabin is captured for young readers.

140. Challand, Helen. *Earthquakes.* Chicago: Children's Press, 1982. 48 pages. ISBN 0-516-01636-9. Accurate and up-to-date information combining photos and diagrams with easy-to-read text.

141. Chase, Richard. *Grandfather Tales: American-English Folk Tales.* Berkeley Williams, Jr., Illustrator. Boston: Houghton Mifflin, 1948. 240 pages. ISBN 0-395-06692-1. Appalachian versions of some well-known and not so well known tales. A great read-aloud.

142. Chase, Richard. *Jack and the Three Sillies.* Joshua Tolford, Illustrator. Boston: Houghton Mifflin, 1950. unpaged ISBN 0-395-19100-9. A humorous American version of a Jack story from England; Jack returns home with a stone after leaving for town with a cow; his wife leaves him but returns when she sees three men as silly as Jack.

143. Chase, Richard. *The Jack Tales.* Berkeley Williams, Jr., Illustrator. Boston: Houghton Mifflin, 1943. 201 pages. ISBN TK A collection of eighteen folk tales from southern Appalachia about Jack and his two brothers, Will and Tom.

144. Cherry, Lynne. *The Great Kapok Tree.* San Diego: Harcourt Brace Jovanovich, 1990. unpaged ISBN 0-15-200520-X. While a young man is asleep, the rain forest comes alive in his dreams, changing his attitudes about the forest forever.

145. Cherry, Lynne. *A River Ran Wild.* Lynne Cherry, San Diego: Harcourt Brace Jovanovich, 1992. unpaged ISBN 0-15200542-0. An uncompromising look at a

river in Massachusetts that came back from the dead because its people cared enough about it.

146. Christelow, Eileen. *Five Little Monkeys Jumping on the Bed.* New York: Clarion, 1989. Unpaged ISBN 0-89919-769-8. A repeating pattern in the tradition of "Ten Little Indians."

147. Clapp, Patricia. *Constance, The Story of Early Plymouth.* New York: Puffin, 1986. 255 pages. ISBN 0-14-032030-X. The story of Constance Hopkins, an original member of Plymouth Colony, as told through her diary.

148. Clark, Margaret Goff. *Freedom Crossing.* New York: Scholastic, 1980. 148 pages. ISBN 0-590-42418-1. A young girl gets caught up, reluctantly, in helping slaves escape from the South.

149. Clavell, James. *The Children's Story.* New York: Dell, 1963, 1981. 96 pages. ISBN 0-440-20468-2. For use with older children, preferably in a read-aloud situation, this novelette tells of a classroom after the country has been defeated in a war.

150. Clavell, James. *Thrump-O-Moto.* New York: Delacorte, 1986. 89 pages. ISBN 0-385-29504-9. Seven-year-old Patricia hooks up with a zany Japanese wizard, and ends up in Japan meeting his family and the evil Nurk-u before she goes on a quest to find a cure for her disability.

151. Claverie, Jean (reteller). *The Three Little Pigs.* New York: North-South Books, 1989. unpaged ISBN 1-55858-004-2. An interesting twist to a classic tale.

152. Cleary, Beverly. *Dear Mr. Henshaw.* New York: Morrow, 1983. 134 pages. ISBN 0-688-02405-X. Leigh Botts writes to an author, Randsom Henshaw, and continues a dialogue with him through his diary.

153. Cleaver, Vera; Bill Cleaver. *Where the Lilies Bloom.* Jim Spanfeller, Illustrator. New York: Harper, 1969. 175 pages. ISBN 0-397-31111-7. Fourteen-year-old Mary Call Luther struggles to keep her family together after her father dies. The Cleavers provide glimpses into the life of sharecroppers and one Appalachian girl's determination to succeed.

154. Clements, Bruce. *The Treasure of Plunderell Manor.* New York: Farrar, Straus and Giroux, 1987. 180 pages. ISBN 0-374-37746-4. Young Laurel, enlisted to spy on her mistress so that she might help an evil lord and lady steal the missing treasure, turns the tables on them with the help of friends.

155. Climo, Shirley. *The Egyptian Cinderella.* Ruth Heller, Illustrator. New York: Crowell, 1989. unpaged ISBN 0-690-04822-X. A Greek slave, Rhodopis, is picked on by her peers but is rewarded for her dancing with a gift of slippers. One of the slippers is taken by a falcon

and dropped into the lap of the pharaoh. The rest is quite predictable.

156. Climo, Shirley. *Someone Saw A Spider: Spider Facts and Folktales.* Dirk Zimmer, Illustrator. New York: Crowell, 1985. 133 pages. ISBN 0-690-04435-6. Stories and information about spiders from around the world.

157. Cobb, Vicki. *Chemically Active! Experiments That You Can Do at Home.* New York: Harper, 1985. 160 pages. ISBN 0-397-32080-9. Plenty of chemical experiments that can safely be conducted at home with easy-to-find ingredients.

158. Cobb, Vicki. *Science Experiments You Can Eat.* Peter Lippman, Illustrator. New York: Harper, 1972. 126 pages. ISBN 0-397-31179-6. Plenty of experiments that illustrate the laws of chemistry and can be eaten afterward.

159. Cobb, Vicki. *Why Doesn't the Earth Fall Up? And Other Not Such Dumb Questions about Motion.* Ted Enick, Illustrator. New York: Lodestar, 1988. 40 pages. ISBN 0-525-67253-2. A series of questions and answers to some of the more perplexing questions about the physical laws of our earth.

160. Cobb, Vicki; Kathy Darling. *Bet You Can't: Science Impossibilities to Fool You.* Martha Weston, Illustrator. New York: Harper, 1980. 128 pages. ISBN 0-688-41905-4. A variety of tricks and

experiments for young scientists. The companion book is *Bet You Can.*

161. Coerr, Eleanor. *Sadako and the Thousand Paper Cranes.* New York: Putnam, 1977. 64 pages. ISBN 0-399-20520-9. The story of Sadako, who contracts leukemia as a result of the atomic bomb drop on Hiroshima.

162. Cohen, Caron Lee. *The Mud Pony: A Traditional Skidi Pawnee Tale.* Shonto Begay, Illustrator. New York: Scholastic, 1988. unpaged ISBN 0-590-41525-5. A young Indian boy becomes a leader of his people through the guidance of a powerful spirit.

163. Cohen, Daniel. *Southern Fried Rat and Other Gruesome Tales.* Peggy Brier, Illustrator. Boston: Houghton Mifflin, 1983. unpaged ISBN 0-87131-400-2. Not for the fainthearted, a collection of gruesome modern American folk tales.

164. Cohlene, Terri. *Little Firefly.* Charles Reasoner, Illustrator. Mahwah: Watermall Press, 1990. 48 pages. ISBN 0-8167-2363-X. A unique combination of an Algonquian legend of a young maiden, ill-treated by her sisters, who marries The Invisible One, with information about the Algonquian people.

165. Cole, Joanna. *Bony-Legs.* Dirk Zimmer, Illustrator. New York: Macmillan, 1983. 48 pages. ISBN 0-02-722970-X. Stories about Baba Yaga, the

Russian witch, in an easy-reader format.

166. Cole, Joanna. *Cut, Breaks, Bruises, and Burns: How Your Body Heals.* True Kelley, Illustrator. New York: Crowell, 1985. 48 pages. ISBN 0-690-04437-2. A book designed in a question-answer format. Most answers are short (about a page) but a few are much longer (How do cuts heal?).

167. Cole, Joanna. *The Magic School Bus Inside the Earth.* Bruce Degen, Illustrator. New York: Scholastic, 1987. unpaged ISBN 0-590-40760-0. A wild journey into earth science, this book follows the format of a fantastic voyage and gives.

real science information.

168. Cole, Joanna. *The Magic School Bus Inside the Human Body.* Bruce Degen, Illustrator. New York: Scholastic, 1988. unpaged ISBN 0-590-41426-7. The Magic School Bus combines information about the body while telling a funny story. The combination of story, information, and illustrations is quite successful.

169. Cole, Joanna. *The Magic School Bus Lost in the Solar System.* Bruce Degen, Illustrator. New York: Scholastic, 1990. unpaged ISBN 0-590-41428-3. Yet another voyage of this marvelous school bus takes its passengers on a fun and fact-filled field trip into space.

170. Cole, Joanna.
My Puppy Is Born.
Photographs by Margaret Miller. New York: Scholastic, 1981. unpaged ISBN 0-590-62023-1. Graphic photographs of the birth and first eight weeks of a Norfolk terrier.

171. Cole, Joanna; Philip Cole.
Big Goof and Little Goof.
M.K. Brown, Illustrator. New York: Scholastic, 1989. unpaged ISBN 0-590-41591-3. Three rib-tickling stories about a couple of real goofy guys.

172. Coleridge, Ann.
The Friends of Emily Culpepper.
Roland Harvey, Illustrator. New York: Putnam, 1983. unpaged ISBN 0-399-21449-6. Emily is an old lady who likes to have her friends around all the time, so she shrinks them and keeps them in jars.

173. Conley, Andrea.
Window on the Deep: The Adventures of Underwater Explorer Sylvia Earle.
New York: Franklin Watts, 1991. 41 pages. ISBN 0-531-11119-9. An engaging account of Sylvia Earle and her exploration of the world's oceans.

174. Conrad, Pam.
Prairie Songs.
New York: Harper & Row, 1985. 176 pages. ISBN 0-06-21336-1. A realistic treatment of the hardships of life on the frontier prairie. The story tells of the upper-class bride of the local doctor trying to adjust to the hardships of the frontier. She does not succeed.

175. Conrad, Pam.
Stonewords.
New York: Harper & Row, 1990. 130 pages. ISBN 0-06-440354-8. Zoe must travel back in time to save her friend Zoe Louise from certain death.

176. Cooney, Barbara.
Miss Rumphius.
New York: Penguin, 1982. unpaged ISBN 0-670-47958-6. A story of how a woman fulfilled all her dreams including her grandfather's charge that she make the world more beautiful.

177. Cooper, Susan.
The Dark Is Rising.
New York: Macmillan, 1973. ISBN 0-689-30317-3. The first book in the *Dark is Rising* sequence in which Will Stanton, his mysterious friend Merriman, and other Old Ones battle to overthrow the evil forces of Dark. *Greenwitch, Grey King,* and *Silver on the Tree* follow.

178. Cooper, Susan.
Dawn of Fear.
San Diego: Harcourt Brace Jovanovich, 1988. 224 pages. ISBN 0-15-266201-4. A group of boys, faced with the death of a friend during a bombing raid, must learn to go on with life in World War II England.

179. Cooper, Susan.
Over Sea, Under Stone.
San Diego: Harcourt Brace Jovanovich, 1966. 256 pages. ISBN 0-15-259034-X. Three young children spend a holiday with their Uncle Merry and become embroiled in a quest to locate the stolen Holy Grail. Considered a prequel to the Dark is Rising sequence.

180. Cooper, Susan (reteller).
The Silver Cow: A Welsh Tale.
Warwick Hutton, Illustrator. New York: Macmillan, 1983. unpaged ISBN 0-689-50236-2. A retelling of the story of an old greedy farmer that inherits a cow from his son.

181. Corbett, Scott.
The Disappearing Dog Trick.
Paul Galdone, Illustrator. New York: Scholastic, 1963. 108 pages. ISBN 0-590-40973-5. Kirby uses his chemistry set to get himself and his faithful pet into trouble.

182. Coville, Bruce.
Jeremy Thatcher, Dragon Hatcher.
New York: Simon & Schuster, 1991. 148 pages. ISBN 0-671-74782-7. Jeremy stumbles upon an odd magic shop while trying to avoid two bullies and ends up raising a baby dragon!

183. Cowcher, Helen.
Antarctica.
New York: Farrar, Straus and Giroux, year 1991, 32 pages. ISBN 0-374-40371-6. A beautiful look at the last uncivilized frontier in the world.

184. Cowcher, Helen.
Rain Forest.
New York: Farrar, Straus and Giroux, 1988. 32 pages. ISBN 0-374-46190-2. A fresh look at a very important part of the earth's ecosystem.

185. Craven, Carolyn.
What the Mailman Brought.
Tomie de Paola, Illustrator. New York: Putnam, 1987. unpaged ISBN 0-399-21290-6. Young William is bored and sick, missing his first week in a new school, until he begins to receive unusual packages from a mysterious mailman.

186. Crews, Donald.
Freight Train.
New York: Greenwillow, 1978. unpaged ISBN 0-688-80165-1. Using terrific illustrations, Crews combines the names of the cars and the names of the colors.

187. Crews, Donald.
Ten Black Dots.
New York: Greenwillow, 1986. unpaged ISBN 0-688-80165-X. A revised and redesigned story that encourages children to want to count along.

188. Crowe, Robert.
Clyde Monster.
Kay Chorao, Illustrator. New York: Dutton, 1976. unpaged ISBN 0-525-29025-1. An excellent story of how Clyde, who is afraid of the dark, learns that people won't scare monsters before they go to sleep at night.

189. Cutting, Michael.
The Crooked Little Christmas Tree.
Ron Broda, Illustrator. New York: Scholastic, 1990. unpaged ISBN 0-590-45204-5. A little Christmas tree learns the meaning of true Christmas spirit when it gives shelter to a dove and her hatchlings, which causes the tree to become hunched over and unwanted.

190. Cuyler, Margery.
That's Good! That's Bad!
David Catrow, Illustrator. New York: Henry Holt, 1992. unpaged ISBN 0-8050-1535-3. A little boy goes on some hair-raising adventures that seem to go from bad to worse until he is saved in the end.

D

191. Dabcovich, Lydia.
Busy Beavers.
New York: Dutton, 1988.
unpaged ISBN 0-025-44384-3. An interesting look at a beaver family and their daily life.

192. Dahl, Roald.
Charlie and the Chocolate Factory.
Quentin Blake, Illustrator. New York: Knopf, 1964. 176 pages. ISBN 0-394-81011-2. A classic story of a young boy who wins the last ticket to see Willy Wonka's mysterious chocolate factory, passes a series of tests, and ends up owning the whole of it.

193. Dahl, Roald.
Danny: Champion of the World.
Jill Bennett, Illustrator. New York: Knopf, 1975. 208 pages. ISBN 0-394-93103-3. A heartwarming story of a nine-year-old boy and his love for his father as they unite to pull off the ultimate scheme to poach all of Mr. Victor Hazel's pheasants.

194. Dahl, Roald.
Fantastic Mr. Fox.
Donals Chaffin, Illustrator. New York: Knopf, 1970. 72 pages. ISBN 0-394-80497-X. The humorous story of a wily fox that outwits three rich farmers who would like to evict him.

195. Dahl, Roald.
George's Marvelous Medicine.
Quentin Blake, Illustrator. New York: Knopf, 1982. 96 pages. ISBN 0-394-94600-6. The hilarious account of George and his attempts to get rid of his mean old grandmother.

196. Dahl, Roald.
James and the Giant Peach.
Nancy Ekholm Burkert, Illustrator. New York: Knopf, 1963. 119 pages. ISBN 0-394-91282-9. The rollicking adventure of James and his unusual friends as they sail across the Atlantic in a peach to New York City.

197. Dahl, Roald.
Matilda.
New York: Viking Kestrel, 1988. ISBN 0-670-82439-9. Matilda is a very precocious girl who has abominable parents and an even more dastardly headmistress. However, Matilda also has the power of telekinesis, which together with her intelligence serve to equalize the struggle.

198. Davidson, Margaret.
Frederick Douglass Fights for Freedom.
New York: Scholastic, 1968. 80 pages. ISBN 0-590-42218-9. The story of a famous African American.

199. Day, Alexandra.
Carl's Christmas.
New York: Scholastic, 1991. unpaged ISBN 0-590-44790-4. While Carl is babysitting for baby, they get into plenty of mischief, including a visit from Santa Claus.

200. Day, Alexandra.
Good Dog, Carl.
Alexandra Day, Illustrator. LaJolla: Green Tiger Press, 1985. unpaged ISBN 0-88138-062-8. Carl's owner goes on a short shopping trip, leaving Carl alone to babysit with humorous results.

201. Dayrell, Elphinstone.
Why the Sun and the Moon Live in the Sky.
Blair Lent, Illustrator. New York: Scholastic, 1968. 28 pages. ISBN 0-590-44475-1. A West African folk tale that explains why the sun and the moon live in the sky.

202. de Angeli, Marguerite.
The Door in the Wall.
New York: Doubleday, 1949. 123 pages. ISBN 0-385-07283-X. Robin, disabled by a crippling disease, courageously saves his friends from an invasion of enemies.

203. de Beer, Hans.
Little Polar Bear.
New York: North-South Books, 1987. unpaged ISBN 1-55858-024-7. Lars, a young polar bear, gets separated from his father and goes on an adventure to a tropical climate.

204. de Regniers, Beatrice Schenk.
Jack and the Beanstalk.
Anne Wilsdorf, Illustrator. New York: Macmillan, 1985. unpaged ISBN 0-689-31174-5. A verse version that adds many ruffles and flourishes to the original with both text and illustrations.

205. de Regniers, Beatrice Schenk.
May I Bring a Friend?
Beni Montresor, Illustrator. New York: Atheneum, 1964. ISBN 0-689-20615-1. A young boy brings an assortment of animal friends to dine with the King and Queen.

206. de Regniers, Beatrice Schenk.
Red Riding Hood.
Edward Gorey, Illustrator.
New York: Aladdin, 1972. unpaged ISBN 0-689-71373-8. This version is told in verse. One of the best versions for reading aloud.

207. de Regniers, Beatrice Schenk.
A Week in the Life of Best Friends and Other Poems of Friendship.
Nancy Doyle, Illustrator. New York: Macmillan, 1986. 48 pages. ISBN 0-689-31179-6. Poems detailing both the good and the bad feelings that can result from friendship. The title poem expresses a universal experience for pre- and early teens.

208. de Regniers, Beatrice Schenk; Eva Moore; Mary Michaels White; Jan Carr.
Sing a Song of Popcorn.
New York: Scholastic, 1988. 142 pages. ISBN 0-590-40645-0. An excellent collection of poetry that is illustrated by Caldecott award-winning authors.

209. DeFelice, Cynthia C.
The Dancing Skeleton.
Robert Andrew Parker, Illustrator. New York: Macmillan, 1989. unpaged ISBN 0-02-726452-1. This folk tale retelling is about a man so ornery he wouldn't believe he was dead but rather just sat in his living room and rocked in his chair. Finally, a fiddler who wants to marry his widow finds a solution.

210. Delaney, A.
The Gunnywolf.
New York: Harper, 1988. unpaged ISBN 0-06-021594-1. In this version of "The Gunnywolf" Little Sister sings the Alphabet song to escape from the wolf. Compare to

"The Wolf and Little Sister" in "The People Could Fly."

211. Denenberg, Barry.
John Fitzgerald Kennedy: America's 35th President.
New York: Scholastic, 1988. 104 pages. ISBN 0-590-41344-9.
A look at one of America's most interesting presidents.

212. Denenberg, Barry.
Nelson Mandela "No Easy Walk to Freedom."
New York: Scholastic, 1991. 194 pages. ISBN 0-590-44154-X. The enthralling story of one of the most influential men in Africa.

213. Denenberg, Barry.
Stealing Home: The Story of Jackie Robinson.
New York: Scholastic, 1990. 117 pages. ISBN 0-590-42560-9. A hero to all people, Jackie Robinson was a brave man who led the way to integrating the major leagues.

214. dePaola, Tomie.
The Art Lesson.
New York: Putnam, 1989. unpaged ISBN 0-399-21688-X. Young Tommy finds that being a creative artist in school can be difficult unless you can compromise.

215. dePaola, Tomie.
The Family Christmas Tree Book.
New York: Holiday House, 1980. unpaged ISBN 0-8234-0416-1. The story of the Christmas tree is told as a family decorates their own tree.

216. dePaola, Tomie.
The Legend of Bluebonnet.
New York: Putnam, 1983. unpaged ISBN 0-399-20938-7. A retelling of the story of a young girl who sacrifices a precious belonging to help save her people.

217. dePaola, Tomie.
The Legend of the Indian Paintbrush.
New York: Putnam, 1988. unpaged ISBN 0-399-21534-4. This legend tells how an Indian artist struggled to find the right colors to paint the sunset and how he finally succeeded when his magically-provided paintbrushes became flowers.

218. dePaola, Tomie.
Nana Upstairs and Nana Downstairs.
New York: Putnam, 1973. unpaged ISBN 0-399-60787-0. Tommy loves his grandmother and learns how to adjust to her death.

219. dePaola, Tomie.
Oliver Button Is a Sissy.
San Diego: Harcourt Brace Jovanovich, 1979. unpaged ISBN 0-15-668140-4. Oliver is harassed by his classmates because he likes to dance instead of playing sports.

220. dePaola, Tomie (reteller).
Strega Nona.
New York: Simon & Schuster, 1975. unpaged ISBN 0-671-66606-1.

221. dePaola, Tomie.
Tomi dePaola's Favorite Nursery Tales.
New York: Putnam, 1986. 128 pages. ISBN 0-399-21319-8. A collection of traditional folk tales, fables, and rhymes for young children.

222. Devlin, Wende; Harry Devlin.
Cranberry Summer.
Harry Devlin, Illustrator. New York: Four Winds, 1992. unpaged ISBN 0-02-729181-2. Maggie and Mr. Wiskers team up to save poor Eliza from mean Mr. Grape in another Cranberryport adventure.

223. Dickens, Charles.
A Christmas Carol.
Mercer Mayer, Illustrator. New York: Macmillan, 1986. unpaged ISBN 0-02730310-1. An abridged version of the classic story that substitutes animals for the characters.

224. Donnelly, Liza.
Dinosaurs' Christmas.
New York: Scholastic, 1991. unpaged ISBN 0-590-44767-1. When Rex and his dog Bones leave to go sledding, they don't realize that they will be helping Santa's elves correctly make dinosaur toys.

225. Dorros, Arthur.
Animal Tracks.
New York: Scholastic, 1991. unpaged ISBN 0-590-43367-9. A creatively designed book in which the reader is asked to predict what animal tracks were left in the sand. The riddle is immediately answered on the next page.

226. Dorros, Arthur.
Rain Forest Secrets.
New York: Scholastic, 1990. unpaged ISBN 0-590-43368-7. A very interesting book about our fast-disappearing rain forests. Full of facts and details that will both educate and interest the reader.

227. Douglass, Barbara.
The Great Town and Country Bicycle Balloon Chase.
Carol Newsom, Illustrator. New York: Lothrop, 1984. unpaged ISBN 0-688-02223-6. Bicyclists chase after a balloon in order to be chosen for a ride themselves.

228. Downer, Ann.
Don't Blink Now!
New York: Franklin Watts, 1991. 40 pages. ISBN 0-531-15225-1. An interesting photographic look at underwater creatures that rely on camouflage, skill, and poisonous defenses to protect them from predators.

229. Dragonwagon, Crescent.
Alligator Arrived with Apples: A Potluck Alphabet Feast.
Jose Aruego and Ariane Dewey, Illustrators. New York: Macmillan, 1992. unpaged ISBN 0-02-733090-7. An alliterative alphabet book describing a wildly diverse Thanksgiving feast for which the Alligator contributed apples and allspice and the Zebra brought Zaftig Zucchini.

230. Duncan, Beverly (collector).
Christmas in the Stable.
San Diego: Harcourt Brace Jovanovich, 1990. 32 pages. ISBN 0-15-217758-2. Beautifully patterned illustrations that frame poems about the Christmas season.

231. Durell, Ann.
The Diane Goode Book of American Folk Tales & Songs.
Diane Goode, Illustrator. New York: Dutton, 1989. 63 pages. ISBN 0-525-44458-0. A nice blend of folk tale and folk song helps to reinforce that both are part of the oral tradition.

232. Durell, Ann; Marilyn Sachs, editors.
The Big Book of Peace.

New York: Dutton, 1990. ISBN 0-525-44605-2. Stories centered on a theme of peace by Newbery and other award-winning authors. Illustrations by Caldecott award winners and other noted illustrators.

233. Duvoisin, Roger. *Petunia.* New York: Knopf, 1962. unpaged ISBN 0-394-90865-1. Petunia is a goose who wants to read a book but can't, resulting in a good deal of trouble.

234. Dyson, John. *Westward with Christopher Columbus.* Photographs by Peter Christopher. New York: Scholastic, 1992. 64 pages. ISBN 0-590-43846-8. A recreation of Columbus's original trip to the New World that is told in the present as well as through the eyes of a young member of Columbus's expedition.

E

235. Earth Works Group. *50 Simple Things Kids Can Do to Save the Earth.* Michele Montez, Illustrator. Kansas City: Andrews and McMeel, 1990. 156 pages. ISBN 0-8362-2301-2. An excellent resource book with 50 activities that can lead students to become more aware of our environment.

236. Eckert, Allan W. *Incident at Hawk's Hill.* John Schoenherr, Illustrator. New York: Little, Brown, 1971. ISBN 0-316-20866-3. Based on a true incident, a boy is lost on the plains of late 1800s Canada and adopted by a badger.

237. Ehlers, Laurie Lattig. *Canoeing.* Gantschev, Illustrator. Natick: Picture Book Studio, 1986. unpaged ISBN 088708-029-4. Vibrant prose that takes the reader dipping and splashing on an early evening canoe ride down the river.

238. Ehlert, Lois. *Color Zoo.* New York: Lippincott, 1989. unpaged ISBN 0-397-32260-7. Ehlert combines color and shapes to create a zoo.

239. Ehlert, Lois. *Eating the Alphabet: Fruits and Vegetables From A to Z.* San Diego: Harcourt Brace Jovanovich, 1989. unpaged ISBN 0-015-224435-2. A luscious romp through the alphabet beginning with an apricot and ending with a zucchini.

240. Ehlert, Lois. *Feathers for Lunch.* San Diego: Harcourt Brace Jovanovich, 1990. unpaged ISBN 0-15-230550-5. A backyard as the cat tries unsuccessfully to dine on twelve common birds for lunch. A full glossary is found in the back.

241. Ehlert, Lois. *Growing Vegetable Soup.* New York: Harcourt Brace Jovanovich, 1987. unpaged ISBN 0-15-232575-1. Everything needed to grow the vegetables and make the soup is labeled.

242. Ehlert, Lois. *Planting a Rainbow.* San Diego: Harcourt Brace Jovanovich, 1988. unpaged ISBN 0-15-262609-3. A mother and her daughter plant bulbs. See what grows before

the reader's eyes into a riot of colorful flowers.

243. Ehrlich, Amy adapted by. *The Random House Book of Fairy Tales.* Diane Goode, Illustrator. New York: Random House, 1985. ISBN 0-394-85693-7. A wonderful retelling of nineteen classic fairy tales that are beautifully illustrated.

244. Eichenberg, Fritz. *Ape in a Cape: An Alphabet of Odd Animals.* New York: Harcourt Brace Jovanovich, 1952. unpaged ISBN 0-15-203722-5. A heavily rhymed alphabet book.

245. Eisenberg, Phyllis Rose. *You're My Nikki.* Jill Kastner, Illustrator. New York: Dial, 1992. unpaged ISBN 0-8037-1129-8. Needing reassurance, Nikki tests her mother to see if she really knows her.

246. Ekoomiak, Normee. *Arctic Memories.* New York: Henry Holt, 1990. unpaged. ISBN 0-8050-1254-0. Author/illustrator Ekoomiak recalls scenes from the lives of the Inuit in northern Canada. Text is in English and Inuktitut.

247. Elkington, John; Julia Hailes; Douglas Hill; Joel Makower. *Going Green: A Kid's Handbook to Saving the Planet.* Tony Ross, Illustrator. New York: Viking, 1990. 112 pages. ISBN 0-14-034597-3. How to save the environment with simple explanations of complex issues and projects that students can do.

248. Ellis, Carol. *A Cry in the Night.* New York: Scholastic, 1990. 154 pages. ISBN 0-590-42845-4. Molly Bishop solves a 300-year old mystery with the help of a ghost only she can see.

249. Emberley, Barbara. *Drummer Hoff.* Ed Emberly, Illustrator. New York: Prentice-Hall, 1967. unpaged ISBN 0-13-220822-9. A cumulative tale retold by Barbara Emberley and given wonderful form by Ed Emberley.

250. Emberley, Ed. *The Wing on a Flea.* Boston: Little, Brown, 1961. unpaged ISBN 0-316-23600-4. An exploration into the shapes that can exist on something as small as a wing of a flea.

251. Emberley, Michael. *Ruby.* Boston: Little, Brown, 1990. unpaged ISBN 0-316-23643-8. A much revised version of Red Riding Hood. The lead is a streetwise little mouse and the wolf becomes a smooth-talking cat.

252. Enright, Elizabeth. *Gone-Away Lake.* New York: Harcourt Brace Jovanovich, 1957. 192 pages. ISBN 0-15-636460-3. Portia and her cousin Julian rediscover a treasure trove of old summer houses in this exciting adventure.

253. Ernst, Lisa Campbell. *Sam Johnson and the Blue Ribbon Quilt.* New York: Morrow, 1992. unpaged ISBN 0-688-11505-5. Sam Johnson, banned from joining the Rosedale Women's

Quilting Club, organizes his own male club with hilarious results when they both compete.

254. Esbensen, Barbara Juster. *The Star Maiden: An Ojibway Tale.* Helen K. Davie, Illustrator. Boston: Little, Brown, 1988. unpaged ISBN 0-316-24951-3. An Ojibway tale that explains how the Star Maiden came down from the sky to be close to the people she loved and became a water lily.

255. Evslin, Bernard. *The Dolphin Rider and Other Greek Myths.* New York: Scholastic, 1976. 139 pages. ISBN 0-590-00128-0. A retelling of a variety of Greek myths for young readers.

256. Evslin, Bernard; Dorothy Evslin; Ned Hoopes. *The Greek Gods.* New York: Scholastic, 1966. 116 pages. ISBN 0-590-41396-1. A rich source of information for younger readers of Greek/Roman mythology.

257. Evslin, Bernard; Dorothy Evslin; Ned Hoopes. *Heroes & Monsters of Greek Myth.* New York: Scholastic, 1967. 112 pages. ISBN 0-590-41072-5. A rich source of information for younger readers of Greek/Roman mythology.

F

258. Farley, Walter. *The Black Stallion.* New York: Random House, 1941. 187 pages. ISBN 0-394-80601-8. A 17 year old boy

frees and befriends an Arabian stallion.

259. *Farm Animals.* New York: Macmillan, 1991. 21 pages. ISBN 0-689-71403-3. Photos and detailed illustrations support descriptions of domestic animals all kids want to know more about.

260. Feelings, Murial. *Jambo Means Hello: Swahili Alphabet Book.* Tom Feelings, Illustrator. New York: Dial, 1974. unpaged ISBN 0-8037-4350-5. A unique alphabet book that illustrates Swahili life.

261. Feelings, Murial. *Moja Means One: Swahili Counting Book.* Tom Feelings, Illustrator. New York: Dial, 1971. unpaged ISBN 0-8037-5776-X. A unique book that teaches counting through the culture of another people, the Swahili.

262. Finzel, Julia. *Large As Life.* New York: Lothrop, 1991. unpaged ISBN 0-688-10653-8. Explores the concept of big and small through colorful illustrations and a hard-to-locate ladybug.

263. Fischer-Nagel, Heiderose; Andreas Fischer-Nagel. *Life of the Ladybug.* Minneapolis: Carolrhoda Books, 1986. 48 pages. ISBN 0-87614-240-4. A pictorial look at one of Mother Nature's smallest friends.

264. Fleischman, Paul. *I Am Phoenix: Poems for Two Voices.* Ken Nutt, Illustrator. New

York: Harper, 1985. ISBN 0-06-021882-7. Poems about birds that were written to be recited by two voices.

265. Fleischman, Paul. *Joyful Noise: Poems for Two Voices.* Eric Beddows, Illustrator. New York: Harper, 1988. ISBN 0-06-021853-3. Award-winning poems about insects that need to be read aloud simultaneously by two people to appreciate their intricacy and rhythm.

266. Fleischman, Sid. *The Scarebird.* Peter Sis, Illustrator. New York: Greenwillow, 1988. unpaged ISBN 0-688-07317-4. A lonely old farmer constructs and makes a friend of a scarecrow but then learns that a human friend is better.

267. Flournoy, Valerie. *The Patchwork Quilt.* Jerry Pickney, Illustrator. New York: Dial, 1985. unpaged ISBN 0-8037-0097-0. Tanya and her grandmother gather scraps of cloth from family members and lovingly turn them into a beautiful quilt.

268. Follett, Ken. *The Mystery Hideout.* New York: Morrow, 1990. 88 pages. ISBN 0-688-18721-3. Mick and Izzie attempt to help save an old film studio in London with thrilling consequences.

269. Forest, Heather. *The Woman Who Flummoxed the Fairies.* Susan Gaber, Illustrator. New York: Harcourt Brace Jovanovich, 1990. unpaged ISBN 0-15-299150-6. A retelling of a Scottish folk tale in which a woman famous for

her baking manages to outwit the king of fairies.

270. Foster, John chosen by. *Never Say Boo to a Ghost and Other Haunting Rhymes.* Korky Paul, Illustrator. New York: Scholastic, 1990. 96 pages. ISBN 0-590-45127-8. A zany collection of poems that will delight children of all ages.

271. Fox, Mem. *Koala Lou.* San Diego: Harcourt Brace Jovanovich, 1989. unpaged ISBN 0-15-200502-1. Koala Lou trains very hard for the Bush Olympics and believes she's a failure when she does not win.

272. Fox, Mem. *Night Noises.* Terry Denton, Illustrator. San Diego: Harcourt Brace Jovanovich, 1989. unpaged ISBN 0-15-200543-9. Ninety-year-old Lilly Laceby dozes by the fire only to be abruptly awakened to a tumultuous surprise from her family.

273. Fox, Mem. *Wilfrid Gordon McDonald Partridge.* Julie Vivas, Illustrator. Brooklyn: Kane/Miller, 1985. unpaged ISBN 0-916291-04-9. The story of a boy who helps an elderly friend find her memories by sharing possessions that evoke emotions.

274. Fox, Paula. *One-Eyed Cat.* New York: Bradbury Press, 1984. 216 pages. ISBN 0-02-735540-3. Young Ned Wallis cannot resist the temptation of the forbidden rifle and must come to terms with the painful results of his actions.

275. Frasier, Debra.
On the Day You Were Born.
San Diego: Harcourt Brace Jovanovich, 1991. unpaged ISBN 0-15-257995-8. A wonderful story of how all creation was prepared for your birth. A terrific way to introduce almost any science topic.

276. Freedman, Russell.
Children of the Wild West.
New York: Clarion, 1983. ISBN 0-89919-143-6. A photojournalistic treatment of children and how they lived in the late nineteenth-century American West.

277. Freedman, Russell.
Cowboys of the Wild West.
New York: Clarion, 1985. ISBN 0-89919-301-3. Journalistic essays on how cowboys lived and worked in the Old West.

278. Freedman, Russell.
Immigrant Kids.
New York: Dutton, 1980. 72 pages. ISBN 0-525-32538-7. Pictures and information about European immigrants coming to the United States between 1880 and 1920.

279. Freedman, Russell.
Indian Chiefs.
New York: Holiday House, 1987. 151 pages. ISBN 0-8234-0625-3. A stirring look at six Native American leaders and their attempts to protect their way of life from the encroachment of American settlers and miners.

280. Freedman, Russell.
Lincoln: A Photobiography.
New York: Clarion, 1987. ISBN 0-89919-380-3. A well written photo history of the sixteenth president of the United States.

281. Freeman, Don.
Corduroy.
New York: Penguin, 1968. unpaged ISBN 0-670-24133-4. Corduroy is a toy bear with a missing button, afraid that no one will buy him.

282. Freeman, Don.
The Seal and the Slick.
New York: Viking, 1974. unpaged ISBN 0-670-62659-7. The story of a young seal caught in an oil slick and the humans who fight to clean him up.

283. Freeman, Mae.
The Real Magnet Book.
Norman Bridwell, Illustrator. New York: Scholastic, 1967. unpaged ISBN TK. Several activities and experiments accompany information about magnets

284. French, Fiona.
Snow White in New York.
Toronto: Oxford University Press, 1986. unpaged ISBN 0-19-279808-1. A parody of a familiar folk tale set in 1920s New York. Great for upper grades.

285. Fritz, Jean.
George Washington's Breakfast.
Paul Galdone, Illustrator. New York: Coward, 1969. ISBN 0-689-30099-8. A young know-it-all thinks he knows all about George Washington—but doesn't.

286. Fritz, Jean.
Shh! We're Writing the Constitution.
New York: Putnam, 1987. 64 pages. ISBN 0-399-21403-7. About the people and events that worked to create the U.S. Constitution.

287. Fritz, Jean.
Where Was Patrick Henry On the 29th of May?
Margot Tomes, Illustrator. New York: Coward-McCann, 1975. ISBN 0-698-20544-8. Factual account of the man who said "Give me liberty or give me death."

288. Fritz, Jean.
Will You Sign Here, John Hancock?
Trina Schart Hyman, Illustrator. New York: Coward-McCann, 1976. ISBN 0-698-20307-0. Story of the man who signed his name so large on the Decleration of Independence.

289. Frost, Robert.
Stopping by Woods on a Snowy Evening.
Susan Jeffers, Illustrator. New York: Dutton, 1978. unpaged ISBN 0-525-40115-6. Superb illustrations bring a classic poem to life.

G

290. Gackenbach, Dick.
Mighty Tree.
San Diego: Harcourt Brace Jovanovich, 1992. unpaged ISBN 0-15-200519-6. The colorful story of three tree seeds that grow to maturity and what happens to them.

291. Gág, Wanda.
The ABC Bunny.
New York: Putnam, 1961. unpaged ISBN 0-698-20000-4. An ageless classic about a bunny, told in abc order.

292. Gág, Wanda.
Millions of Cats.
New York: Coward-McCann, 1928. unpaged ISBN 0-698-20091-8. A classic story of an old couple who wanted a cat but encounter millions of cats.

293. Gág, Wanda.
Tales from Grimm.
New York: Coward, McCann & Geoghegan, 1981. 238 pages. ISBN 0-698-20533-2. Sixteen tales from the Grimms, translated and illustrated by the author of *Millions of Cats.*

294. Galdone, Paul.
The Gingerbread Boy.
New York: Clarion, 1975. unpaged ISBN 0-89919-163-0. A cumulative tale that is a favorite among younger students. In this version the fox is the ultimate winner.

295. Galdone, Paul.
Over in the Meadow: An Old Nursery Counting Rhyme.
New York: Simon & Schuster, 1989. unpaged ISBN 0-671-67837-X. An excellent recreation of an old nursery rhyme featuring ten different animal families.

296. Galdone, Paul.
The Three Billy Goats Gruff.
New York: Clarion, 1973. unpaged ISBN 0-395-28812-6. A perennial favorite of the K-1 classes that uses strong language and repeating motifs.

297. Galdone, Paul.
The Three Little Pigs.
New York: Clarion, 1970. unpaged ISBN 0-395-28813-4. A good edition of the story for younger students.

298. Gardiner, John Reynolds.
Stone Fox.
New York: Crowell, 1980. 81 pages. ISBN 0-690-03983-2. Little Willy and his dog Searchlight run race of to try to save his grandpa's farm.

299. Gardner, Robert.
The Whale Watchers' Guide.

Don Sineti, Illustrator. Messner, 1984. 170 pages. ISBN 0-671-45811-6. Originally published as a whale-watching guide, this is an excellent classroom resource.

300. Gates, Doris.
The Blue Willow.
New York: Penguin, 1940. 154 pages. ISBN 0-670-17557-9. Janey Larkin, the daughter of a migrant worker during the depression, almost loses the only treasure she has left to remember her mom by.

301. George, Jean Craighead.
Julie of the Wolves.
John Schoenherr, Illustrator. New York: Harper, 1972. 170 pages. ISBN 0-06-021943-2. Julie is an Eskimo girl alone on the Tundra whose only hope of survival depends on befriending a wolf pack.

302. George, Jean Craighead.
On the Far Side of the Mountain.
New York: Dutton, 1990. ISBN 0-525-44563-3. In this sequel to *My Side of the Mountain*, Sam loses and regains and finally releases his falcon.

303. George, Jean Craighead.
Who Really Killed Cock Robin?
New York: Dutton, 1971. 149 pages. ISBN 0-525-42700-7. An ecological thriller of a group of students and their attempt to solve the mystery of who killed cock robin.

304. Gibbons, Gail.
Check It Out!
The Book about Libraries.
San Diego: Harcourt Brace Jovanovich, 1985. unpaged ISBN 0-15-216400-6. A colorful book about the library and its various parts and services.

305. Gibbons, Gail.
Dinosaurs.
New York: Holiday House, 1987. unpaged ISBN 0-8234-0657-1. A colorfully illustrated description of a variety of dinosaurs.

306. Gibbons, Gail.
Flying.
New York: Holiday House, 1986. unpaged ISBN 0-8234-0599-0. Gibbons tells about flying, from balloons to space shuttles.

307. Gibbons, Gail.
From Seed to Plant.
New York: Holiday House, 1991. unpaged ISBN 0-8234-0872-8. A comprehensive look at plants and how they begin as seeds and grow.

308. Gibbons, Gail.
Monarch Butterfly.
New York: Holiday House, 1989. unpaged ISBN 0-8234-0773-X. The monarch butterfly is brought to life with excellent illustrations and clear text.

309. Gibbons, Gail.
Thanksgiving Day.
New York: Holiday House, 1983. unpaged ISBN 0-8234-0576-1. A colorful book about the origins, customs, and traditions of Thanksgiving and how it is celebrated today.

310. Gibbons, Gail.
Things To Make and Do on Columbus Day.
New York: Franklin Watts, 1977. unpaged ISBN 0-531-01274-3. Plenty of do-able projects for primary children that teach about Christopher Columbus.

311. Gibbons, Gail.
Weather Words and What They Mean.
New York: Holiday House, 1990. unpaged. ISBN 0-8234-0805-1 Informative illustrations and text explain weather and the words that are used to describe it.

312. Gibbons, Gail. *Zoo.* New York: Harper, 1987. unpaged ISBN 0-690-04631-6. A description of a city zoo and the people who work there.

313. Giff, Patricia Reilly.
Laura Ingalls Wilder: Growing Up in the Little House.
Eileen McKeating, Illustrator. New York: Puffin, 1987. 56 pages. ISBN 0-14-032074-1. Giff tells Wilder's story using her books as threads.

314. Giganti, Paul Jr.
Each Orange Had 8 Slices.
Donald Crews, Illustrator. New York: Greenwillow, 1992. unpaged ISBN 0-688-10428-2. A unique picture book that combines counting with simple addition.

315. Gilman, Phoebe.
Jillian Jiggs.
New York: Scholastic, 1988. 36 pages. ISBN 0-590-41340-6. The story of a young girl and her very active imagination, told in delightful verse.

316. Glimmerveen, Ulco.
A Tale of Antarctica.
New York: Scholastic, 1989. 32 pages. ISBN 0-590-43360-1. The potential ecological damage that man's encroachment can do to this pristine environment.

317. Goble, Paul.
Crow Chief.
New York: Orchard, 1972. unpaged ISBN 0-531-05947-2. The story of how the Crow Chief, who wanted to rule over everyone, was punished for keeping the people from hunting the buffalo.

318. Goble, Paul.
Scarsdale: Bradbury Press, 1980. unpaged ISBN 0-02-736560-3. A story about a boy who brings horses to his people.

319. Goble, Paul.
The Girl Who Loved Wild Horses.
Paul Goble, Illustrator. Scarsdale, New York: Bradbury Press, 1979. unpaged ISBN 0-02-736570-0. A story woven from the legends of the Plains Indians of a young girl and her love for a black stallion.

320. Goble, Paul.
Iktomi and the Berries.
Paul Goble, Illustrator. New York: Orchard Books, 1989. unpaged ISBN 0-531-05819-0. Iktomi the trickster is again causing trouble, this time with buffalo berries.

321. Goble, Paul.
Iktomi and the Boulder.
New York: Orchard Books, 1988. unpaged ISBN 0-531-05760-7. This pourquoi story tells of Iktomi's run-in with a boulder and his eventual escape by tricking the bats into helping him.

322. Goble, Paul.
Iktomi and the Ducks.
New York: Orchard Books, 1990. unpaged ISBN 0-531-08483-3. A retelling of the trickster Iktomi and his plan to enjoy a duck dinner that is

interrupted by several unforeseen intrusions.

323. Goble, Paul.
Star Boy.
New York: Bradbury Press, 1983. unpaged ISBN 0-02-722660-3. A young boy must journey far to the Sky World in order to gain forgiveness for his mother's disobedience.

324. Goldin, Augusta.
Spider Silk.
Joseph Low, Illustrator. New York: Crowell, 1964. 36 pages. ISBN 0-690-76075-2. An interesting book about spiders.

325. Gomi, Taro.
Hi, Butterfly!
New York: Morrow, 1983. unpaged ISBN 0-688-04138-X. A young boy chases an elusive butterfly over hill and dale with humorous results.

326. Goodall, John S.
Little Red Riding Hood.
New York: McElderry, 1988. Unpaged ISBN 0-689-50457-8. A wordless adaptation of Red Riding Hood with the lead character played by a mouse. Goodall uses split-page illustrations to enhance the retelling.

327. Goor, Ron; Nancy Goor.
Insect Metamorphosis.
New York: Atheneum, 1990. 26 pages. ISBN 0-689-31445-0. The story of metamorphosis colorfully told through photos and text.

328. Graham-Barber, Lynda.
Gobble! The Complete Book of Thanksgiving Words.
Betsy Lewin, Illustrator. New York: Bradbury Press, 1991. 122 pages. ISBN 0-02-708332-2. An excellent

reference that defines words associated with Thanksgiving.

329. Greenfield, Eloise.
Night on Neighborhood Street. Jan Spivey Gilchrist, Illustrator. New York: Dial, 1991. unpaged ISBN 0-8037-0777-0. Greenfield depicts scenes from a community, most centered on the family. The whole range of emotions is explored but most are infused with the warmth and strength of family.

330. Grifalconi, Ann.
Osa's Pride.
Boston: Little, Brown, 1990. unpaged ISBN 0-316-32865-0. A girl in an African village makes up stories about her missing father until her grandmother helps her.

331. Griffin, Judith Berry.
Phoebe the Spy.
New York: Scholastic, 1977. 47 pages. ISBN 0-590-42432-7. The story of a brave young African-American girl and her help during the revolutionary war.

332. Grimm, Jacob; Willhelm Grimm.
Snow White.
Trina Schart Hyman, Illustrator. Boston: Little, Brown, 1974. unpaged ISBN 0-316-35450-3. The classic tale of the jealous stepmother's attempts to destroy Snow White. Hyman's illustrations should be compared to those of Burkert.

333. Grimm, Jacob; Willhelm Grimm.
Snow-White and the Seven Dwarfs.
Nancy Ekholm Burkert, Illustrator. New York: Farrar, Straus and Giroux, 1972.

Unpaged ISBN 374-46868. This classic tale is well told, and the use of two-page-spread illustrations alternating with two of text is effective. The story is greatly enhanced when read aloud.

334. Grimm, Jacob; Wilhelm Grimm.
Hansel and Gretel. Lisbeth Zwerger, Illustrator. New York: Morrow, 1979. unpaged ISBN 0-688-22198-X. A traditional tale with some new touches (the gingerbread house is now made of bread, topped with cakes, and has windows made of sugar) and children typical of Lisbeth Zwerger.

335. Grimm, Jacob; Wilhelm Grimm.
Little Red Cap.
Lisbeth Zwerger, Illustrator. New York: Morrow, 1983. unpaged ISBN 0-688-01715-0. A very traditional rendition of the German Red Riding Hood story. Zwerger's illustrations make it worth adding to a classroom collection.

336. Gross, Ruth Belov.
You Don't Need Words!
Susan Ryan, Illustrator. New York: Scholastic, 1991. 48 pages. ISBN 0-590-43897-2. A celebration of all kinds of nonverbal gestures and signs that we use to communicate daily.

337. Guarino, Deborah.
Is Your Mama a Llama.
Steven Kellogg, Illustrator. New York: Scholastic, 1989. unpaged ISBN 0-590-41387-2. Lloyd wanders around asking his friends "Is your mama a llama?" with some predictable results.

338. Guccione, Leslie Davis.
Nobody Listens to Me.
New York: Scholastic, 1991. 167 pages. ISBN 0-590-43106-4. Mendy's concern that whale-watching may endanger whales erupts into a full-scale war between herself and her father and members of their New England seacoast town after her favorite humpback whale, Daisy, is killed.

339. Gwynne, Fred.
A Chocolate Moose for Dinner.
New York: Simon & Schuster, 1990. unpaged ISBN 0-671-66685-1. A humorous collection of homonyms that become a play on words.

340. Hahn, Mary Downing.
The Doll in the Garden: A Ghost Story. New York: Clarion, 1989. 128 pages. ISBN 0-89919-848-1. Ashley follows a beautiful white cat through the hedge and finds herself in the middle of an old mystery that was covered by a lie.

H

341. Hahn, Mary Downing.
Wait Till Helen Comes: A Ghost Story.
New York: Clarion, 1987. 184 pages. ISBN 0-89919-453-2. Molly and Michael must overcome an unnatural force to save Heather from trouble.

342. Hale, Sarah Josepha.
Mary Had a Little Lamb.
Photoillustrations by Bruce McMillan. New York: Scholastic, 1990. unpaged ISBN 0-590-43773-9. A retelling of the famous eighteenth-century poem illustrated with contemporary photographs.

343. Haley, Gail E.
Jack and the Bean Tree.
New York: Crown, 1986.
unpaged ISBN 0-517-55717-7. A retelling of "Jack and the Beanstalk" as it is told in Appalachia. The storyteller's beginning adds to the richness of the book.

344. Haley, Gail E.
A Story a Story.
New York: Atheneum, 1970. unpaged ISBN 0-689-20511-2. An African folk tale that explains how Ananse obtained the golden box of stories from the sky god.

345. Hall, Donald.
Ox-Cart Man.
New York: Penguin, 1979. unpaged ISBN 0-670-53328-9. A historical account of a family and the effort involved to bring their produce to market.

346. Hall, Lynn.
Danza.
New York: Scribner, 1981. 186 pages. ISBN 0-684-17158-9. A young Puerto Rican boy helps to nurse a horse back to health after it has become sick because of his carelessness. He later has to save the horse from an abusive trainer.

347. Hall, Nancy Christensen.
Macmillan Fairy Tale Book.
John O'Brian, Illustrator. New York: Macmillan, 1983. unpaged ISBN 0-02-741960-6. Scenes from a variety of folk tales are used as a backdrop for words beginning with each letter of the alphabet.

348. Hamanaka, Sheila.
The Journey.
Designed by Steve Frederick. New York: Orchard, 1990.

ISBN 0-531-05849-2. The struggles of Japanese immigrants to the United States depicted through written vignettes and views of an original five-panel mural.

349. Hamilton, Morse.
Little Sister for Sale.
Gioia Faimmenghi, Illustrator. New York: Dutton, 1992. unpaged ISBN 0-525-65078-4. Faced with a pesky sister, Kate sells her to her next-door neighbor only to find that she really misses the little pest.

350. Hamilton, Virginia.
Anthony Burns: The Defeat and Triumph of a Fugitive Slave.
New York: Knopf, 1988. 193 pages. ISBN 0-394-88185-0. Young Anthony Burns stows away on a ship to Boston to gain his freedom. Little does he know that that is only the beginning of his troubles.

351. Hamilton, Virginia.
In the Beginning: Creation Stories from Around the World.
Barry Moser, Illustrator. New York: Harcourt Brace Jovanovich, 1988. 161 pages. ISBN 0-15-238740-4. Stories of many cultures that attempt to explain how people, the Earth, and the universe began.

352. Hamilton, Virginia.
The People Could Fly: American Black Folk tales.
Leo and Diane Dillon, Illustrators. New York: Knopf, 1985. 178 pages. ISBN 0-394-86925-7. This anthology contains tales that may be unfamiliar to many people, but they contain motifs and story types that will be familiar. The rich language and pictures make it all the better.

353. Harrison, Sarah.
In Granny's Garden.
Mike Wilks, Illustrator. New York: Holt, Rinehart and Winston, 1980. unpaged ISBN 0-03-050876-2. A young boy's recollections of his grandmother's jungly, wild garden in which he meets a brontosaurus, among other animals.

354. Haskins, Jim.
The Day Martin Luther King Jr. Was Shot.
New York: Scholastic, 1992. 96 pages. ISBN 0-590-43661-9. A photo history of the civil rights movement in America with an up-to-date time line.

355. Hatchett, Clint.
The Glow-in-the-Dark Night Sky Book.
Stephen Marchesi, Illustrator. New York: Random House, 1988. unpaged ISBN 0-394-89113-9. A hands-on book with glow-in-the-dark outlines of the major star constellations.

356. Haviland, Virginia.
The Fairy Tale Treasury.
Raymond Briggs, Illustrator. New York: Puffin, 1974, 1984. 192 pages. ISBN 014-050-103-7. A collection of folk tales and literary fairy tales from around the world, although most are European.

357. Hawes, Judy.
Bees and Beelines.
Aliki, Illustrator. New York: Crowell, 1964. 32 pages. ISBN 0-690-12739-1. An entertaining book about bees.

358. Hayman, Leroy.
The Death of Lincoln: A Picture History of the Assassination.
New York: Scholastic, 1968. 128 pages. ISBN 0-590-

40639-6. A picture history of the assassination of Abraham Lincoln and its aftermath.

359. Haynes, Betsy.
Spies on the Devil's Belt.
New York: Scholastic, 1974. 158 pages. ISBN 0-590-40567-5.

360. Heller, Ruth.
A Cache of Jewels.
New York: Grosset & Dunlap, 1987. unpaged ISBN 0-448-19211-X. A riot of collective nouns that are brought to life with dazzling illustrations.

361. Heller, Ruth.
Chickens Aren't the Only Ones.
New York: Grosset & Dunlap, 1981. unpaged ISBN 0-448-01872-1. A book about all the different types of animals that lay eggs.

362. Heller, Ruth.
Kites Sail High: A Book about Verbs.
New York: Grosset & Dunlap, 1988. unpaged ISBN 0-448-10480-6. A wonderful book about our language.

363. Heller, Ruth.
Many Luscious Lollipops.
New York: Grosset & Dunlap, 1989. unpaged ISBN 0-448-03151-5. A wonderful book about our language

364. Heller, Ruth.
Merry-Go-Round: A Book about Nouns.
New York: Grosset, 1990. unpaged ISBN 0-448-40085-5. Everything you wanted to know about nouns in a colorfully illustrated presentation.

365. Heller, Ruth.
Plants That Never Ever Bloom.

New York: Grosset & Dunlap, 1984. unpaged ISBN 0-448-18964-X. Beautiful illustrations of the other kinds of plants that inhabit our earth.

366. Heller, Ruth.
The Reason for a Flower.
New York: Grosset & Dunlap, 1983. unpaged ISBN 0-448-14495-6. A beautifully illustrated explanation of where flowers come from and their many uses.

367. Henkes, Kevin.
Jessica.
New York: Puffin, 1989. unpaged ISBN 0-14-054194-2. Jessica is Ruthie's imaginary friend who shares Ruthie's every moment until she goes to kindergarten and meets a real friend.

368. Hepworth, Cathi.
Antics!
New York: Putnam, 1992. unpaged ISBN 0-399-21862-9. A brilliANT alphabet book that illustrates ANTS and their jubilANT ANTics.

369. Herriot, James.
The Christmas Day Kitten.
Ruth Brown, Illustrator. New York: St. Martin's Press, 1986. unpaged ISBN 0-312-13407-X. Debbie, a stray cat, gives birth to a Christmas day kitten that brings joy and entertainment to the Pickerings.

370. Herriot, James.
Moses the Kitten.
Peter Barrett, Illustrator. New York: St. Martin's Press, 1984. unpaged ISBN 0-312-54905-9. A shiny black kitten is found abandoned and is given to the Butlers who provide him with a nice comfortable home.

371. Herriot, James.
Oscar, Cat-About-Town.
Ruth Brown, Illustrator. New York: St. Martin's Press, 1990. unpaged ISBN 0-312-05137-9. A warm story about a stray cat, adopted by the Herriots, who keeps wandering away only to return after visiting every social event in town.

372. Himmelman, John.
Ibis: A True Whale Story.
New York: Scholastic, 1990. unpaged ISBN 0-590-42848-9. The true story of a young whale's fight to stay alive and the help it received from humans.

373. Hirschfelder, Arlene.
Happily May I Walk: American Indians and Alaska Natives Today.
New York: Scribner, 1985. 152 pages. ISBN 0-684-18624-1. This should serve as a classroom reference book as it helps to remind us that Native American peoples are part of the modern world and not just part of our past.

374. Hirschi, Ron.
Who Lives in the Mountains.
Photographs by Galen Burrell. New York: Putnam, 1989. unpaged ISBN 0-399-21900-5. Very simple text and full-color photographs depict the animals going about their lives in the mountains.

375. Hirschi, Ron.
Winter.
Photographs by Thomas D. Mangelsen. New York: Dutton, 1990. unpaged ISBN 0-525-65026-1. A variety of wild animals and birds are captured in winter settings.

376. Hoban, Russell.
A Baby Sister for Frances.
Lillian Hoban, Illustrator. New York: Harper & Row, 1964. ISBN 0-06-022335-9. Frances is a badger who acts very much like a human child with the same emotions and problems.

377. Hoberman, Mary Ann.
A House Is a House for Me.
Betty Fraser, Illustrator. New York: Penguin, 1982. unpaged ISBN 0-670-38016. A rhyming collection of shelters for a variety of animals, plants, and other things. A poetic look at houses and homes for animals, and inanimate objects with a wonderful repeating refrain.

378. Hodges, Margaret.
The Kitchen Knight: A Tale of King Arthur.
Trina Schart Hyman, Illustrator. New York: Holiday House, 1990. unpaged ISBN 0-8234-0787-X. A retelling of the story of Sir Gareth's becoming a knight that is faithful to the original tale and enriched by the illustrations.

379. Hodges, Margaret.
Saint George and the Dragon.
Trina Schart Hyman, Illustrator. Boston: Little, Brown, 1984. unpaged ISBN 0-316-36789-3. St. George, as the Knight of the Red Cross, must fight the dragon that is destroying a princess's land. The battle continues for three days.

380. Hoff, Syd.
Julius.
New York: Harper, 1959. 64 pages. ISBN 0-06-022491-4. Julius is a King Kong-sized gorilla with the personality of Ferdinand the Bull.

381. Hoffman, Mary.
Amazing Grace.
Caroline Birch, Illustrator. New York: Dial, 1991. unpaged ISBN 0-8037-1040-2. Grace loves stories and acts them out in marvelous scenes. She wants to play Peter Pan in the class play, but is told she is the wrong gender and color. She gets help from Grandma.

382. Hooks, William H.
Moss Gown.
Donald Carrick, Illustrator. New York: Clarion, 1987. unpaged ISBN 0-89919-460-5. This traditional story set in the south contains the Cinderella motif. It can be compared to *Tattercoats.*

383. Hooks, William H.
The Three Little Pigs and the Fox.
S. D. Schindler, Illustrator. New York: Macmillan, 1989. unpaged ISBN 0-02-744431-7. A rendition of the three little pigs that is based on the oral versions that have been told for over 300 years in the Great Smoky Mountains.

384. Hopkins, Lee Bennett.
Animals from Mother Goose.
Kathryn Hewitt, Illustrator. San Diego: Harcourt Brace Jovanovich, 1989. unpaged ISBN 0-15-200406-8. An interesting flap-page book that poses questions with answers about familiar animals from Mother Goose.

385. Hopkins, Lee Bennett.
People from Mother Goose.
Kathryn Hewitt, Illustrator. San Diego: Harcourt Brace Jovanovich, 1989. unpaged ISBN 0-15-200406-8. An interesting flap-page book that poses questions with answers

about familiar characters from Mother Goose.

386. Horner, John R.; James Gorman.
Maia: A Dinosaur Grows Up.
Doug Henderson, Illustrator. Philadelphia: Running Press, 1989. 56 pages. ISBN 0-89471-522-6. Based on scientific information, this is a story of the life of a Maiasaura in prehistoric Montana.

387. Hort, Lenny (reteller).
The Boy Who Held Back the Sea.
Thomas Locker, Illustrator. New York: Dial, 1987. unpaged ISBN 0-8037-0406-2. A retelling of a classic Dutch story that is handsomely illustrated in the Dutch Masters tradition.

388. Horton, Casey.
Insects.
New York: Franklin Watts, 1984. 37 pages. ISBN 0-531-03476-3. An informative look at a wide variety of insects from around the world.

389. Houghton, Eric.
Walter's Magic Wand.
New York: Orchard, 1989. ISBN 0-531-05851-4. Walter visits the library with his "magic wand" and finds many adventures in the books.

390. Howard, Jane R.
When I Am Sleepy.
Lynne Cherry, Illustrator. New York: Dutton, 1985. unpaged ISBN 0-525-44204-9. A young girl imagines what it would be like to fall asleep with some of her favorite animals.

391. Howe, James.
The Day the Teacher Went Bananas.
Lillian Hoban, Illustrator.

New York: Dutton, 1984. unpaged ISBN 0-525-44107-7. When the class gets a new teacher, they are surprised to find it's a gorilla.

392. Howe, James.
What Eric Knew: A Sebastian Barth Mystery.
New York: Atheneum, 1986. 138 pages. ISBN 0-689-31159-1. Sebastian Barth uncovers a mystery in shady…

393. Huck, Charlotte reteller.
Princess Furball.
Anita Lobel, Illustrator. New York: Greenwillow, 1989. unpaged ISBN 0-688-07837-0. A clever princess prevails in the end in a variation of Cinderella.

394. Huntington, Harriet.
Let's Look at Insects.
Photographs by the author. New York: Doubleday, 1969. 60 pages. Illustrated with black and white photographs, this book provides valuable information to students by looking at the individual parts of an insect.

395. Hutchins, Pat.
The Doorbell Rang.
New York: Greenwillow, 1986. unpaged ISBN 0-688-05251-7. Ma's large plate of cookies keeps getting smaller and smaller as more visitors arrive to help Victoria and Sam eat them.

I

396. Innocenti, Roberto.
Rose Blanche.
New York: Stewart, Tabori & Chang, 1985, 1990. Unpaged ISBN 1-55670-207-8. A troubling story of a girl's encounter with the concentration camps during

World War II. The ending may be disturbing to some children, but may lead to productive discussions.

J

397. Jacobs, Joseph.
English Fairy Tales.
John D. Batten, Illustrator. New York: Dover, 1967. 261 pages. ISBN 486-21818-X. This reprint of the original 1898 edition contains earlier versions of "The Three Bears" and "The Three Pigs." Children especially love hearing the pre-Goldilocks version of "The Three Bears."

398. Jacobs, Joseph.
Tattercoats.
Margot Tomes, Illustrator. New York: Putnam, 1989. unpaged ISBN 0-399-21584-0. An English variant of Cinderella, collected and edited by one of the noted folklorists of his time. In this tale, Tattercoats is banished to the kitchen by her father but is able to win the heart of the prince through the musical intervention of the gooseherd.

399. James, Simon.
Dear Mr. Blueberry.
New York: McElderry Books, 1991. unpaged ISBN 0-689-50529-9. Emily sees a whale in her pond and begins a correspondence with her teacher about the whale and how to take care of it.

400. Jaquith, Priscilla (reteller).
Bo Rabbit Smart for True: Folk tales from the Gullah.
Ed Young, Illustrator. New York: Putnam, 1981. unpaged ISBN 0-399-61179-7. Four folk tales that originated on the islands off the coast of Georgia and South Carolina,

retold as they were told during slave days.

401. Jarrell, Randall.
The Bat Poet.
Maurice Sendak, Illustrator. New York: Macmillan, 1964. 64 pages. ISBN 0-02-747640-5. A bat finds that he would rather write poetry than do "batty" things.

402. Jeffers, Susan adapted by.
The Three Jovial Huntsmen.
Scarsdale: Bradbury Press, 1984. unpaged ISBN 0-87888-023-2. The forest comes alive in a retelling of a Mother Goose rhyme in which three huntsman find only a sailing ship, a piece of cheese, and a pin cushion while hunting.

403. Jeunesse, Galimard; Pascale de Bourgoing.
Colors.
P.M. Valet and Sylvaine Perols, Illustrators. New York: Scholastic, 1991. unpaged ISBN 0-590-45236-3. An imaginative look at the primary colors and the many combinations that result because of them.

404. Jeunesse, Galimard; Pascale de Bourgoing.
The Egg.
Rene Mettler, Illustrator. New York: Scholastic, 1992. unpaged ISBN 0-590-45266-5. Eggs of all kinds are illustrated as the reader follows the development of a chick, from the egg to it's birth.

405. Jeunesse, Galimard; Pascale de Bourgoing.
Fruit.
P.M. Valet, Illustrator. New York: Scholastic, 1989. unpaged ISBN 0-590-45233-9. Watch an apple seed grow

to maturity and learn about other fruit as well.

406. Jeunesse, Galimard; Pascale de Bourgoing. *The Ladybug and Other Insects.* Sylvia Perols, Illustrator. New York: Scholastic, 1991. unpaged ISBN 0-590-45235-5. A delightful presentation of information through text and colorful overlays that entice the reader to follow along as a ladybug lays her eggs.

407. Jeunesse, Galimard; Pascale de Bourgoing. *The Tree.* Christian Broutin, Illustrator. New York: Scholastic, 1992. unpaged ISBN 0-590-45265-7. All kinds of trees are carefully detailed and explained for young readers.

408. Jeunesse, Galimard; Pascale de Bourgoing. *Weather.* Sophie Kniffke, Illustrator. New York: Scholastic, 1991. unpaged ISBN 0-590-45234-7. A colorful look at weather and the seasons.

409. Johnston, Tony. *The Quilt Story.* Tomi de Paola, Illustrator. New York: Scholastic, 1985. unpaged ISBN 0-590-43890-5. A story about a quilt and two young girls from different generations who find comfort and warmth in it.

410. Jonas, Ann. *Aardvarks, Disembark!* New York: Greenwillow, 1990. unpaged ISBN 0-668-07206-2. After the flood Noah releases the animals from the ark, beginning with the zebra and ending with the aardvark.

411. Juster, Norman. *As: A Surfeit of Similes.* David Small, Illustrator. New York: Morrow, 1989. unpaged ISBN 0-688-08139-8. A wonderful book that is sharp as a stick and clear as a bell.

K

412. Kaizuki, Kiyonori. *A Calf Is Born.* New York: Orchard, 1988. unpaged ISBN 0-531-05862-X. Wonderful, realistic illustrations showing the birth of a calf.

413. Kalan, Robert. *Jump, Frog, Jump!* Byron Barton, Illustrator. New York: Greenwillow, 1981. unpaged ISBN 0-688-80271-0. An amusing cumulative rhyme that involves a frog's escapades to escape capture.

414. Kalas, Sybille. *The Goose Family Book.* Photographs by TK. Natick: Picture Book Studio, 1986. unpaged ISBN 0-88708-019-7. A graceful photo story of a family of wild grey geese as told through the eyes of the author's young child.

415. Kassem, Lou. *A Haunting in Williamsburg.* New York: Avon, 1990. 104 pages. ISBN 0-380-75892-X. A ghost named Sally Custis helps Jayne undo a 200-year-old wrong.

416. Kaye, Marilyn. *The Real Tooth Fairy.* Helen Cogancherry, Illustrator. San Diego: Harcourt, 1990. unpaged ISBN 0-15-265780-0. A young girl finally sees the real tooth fairy and is enchanted.

417. Keats, Ezra Jack. *John Henry the American Legend.* New York: Knopf, 1965. unpaged ISBN 0-394-99052-8. A retelling of a popular American tall tale.

418. Keats, Ezra Jack. *Maggie and the Pirate.* New York: Four Winds, 1979,1987. unpaged ISBN 0-02-749710-0. Maggie's pet cricket, kidnapped by a mysterious pirate, meets an untimely end when Maggie struggles to regain her pet. A moving story of sorrow turned to friendship.

419. Keats, Ezra Jack. *Pet Show.* New York: Macmillan, 1972. unpaged ISBN 0-02-749620-1. Peter's cat is missing for the pet show and he must make do with a most unusual substitute.

420. Keats, Ezra Jack. *Peter's Chair.* New York: Harper, 1967. unpaged ISBN 0-06-023112-2. Pete, feeling threatened by all of his furniture being painted pink for his new baby sister, eventually gives up the chair that he also tried to keep from being painted.

421. Keats, Ezra Jack. *The Snowy Day.* New York: Viking, 1962. unpaged ISBN 0-670-65400-0. A child's eye-view of a walk through the snow. Pictures and text combine to bring a sense of wonder to the familiar.

422. Keats, Ezra Jack. *Whistle for Willie.* New York: Penguin, 1964. ISBN 0-670-76240-7. A whimsical story of young Peter's valiant effort to learn to whistle.

423. Kellogg, Steven. *Aster Aardvark's Alphabet Adventures.* New York: Morrow, 1987. unpaged ISBN 0-688-07257-7. A very different alphabet book where each letter is developed in a short story.

424. Kellogg, Steven. *Best Friends.* New York: Dial, 1986. unpaged ISBN 0-8037-0829-7. A touching story of the joy and sorrow of being best friends.

425. Kellogg, Steven. *The Mysterious Tadpole.* New York: Dial, 1977. unpaged ISBN 0-8037-6245-3. A little tadpole from Scotland surprises and delights everyone when it turns into a very famous water creature.

426. Kendall, Russ. *Eskimo Boy: Life in an Inupiaq Eskimo Village.* Photographs by Russ Kendall. New York: Scholastic, 1992. 40 pages. ISBN 0-59043695-3. The author's personal photo-essay of an Eskimo boy and the life and customs of the "first people."

427. Kennedy, Jimmy. *The Teddy Bears' Picnic.* Michael Hague, Illustrator. New York: Henry Holt, 1992. unpaged ISBN 0-8050-1008-4. A little boy dressed in a teddy bear suit, joins the other teddy bears at their picnic in this illustrated version of an old song.

428. Kennedy, X. J. ; Dorothy M. Kennedy. *Knock at a Star: A Child's Introduction to Poetry.* Boston: Little, Brown, 1982,

1985. ISBN 0-316-48854-2. The Kennedys talk about poetry and provide many examples. A nice book for middle graders.

429. Kent, Jack.
The Caterpillar and the Polliwog.
Englewood Cliffs: Prentice-Hall, 1982. unpaged ISBN 0-13-120469-6. While the caterpillar exalts at being different because it doesn't stay the same, the polliwog's disappointment soon turns to joy when it also begins to change. -

430. Kessler, Leonard.
Here Comes the Strikeout.
New York: HarperCollins, 1992. 64 pages. ISBN 0-06023155-6. Bobby learns the value of hard work when he goes from a laughing stock to the star hitter on his baseball team.

431. Kimmel, Eric (reteller).
Anasi and the Moss-Covered Rock.
Janet Stevens, Illustrator. New York: Holiday House, 1988. unpaged ISBN 0-8234-0689-X. Anasi the trickster is up to his old tricks until the unassuming Little Bush Deer turns the table on him.

432. Kimmel, Eric.
Hershel and the Hanukkah Goblins.
Trina Schart Hyman, Illustrator. New York: Holiday House, 1989. unpaged ISBN 0-8234-0769-1. A folk tale-like story that tells how Hershel was able to trick the goblins haunting the synagogue every Hanukkah.

433. King, Elizabeth.
The Pumpkin Patch.
Photographs by author. New

York: Dutton, 1990. unpaged ISBN 0-525-44640-0. A photographic look at pumpkins from seeds to maturity during the Halloween season.

434. Kitamura, Satoshi.
From Acorn to Zoo and Everything in Between in Alphabetical Order.
Satoshi Kitamura. New York: Farrar, Straus and Giroux, 1992. 32 pages. ISBN 0-374-32470-0. An alphabet book with plenty of visual pictures for young readers.

435. Kitamura, Satoshi.
What's Inside: The Alphabet Book.
New York: Farrar, Straus and Giroux, 1985. unpaged ISBN 0-374-38306-5. A delightful alphabet book that is different from most books because of its unique way of looking at things.

436. Kitamura, Satoshi.
When Sheep Cannot Sleep: The Counting Book.
New York: Farrar, Straus and Giroux, 1986. unpaged ISBN 0-374-38311-1. When a sheep can't sleep what should it do? Go for a walk and see what it can see.

437. Klasky, Charles.
Rugs Have Naps (But Never Take Them).
Mike Venezia, Illustrator. Chicago: Children's Press, 1984. 32 pages. ISBN 0-516-03571-1. A zany look at homonyms and the confusion that they can cause.

438. Konigsburg, E. L.
Up From Jericho Tell.
New York: Atheneum, 1986. 192 pages. ISBN 0-689-31194-X. Two latch-key children are given powers of

invisibility in order to find who stole Talullah's necklace the day she died.

439. Koral, April.
Our Global Greenhouse.
New York: Franklin Watts, 1989. 64 pages. ISBN 0-531-10745-0.
A frank discussion on the origins, possible results, and potential remedies to the greenhouse effects to our planet.

440. Korman, Gordon.
The Zucchini Warriors.
New York: Scholastic, 1988. 198 pages. ISBN 0-590-41335-X. Boots and Bruno develop an ingenious plan to get a rec hall for their boys' school and to not have to eat any zucchini sticks.

441. Kraus, Robert.
Whose Mouse Are You?
Jose Aruego, Illustrator. New York: Macmillan, 1970. ISBN 0-02-751190-1. A very simple story of a mouse who rescues his family.

442. Krensky, Stephen.
Four Against the Odds: The Struggle to Save Our Environment.
New York: Scholastic, 1992. 105 pages. ISBN 0-590-44743-2. The biographies of four courageous people and their lonely fight to save the environment from the encroachment of humans and pollution; with a comprehensive bibliography.

443. Krensky, Stephen.
George Washington: The Man Who Would Not Be King.
New York: Scholastic, 1991. 116 pages. ISBN 0-590-43730-5. The biography of our nation's first president.

444. Kuskin, Karla.
Soap Soup.
New York: HarperCollins, 1992. 64 pages. ISBN 0-06-023571-3. Delightful verse that celebrates the simple things around us.

L

445. La Fontaine.
The Lion and the Rat
Brian Wildsmith, Illustrator. New York: Oxford, 1963. unpaged ISBN 0-19-279607-0. A retelling of the story of a rat that was able to do what the mighty lion couldn't.

446. Langstaff, John.
Frog Went A-Courtin'.
Feodor Rojankovsky, Illustrator. San Diego: Harcourt Brace Jovanovich, 1955. unpaged ISBN 0-15-230215-X. An award-winning rendition of a folk song set to pictures.

447. Langstaff, John.
Over in the Meadow.
Feodor Rojankovsky, Illustrator. San Diego: Harcourt Brace Jovanovich, 1957. unpaged ISBN 0-15-258854-X.
An old counting song accompanied by illustrations.

448. Lansky, Vicki.
Microwave Cooking for Kids.
New York: Scholastic, 1991. 48 pages. ISBN 0-590-44203-1. Twenty-seven mouth-watering recipes with simple yet explicit step-by-step directions for young cooks.

449. Larrick, Nancy.
Cats Are Cats.
Ed Young, Illustrator. New York: Putnam, 1988. 80 pages. ISBN 0-399-21517-4. Poems about cats selected by

Larrick, with rich pastel illustrations by Ed Young.

450. Larrick, Nancy (selector). *I Heard a Scream in the Street: Poems by Young People in the City.* New York: Dell, 1970. Poems that express the thoughts and feelings of children of the city.

451. Lasky, Kathryn. *The Bone Wars.* New York: Morrow, 1988. 370 pages. ISBN 0-688-07433-2. Homeless and alone, Jim uses his tracking skills to locate dinosaur bones in the western United States.

452. Lasky, Kathryn. *The Night Journey.* New York: Penguin, 1981. 150 pages. ISBN 0-670-80935-7. Rachel learns the history of her family and their escape from Russia during her visits with her great-grandmother Nana Sashie.

453. Lasky, Kathryn. *Sea Swan.* Catherine Stock, Illustrator. New York: Macmillan, 1988. unpaged ISBN 0-02-751700-4. Elzibah Swan decides to learn to swim on her seventy-fifth birthday, thereby setting off a chain of events leading to her own personal independence and a new life.

454. Lasky, Kathryn. *Sugaring Time.* Photographs by Christopher Knight. New York: Macmillan, 1983. unpaged ISBN 0-02751680-6. A comprehensive look at the process of turning maple sap into maple syrup.

455. Lauber, Patricia. *Dinosaurs Walked Here & Other Stories Fossils Tell.*

New York: Bradbury Press, 1987. 56 pages. ISBN 0-02-754510-5. A combination of photos and full-color drawings that lead the reader through an explanation of fossils and the secrets they can unlock about previous life forms.

456. Lauber, Patricia. *Living with Dinosaurs.* Douglas Henderson, Illustrator. New York: Bradbury Press, 1991. 48 pages. ISBN 0-02-754521-0. A marvelous rendition of how dinosaurs may have looked and lived over 75 million years ago.

457. Lauber, Patricia. *Lost Star, The Story of Amelia Earhart.* New York: Scholastic, 1988. 106 pages. ISBN 0-590-41615-4. A refreshing look at one of America's most famous missing persons.

458. Lauber, Patricia. *The News about Dinosaurs.* New York: Bradbury Press, 1989. 48 pages. ISBN 0-02-754520-2. A frank discussion of the latest theories about dinosaurs, with accompanying illustrations.

459. Lauber, Patricia. *Seeing Earth from Space.* New York: Orchard, 1990. 80 pages. ISBN 0-531-08502-3. Lauber uses both photographs and infrared and radar images in this photo album of Earth. The images are spectacular and varied, including pictures of the hole in the ozone layer at the South Pole.

460. Lauber, Patricia. *Volcano: The Eruption and Healing of Mount St. Helens.* New York: Bradbury Press, 1987. 64 pages. ISBN 0-02-

754500-8. A description of the effects of the eruption and how nature has been restoring the area.

461. Lauber, Patricia. *Volcanoes and Earthquakes.* New York: Scholastic, 1985. 76 pages. ISBN 0-590-42592-7. A comprehensive look through photos and text at two of the most destructive forces at work in nature.

462. Leach, Maria. *How the People Sang the Mountains Up: How and Why Stories.* Glen Rounds, Illustrator. New York: Viking, 1967. 159 pages. ISBN TK. From Maria Leach's introduction: "The stories in this book are why and how stories. They come to us from all over the world, from wherever the first thinkers, the first questioners looked at the stars or the hills or the sea or listened to their own hearts beat, and stopped to say 'Why?—How?'"

463. Lear, Edward. *An Edward Lear Alphabet.* Carol Newsom, Illustrator. New York: Lothrop, 1983. unpaged ISBN 0-688-00965-4. Interesting illustrations accompany some very famous nonsense poetry.

464. Lear, Edward. *The Owl and the Pussycat.* Jan Brett, Illustrator. New York: Putnam, 1991. unpaged ISBN 0-399-21925-0. A colorful rendition of one of Lear's famous poems.

465. Leedy, Loreen. *Messages in the Mailbox: How to Write a Letter.* New York: Holiday House, 1991. unpaged ISBN 0-8234-0889-2. Mrs. Gator teaches

her class of children and animals how to write different types of letters and what to put into each.

466. LeGuin, Ursula K. *A Wizard of Earthsea.* Boston: Houghton Mifflin, 1968. 183 pages. ISBN 0-395-27653-5. The first of a four-book series in which Ged must confront an evil force that he released into the world.

467. Lehr, Norma. *The Shimmering Ghost of Riversend.* Minneapolis: First Avenue, 1991. 168 pages. ISBN 0-8225-9589-3. Kathy spends the summer in an old mysterious house with her aunt and becomes embroiled in an old family mystery.

468. L'Engle, Madeleine. *Meet the Austins.* New York: Dell, 1961. 192 pages. ISBN 0-440-95777-X. A large family is forced to readjust when they take in a spoiled relative who has lost her family.

469. L'Engle, Madeleine. *A Wind in the Door.* New York: Farrar, Straus & Giroux, 1973, 1976. 224 pages. ISBN 0-374-38443-6. Charles Wallace has become ill as the forces of evil in the universe attack the mitochondria in his cells. His sister helps to overcome them with a bit of supernatural help.

470. Lerner, Carol. *Moonseed and Mistletoe: A Book of Poisonous Wild Plants.* New York: Morrow, 1988. 32 pages. ISBN 0-688-07307-7. Lerner tells of plants that are harmful to touch and to eat.

471. Leslie, Clare Walker. *Nature All Year Long.* New York: Greenwillow, 1991. 56 pages. ISBN 0-688-09183-0. A cleverly constructed treasure hunt of things to do and see in nature the year round.

472. Lesser, Rika. *Hansel and Gretel.* Paul O. Zelinsky, Illustrator. New York: Putnam, 1984. unpaged ISBN 0-399-21733-9. Zelinsky's illustrations and Lesser's retelling work to earn this version a place with those of Sendak and Zwerger.

473. Lester, Helen. *A Porcupine Named Fluffy.* Lynn Munsinger, Boston: Houghton Mifflin, 1986. unpaged ISBN 0-395-42636-7. An anything but fluffy porcupine learns that his name isn't quite so bad when he meets a rhino named Hippo.

474. Lester, Helen. *Tacky the Penguin.* Lynn Munsinger, Boston: Houghton Mifflin, 1988. unpaged ISBN 0-395-56233-3. A very funny story of Tacky, the nonconformist penguin, who uses his wits to scare off the evil hunters.

475. Lester, Julius. *The Knee-High Man and Other Tales.* Ralph Pinto, Illustrator. New York: Dial, 1972. unpaged ISBN 0-8037-4593-1. A collection of six African-American tales involving animals.

476. Lester, Julius. *More Tales of Uncle Remus: Further Adventures of Brer Rabbit, His Friends, Enemies, and Others.* Jerry Pinkney, Illustrator. New York: Dial, 1988. 143 pages. ISBN 0-8037-0420-8. A collection of thirty-seven tales in which Lester retells the Uncle Remus tales with a storyteller's voice.

477. Lester, Julius. *To Be a Slave.* Tom Feeling, Illustrator. New York: Dial, 1968. 160 pages. ISBN 0-8037-8955-6. First person accounts of what it was like to be a slave in the United States.

478. Levine, Ellen. *Ready, Aim, Fire! The Real Adventures of Annie Oakley.* New York: Scholastic, 1989. 132 pages. ISBN 0-590-41877-7. An interesting biographical description of one of the old West's leading ladies.

479. Levitin, Sonia. *The Man Who Kept His Heart in a Bucket.* Jerry Pickney, Illustrator. New York: Dial, 1991. unpaged ISBN 0-8037-1030-5. Jack, his heart once broken, must solve a riddle in order to get his heart back from a beautiful young maiden.

480. Lewin, Hugh. *Jafta.* Lisa Kopper, Illustrator. Minneapolis: Carolrhoda Books, 1983. unpaged ISBN 0-87614-494-6. A young South African boy describes his emotions though comparisons with native animals.

481. Lewis, Claudia. *Long Ago in Oregon.* Joel Fontaine, Illustrator. New York: Harper, 1987. 56 pages. ISBN 0-06-023839-9. Striking descriptions drawn through words and pictures of life at the turn of the twentieth century.

482. Lewis, Rob. *Friska the Sheep That Was Too Small.* Rob Lewis, Illustrator. New York: Farrar, Straus and Giroux, 1987. unpaged ISBN 0-374-42463-2. A story of a small but clever sheep who overcomes the taunts of the other sheep to save them from the wolf.

483. Lindbergh, Reeve. *The Midnight Farm.* Susan Jeffers, Illustrator. New York: Dial, 1987. unpaged ISBN 0-8037-0331-7. A beautifully illustrated lullaby of wild and domestic animals found around a farm.

484. Lionni, Leo. *Frederick.* New York: Pantheon, 1967. unpaged ISBN 0-394-910040-0. A version of "The Grasshopper and the Ant" in which Frederick the mouse saves his family with his words that have been his work.

485. Lionni, Leo. *Fredrick's Fables.* New York: Pantheon, 1983. 132 pages. ISBN 0-394-87710-1. A collection of thirteen of Lionni's previously published fables.

486. Lionni, Leo. *Inch by Inch.* New York: Astor-Honor, 1962. unpaged ISBN 0-8392-3010-9. An inchworm captured by a robin, measures different birds before inching out of danger.

487. Lionni, Leo. *Mathew's Dream.* New York: Knopf, 1991. unpaged ISBN 0-679-81075-7. Mathew, inspired by a trip to an art museum, decides that he will grow up to be a painter.

488. Lister, Robin (reteller). *The Legend of King Arthur.* Alan Baker, Illustrator. New York: Doubleday, 1988. 96 pages. ISBN 0-385-26369-4. A retelling of the tales of the legend of King Arthur in picture book format.

489. Littledale, Freyda. *Peter and the North Wind.* Troy Howell, Illustrator. New York: Scholastic, 1988. unpaged ISBN 0-590-40756-2. A resourceful lad receives fabulous gifts from the North Wind as repayment for flour the wind has blown away. However, he has to outwit an evil innkeeper in order to keep his gifts.

490. Livingston, Myra Cohn. *A Circle of Seasons.* Leonard Everett Fisher, Illustrator. New York: Holiday House, 1982. ISBN 0-8234-0452-8. Poems that celebrate the passing of the seasons.

491. Livingston, Myra Cohn. *Earth Songs.* Leonard Everett Fisher, Illustrator. New York: Scholastic, 1986. unpaged ISBN 0-590-44670-3. A lyrical celebration of the earth and its many wonders.

492. Lobel, Anita. *The Dwarf Giant.* New York: Holiday House, 1991. unpaged ISBN 0-8234-0852-3. Prince Mainichi and Princess Ichinichi's hospitality is put to the test by a mean-spirited dwarf who causes all kinds of trouble before it is

defeated by a many-armed giant.

493. Lobel, Anita.
The Pancake.
New York: Dell, 1978. 48 pages. ISBN 0-440-40624-2. A retelling of the "Runaway Pancake" tale.

494. Lobel, Arnold.
The Book of Pigericks.
New York: Harper, 1983. 48 pages. ISBN 0-06-323982-4. Limericks about pigs. Great for beginning a limerick writing lesson.

495. Lobel, Arnold.
Fables.
New York: Harper, 1980. 41 pages. ISBN 0-06-023973-5. Wonderfully illustrated fables for children.

496. Lobel, Arnold.
Frog and Toad All Year.
New York: Harper & Row, ISBN 0-06-023950-6. More stories for early readers about two memorable friends.

497. Lobel, Arnold.
Frog and Toad Are Friends.
New York: Harper & Row, 1970. ISBN 0-06-023957-3. A "chapter book" suitable for beginning readers containing 5 elegant yet simple stories.

498. Lobel, Arnold.
Frog and Toad Together.
New York: Harper & Row, ISBN 0-06-023959-X. Each chapter is a new story about these two friends.

499. Lobel, Arnold.
Grasshopper on the Road.
New York: HarperCollins, 1978. 64 pages. ISBN 0-06-02361-1. A series of easy-to-read stories that entertain and contain a message.

500. Lobel, Arnold.
Mouse Tales.
New York: Harper & Row, 1972. ISBN 0-06-023941-7. Papa Mouse tells his children seven bedtime stories. This is a good beginning chapter book for the early grades.

501. Lobel, Arnold.
The Random House Book of Mother Goose.
Arnold Lobel, Illustrator. New York: Random House, 1986. 176 pages. ISBN 0-394-86799-8. A collection of familiar and some not-so-familiar nursery rhymes.

502. Locker, Thomas.
Family Farm.
New York: Dial, 1988. unpaged ISBN 0-8037-0489-5. The story of a family and the hardships they face in order to survive on a small farm in modern-day middle America.

503. Locker, Thomas.
The Land of the Gray Wolf.
New York: Dial, 1991. unpaged ISBN 0-0837-0936-6. A haunting story about a small Eastern Woodland Native American tribe and its quest to survive the arrival of the white man.

504. Locker, Thomas.
Sailing with the Wind.
New York: Dial, 1986. unpaged ISBN 0-8037-0311-2. Uncle Jack and Elizabeth spend a wonderful day sailing to the ocean and back. A beautifully illustrated story.

505. Locker, Thomas.
Where the River Begins.
New York: Dial, 1984. unpaged ISBN 0-8037-0090-3. Two boys and their grandfather go exploring for the source of a river.

506. Louie, Ai-Ling (reteller).
Yeh-Shen.
Ed Young, Illustrator. New York: Philomel, 1982. unpaged ISBN 0-399-20900-X. A young Chinese girl overcomes her wicked stepmother and stepsister to marry a prince. A retelling that predates the European version of Cinderella by over 1,000 years.

507. Lovik, Craig.
Andy and the Tire.
Mark Alan Weatherby, Illustrator. New York: Scholastic, 1987. unpaged ISBN 0-570-41323-6. Andy is new and has trouble making friends until he hits upon a unique method of getting attention that leads to making new friends.

508. Lunn, Janet.
The Root Cellar.
New York: Macmillan, 1981, 1983. 247 pages. ISBN 0-684-17855-9. A young girl goes to live with a relative in Canada and stumbles into a cellar that leads to Canada during the American Civil War.

M

509. Maass, Robert.
When Autumn Comes.
New York: Henry Holt, 1990. unpaged ISBN 0-8050-1259-1. A photographic look at the beauty of autumn.

510. Macauley, David.
Black and White.
Boston: Houghton Mifflin, 1990. unpaged ISBN 0-395-52151-3. Macauley tells four parallel stories that finally intersect.

511. Macauley, David.
Castle.
Boston: Houghton Mifflin,

1989. 80 pages. ISBN 0-395-25784-0. The comprehensive story of a fictional castle and its construction and use.

512. Macauley, David.
The Motel of the Mysteries.
Boston: Houghton Mifflin, 1979. pages. ISBN 0-395-28424-4. A parody that shows future archaeologists excavating an old civilization that looks similar to the United States. A motel becomes an ancient temple and burial chamber.

513. Macauley, David.
The Way Things Work.
Boston: Houghton Mifflin, 1988. 400 pages. ISBN 0-395-42857-2. Macauley explains how many common, and some not-so-common, things work. His illustrations are both very clear and informative while containing the full measure of his unique humor.

514. MacLachlan, Patricia.
Sarah, Plain and Tall.
New York: Harper & Row, 1985. 58 pages. ISBN 0-06-024102-0. Sarah answers a farmer's letter and moves to the Plains from the New England seacoast to be his wife.

515. Maestro, Betsy.
A Sea Full of Sharks.
Giulio Maestro, Illustrator. New York: Scholastic, 1990. unpaged ISBN 0-590-43100-5. A colorful introduction to the world of sharks.

516. Maestro, Betsy;
Giulio Maestro.
A More Perfect Union: The Story of Our Constitution.
Giulio Maestro, Illustrator. New York: Mulberry Books, 1990. 48 pages. ISBN 0-688-10192-5. An informative view

of the U. S. Constitution for older readers.

517. Mahy, Margaret.
The Blood-and-Thunder Adventure on Hurricane Peak.
Wendy Smith, Illustrator. New York: McElderry, 1989. 132 pages. ISBN 0-689-50488-8. A preposterous story about an unscrupulous industrialist, a beautiful female scientist, a love- struck magician, a school whose headmistress has been missing for years, and talking cats.

518. Mahy, Margaret.
A Lion in the Meadow.
Jenny Williams, Illustrator. Woodstock: Overlook Press, 1992. unpaged ISBN 0-87951-446-9. A little boy, afraid of the imaginary lion and dragon in the meadow outside his house, overcomes his fears and makes friends with them.

519. Mannetti, William.
Dinosaurs in Your Backyard.
New York: Atheneum, 1982. 147 pages. ISBN 0-689-30906-6. Touching on many aspects of dinosaurs—what defines a dinosaur, whether they were warm or cold blooded, etc.—Mannetti shows us that the study of dinosaurs has been important in science. He also claims that dinosaurs are ancestral to birds. (Others are not as sure.)

520. Manushkin, Fran.
Latkes and Applesauce: A Hanukkah Story.
Robin Spowart, Illustrator. New York: Scholastic, 1990. unpaged ISBN 0-590-42261-8. An untimely storm leaves the Menashe family with very little food for Hanukkah, and they receive help from an unexpected source.

521. Marshak, Samuel.
Month-Brothers: A Slavic Tale.
Diane Stanley, Illustrator. New York: Morrow, 1983. unpaged ISBN 0-688-01509-3. A young girl, sent to find flowers in the middle of winter, encounters the Months of the year who help her. Later her stepsister tries to get gifts from them but is punished instead. Compare to *The Talking Eggs.*

522. Marshall, James (reteller).
Goldilocks and the Three Bears.
Dial: New York, 1988. unpaged ISBN 0-8037-0543-3. A retelling of the Goldilocks story with James Marshall's distinctive style of hilarious characters. This retelling explains how Goldilocks happened upon the Bears' home.

523. Marshall, James.
Red Riding Hood.
New York: Dial, 1987. unpaged ISBN 0-8037-0344-9. A retelling of Red Riding Hood that is slapstick in its language and illustrations.

524. Marshall, James.
Three Little Pigs.
New York: Dial, 1989. unpaged ISBN 0-8037-0591-3. Another of James Marshall's irreverent retellings of traditional tales. This version includes the rest of the story that takes place after the wolf realizes he's not going to blow down a brick house.

525. Martin, Bill Jr.
Brown Bear, Brown Bear What Do You See?
Eric Carle, Illustrator. New York: Henry Holt, 1983.

unpaged ISBN 0-8050-0201-4. An ageless classic that leads the reader to play with our language.

526. Martin, Bill Jr.; John Archambault.
The Ghost Eye Tree.
Ted Rand, Illustrator. New York: Henry Holt, 1985. unpaged ISBN 0-8050-0947-7. A sister and her brother confront the fearsome Ghost Eye when they fetch a pail of milk for their mother.

527. Martin, Bill Jr.; John Archambault.
Here Are My Hands.
Ted Rand, Illustrator. New York: Henry Holt, 1985. unpaged ISBN 0-8050-0328-2. A celebration of the human body and the uses of its various parts.

528. Martin, Bill Jr.; John Archambault.
Knots on a Counting Rope.
Ted Rand, Illustrator. New York: Henry Holt, 1987. unpaged ISBN 0-8050-0571-4. Grandfather tells a young Indian boy about the boy's race; each time he tells it, he puts another knot in a rope. A story designed to be read by two voices.

529. Martin, Bill Jr.; John Archambault.
Listen to the Rain.
James Endicot, Illustrator. New York: Henry Holt, 1988. unpaged ISBN 0-8050-0682-6. Rhythmic language that captures the cadence of the rain.

530. Martin, Bill Jr.; John Archambault.
The Magic Pumpkin.
Robert J. Lee, Illustrator. New York: Henry Holt, 1989. unpaged ISBN 0-8050-1124-

2. A pumpkin comes alive on Halloween night to lead a band of mischief makers only to get snuffed out.

531. Martin, Rafe.
Foolish Rabbit's Big Mistake.
Ed Young, Illustrator. New York: Putnam, 1985. unpaged ISBN 0-399-21178-0. An Asian Jataka tale about a rabbit who thinks the earth is breaking up. He panics all the animals in turn until they reach lion. Compare to *Chicken Little.*

532. Martin, Rodney.
The Making of a Picture Book.
John Siow, Illustrator. Milwaukee: Gareth Stevens Children's Books, 1989. 32 pages. ISBN 0-55532-958-6. A comprehensive look at the step-by- step process of how picture books are created.

533. Maruki, Toshi.
Hiroshima No Pika.
New York: Lothrop, 1980. unpaged ISBN 0-688-01297-3. A book that needs to be carefully used with a class or a select group of children. It's a graphic account of the first atomic bomb drop and the resulting devastation.

534. Marzollo, Jean.
In 1492.
Steve Bjorkman, Illustrator. New York: Scholastic, 1991. unpaged ISBN 0-590-44413-1. A humorous account of Columbus's famous journey told in rhyming couplets.

535. Marzollo, Jean.
Pretend You're A Cat.
Jerry Pinkney, Illustrator. New York: Dial, 1990. unpaged ISBN 0-8037-0773-8. A delightful invitation for

children to set their imaginations free through active play.

536. Marzollo, Jean.
The Silver Bear.
Susan Meddaugh, Illustrator. New York: Dial, 1987. unpaged ISBN 0-8037-0368-6. A gazebo provides two young boys with active imaginations a source of wonderment and entertainment as they see a variety of animals appear from it.

537. Mathews, Louise.
Bunches and Bunches of Bunnies.
Jeni Bassett, Illustrator. New York: Putnam, 1978. unpaged ISBN 0-396-07601-7. A book about counting and multiplication with, appropriately enough, bunnies.

538. Mathis, Sharon Bell.
The Hundred Penny Box.
Leo and Diane Dillon, Illustrators. New York: Penguin, 1975. ISBN 0-670-38787-8. A young boy loves to listen to his grandmother's stories that correspond with the dates on her 100 pennies, but mom and grandmother don't get along.

539. Matsutani, Miyoko (reteller); Alvin Tresselt.
The Crane Maiden.
Iwasaki, Chihiro, Illustrator. New York: Parents' Magazine, 1968. unpaged A poor old man's kindness toward a trapped crane is rewarded when a young lady comes to live with them and weaves beautiful cloth for them.

540. Matthews, Rupert.
The Dinosaur Age.

Colin Newman, Illustrator. New York: Bookwright Press, 1989. 32 pages. ISBN 0-531-18280-0. A variety of dinosaurs from various ages are brought to life through vivid illustrations and text.

541. Mayer, Marianna.
Beauty and the Beast.
New York: Macmillan, 1978. unpaged ISBN 0-02-765270-X. Another version of a classic tale punctuated with excellent illustrations by the author.

542. Mayer, Marianna.
The Black Horse.
Kate Thamer, Illustrator. New York: Dial, 1984. 40 pages. ISBN 0-8037-0075-X. A young prince rescues a princess from an evil king with the help of a magical horse.

543. Mayer, Marianna.
The Prince and the Princess: A Bohemian Fairy Tale.
Jacqueline Rogers, Illustrator. New York: Bantam, 1989. 64 pages. ISBN 0-553-05843-6. A young prince, with the help of three extraordinary people, overcomes an evil sorcerer to save the beautiful princess.

544. Mayer, Marianna.
The Unicorn and the Lake.
Michael Hague, Illustrator. New York: Dial, 1982. unpaged ISBN 0-8037-9337-5. The story of the last unicorn and its battle to stop the evil serpent from destroying the animals from the Lake.

545. Mayer, Mercer.
East of the Sun & West of the Moon.
New York: Four Winds Press, 1980. unpaged ISBN 0-590-07538-1. A young maiden, after rebuffing the request of a

noble youth, searches for him before he marries an evil troll princess.

546. Mayle, Peter.
What's Happening to Me?
Arthur Robbins, Illustrator. Secaucus: Lyle Stuart, 1975. unpaged ISBN 0-8184-0221-0. An honest, unabashed look at the changes, both physical and emotional, that happen during puberty.

547. Mayle, Peter.
Where Did I Come From?
Arthur Robbins, Illustrator. Secaucus: Lyle Stuart, 1973. unpaged ISBN 0-84-0161-3. An honest and unabashed description of human reproduction.

548. Mayo, Gretchen Will.
Star Tales: North American Indian Stories about the Stars.
New York: Walker, 1987. 96 pages. ISBN 0-8027-6673-0. A collection of stories explaining how stars and constellations came to be.

549. McCloskey, Robert.
Blueberries for Sal.
New York: Penguin, 1948. unpaged ISBN 0-670-17591-9. Sal goes blueberry picking one sunny day with her mother and ends up following a mother bear who is also blueberry picking with her cub.

550. McCloskey, Robert.
Make Way for Ducklings.
New York: Penguin, 1941. unpaged ISBN 0-670-45149-5. A classic story of a family of ducks living in the heart of Boston.

551. McCloskey, Robert.
One Morning in Maine.
New York: Penguin, 1952.

unpaged ISBN 0-670-52627-4. Sal's joy of losing her first tooth is captured in blue-pencil drawings by an award-winning author-illustrator.

552. McCloskey, Robert.
Time of Wonder.
New York: Penguin, 1957. unpaged ISBN 0-670-71512-3. A magical look at the coast of Maine and the effects of a hurricane that invades it one summer.

553. McCord, David.
All Small.
Madelaine Gill Linden, Illustrator. Boston: Little, Brown, 1986. 32 pages. ISBN 0-316-55519-3. Great little poems to fill a moment and to think about for hours.

554. McDermott, Gerald.
Anansi the Spider.
New York: Henry Holt, 1972. unpaged ISBN 0-8050-0310-X. Ananasi, the trickster, and his sons quarrel, resulting in the moon being put up in the sky.

555. McDermott, Gerald.
Arrow to the Sun.
New York: Penguin, 1974, 1977. unpaged ISBN 0-670-13369-8. A Pueblo Indian tale of the son of the Sun. Illustrations won the Caldecott medal.

556. McDonald, Megan.
The Great Pumpkin Switch.
Ted Lewin, Illustrator. New York: Orchard Books, 1992. unpaged ISBN 0-531-05450-0. Grampa tells his grandchildren a story of how he and his friend Otto had to find a quick replacement after they accidently smashed his sister's prize Halloween pumpkin.

557. McGill, Marci Ridlon. *The Story of Louisa May Alcott: Determined Writer.* New York: Dell, 1988. 92 pages. ISBN 0-440-40022-8. The story of America's first famous female author.

558. McGovern, Ann. *The Pilgrims' First Thanksgiving.* Joe Lasker, Illustrator. New York: Scholastic, 1973. 48 pages. ISBN 0-590-40617-5. A look at the first year that the Pilgrims spent in the New World, culminating in the first American Thanksgiving.

559. McGovern, Ann. *Robin Hood of Sherwood Forest.* New York: Scholastic, 1968. 128 pages. ISBN 0-590-40842-9. A retelling of the legend that surrounds one of England's most famous outlaws.

560. McGovern, Anne. *The Secret Soldier: The Story of Deborah Sampson.* New York: Macmillan, 1975. 64 pages. ISBN 0-02-765-780-9. The story of a young woman and her determination to fight during the revolutionary war.

561. McGovern, Ann. *Sharks.* Murry Tinkelman, Illustrator. New York: Scholastic, 1976. 48 pages. ISBN 0-590-41360-0. Thirteen interesting questions and answers about sharks are presented in this book.

562. McGovern, Anne; Eugenie Clarke. *The Desert Beneath the Sea.* Craig Phillips, Illustrator. New York: Scholastic, 1991. 48 pages. ISBN 0-590-42638-9.

A marine biologist and an underwater enthusiast bring underwater plants and animals to life in a remarkable book about one of the last frontiers of our world.

563. McGraw, Eloise Jarvis. *Moccasin Trail.* New York: Peter Smith, 1952. 247 pages. ISBN 0-8446-6346-8. Jim Keith, having spent six years living with the Crow Indians, must face prejudice and mistrust as he leads his natural family to the Oregon Territory.

564. McKinley, Robin. *The Hero and the Crown.* New York: Greenwillow, 1984. 256 pages. ISBN 0-688-02593-5. Aerin should be the next ruler of the kingdom, but she is not trusted. Instead, she becomes a dragon killer and eventually wins back the hero's crown for her country.

565. McKissack, Patricia. *Jesse Jackson.* New York: Scholastic, 1989. 108 pages. ISBN 0-590-43181-1. An interesting and extremely readable biography of a famous American.

566. McKissack, Patricia. *Mirandy and Brother Wind.* Jerry Pinkney, Illustrator. New York: Knopf, 1988. unpaged ISBN 0-394-88765-4. Brother Wind is up to his mischievous tricks as Mirandy is preparing for the big social event of her young life.

567. McLerran, Alice. *I Want to Go Home.* Jill Kastner, Illustrator. New York: Tambourine, 1992. unpaged ISBN 0-688-10144-5. Marta was sure she would not like the new house until her mom brought home a cat

that experienced the same difficult time adjusting as its new master.

568. McMillan, Bruce. *Eating Fractions.* New York: Scholastic, 1991. unpaged ISBN 0-509-43778-4. A tasty introduction to basic fraction concepts of halves, thirds, and fourths.

569. McMillan, Bruce. *Growing Colors.* Photographs by Bruce McMillan. New York: Lothrop Lee & Shepard, 1988. ISBN 0-688-07844-3. Glorious photographs displaying the vivid colors of selected fruits and vegetables.

570. McNulty, Faith. *Orphan: The Story of a Baby Woodchuck.* Darby Morrell, Illustrator. New York: Scholastic, 1992. 40 pages. ISBN 0-590-43838-7. The true story of the author's adventure of raising an abandoned baby woodchuck.

571. McPhail, David. *Ed and Me.* San Diego: Harcourt Brace Jovanovich, 1990. unpaged ISBN 0-15-224888-9. A heartwarming story of a young girl and her father's special relationship with an all purpose truck they call Ed.

572. Meigs, Cornelia. *Invincible Louisa.* Boston: Little, Brown, 1933. 247 pages. ISBN 0-316-56590-3. The story of America's first famous female author.

573. Mendez, Phil. *The Black Snowman.* Carole Byard, Illustrator. New York: Scholastic, 1989.

unpaged ISBN 0-590-40552-7. Young Jacob does not appreciate his African heritage until a magical *kente* brings a black snowman to life, causing him to reassess his beliefs.

574. Micucci, Charles. *The Life and Times of the Apple.* New York: Orchard, 1992. 32 pages. ISBN 0-531-05939-1. A cleverly crafted book that tells almost everything there is to know about apples.

575. Miles, Bernard. *Favorite Tales from Shakespeare.* Victor Ambrus, Illustrator. New York: Macmillan, 1988. 125 pages. ISBN 0-02-689-024-0. Five of Shakespeare's famous works specially retold for upper elementary- and middle-school readers.

576. Miles, Miska. *Annie and the Old One.* Peter Parnell, Illustrator. Boston: Little, Brown, 1971. unpaged ISBN 0-316-57120-2. Annie tries to prevent her grandmother's death, but learns from her that all things are of the earth, and must return to the earth.

577. Mills, Lauren. *The Rag Coat.* Boston: Little, Brown, 1991. unpaged ISBN 0-316-57407-4. Minna's coat, at first an object of scorn, tells the story of her new classmates in a beautifully told and illustrated story from Appalachia.

578. Milton, Nancy. *The Giraffe that Walked to Paris.* Roger Roth, Illustrator. New York: Crown, 1992. unpaged ISBN 0-517-58123-9. A

historical account of the journey of a giraffe that was given to the king of France by the pasha of Egypt.

579. Minarik, Else Holmelund.
Little Bear.
Maurice Sendek, Illustrator. New York: Harper, 1957. 64 pages. ISBN 0-06-024241-8. The first of a series of adventures featuring Little Bear and Mother Bear.

580. Minarik, Else Holmelund.
Little Bear's Visit.
Maurice Sendak, Illustrator. New York: Harper, 1961. 64 pages. ISBN 0-06-024265-5. The continuing story of Little Bear, featuring his visit to his grandparents and the fun they have. Others in the series include *Little Bear's Friends* and *A Kiss for Little Bear.*

581. Moche, Dinah.
What's Up There?
Tom Huffman, Illustrator. New York: Scholastic, 1990. 64 pages ISBN 0-590-44056-X. A question-and-answer format that uses photos and drawings to explain the complex universe around us.

582. Moore, Clement C.
The Night Before Christmas.
James Marshall, Illustrator. New York: Scholastic, 1985. unpaged ISBN 0-590-45075-1. Marshall's zany illustrations breathe new life into a Christmas classic.

583. Morey, Walt.
Kavik the Wolf Dog.
New York: Dutton, 1968. 192 pages. ISBN 0-525-33093-3. A young boy's love for a dog is tested when he must return the dog to its owner after he had nursed it back to life.

584. Morimoto, Junko.
My Hiroshima.
New York: Viking, 1990. unpaged ISBN 0-670-83181-6. A story that tells of the first atom bomb which was dropped on Hiroshima.

585. Morozumi, Atsuko.
One Gorilla.
New York: Farrar, Straus and Giroux, 1990. unpaged Count along as a playful gorilla takes a walk through the jungle.

586. Morris, Ann.
Bread Bread Bread.
Photographs by Ken Heyman. New York: Lothrop, 1989. 32 pages. ISBN 0-688-06334-9. Breads of all different types and uses are pictured. The index gives the country of origin for each photograph.

587. Mosel, Arlene (reteller).
Tikki Tikki Tembo.
Blair Lent, Illustrator. New York: Henry Holt, unpaged. ISBN 0-8050-0662-1. The story of why Chinese parents no longer give their firstborn children long names. A marvelous story for reading aloud, just to hear the wonderful sounds of the boy's long name.

588. Moss, Jeff.
The Butterfly Jar.
Chris Demarest, Illustrator. New York: Bantam, 1989. 115 pages. ISBN 0-553-05704-9. A variety of verse that is fun and lively to read, privately or aloud.

589. Mowat, Farley.
Lost in the Barrens.
Boston: Little, Brown, 1982. 192 pages. ISBN 0-316-58638-2. Two young men are separated from their hunting party and must survive the onslaught of winter in

northern Canada while trying to find their way back home.

590. Munro, Roxie.
The Inside-Outside Book of Paris.
New York: Dutton, 1992. unpaged ISBN 0-525-44863-2. A variety of landmarks and sights found in the "City of Lights" are illustrated and explained in a delightful combination of pictures and text.

591. Munsch, Robert.
The Paper Bag Princess.
Michael Martchenko, Illustrator. Toronto: Firefly Books, 1980. unpaged ISBN 0-920236-16-2. Elizabeth the princess sets out to save her future husband, the prince, from the evil dragon, and discovers that the prince is not her type.

592. Murphy, Jim.
The Boys War.
New York: Scholastic, 1990. 110 pages. ISBN 0-590-45604-0. A graphic photo-history of the young men and boys that fought in the Civil War.

593. Murphy, Joanne Brisson.
Feelings.
Heather Collins, Illustrator. Windsor: Black Moss Press, 1985. unpaged ISBN 0-88753-129-6. A wonderful book that probes and illustrates the feelings all young children confront as they grow and change.

594. Musgrove, Margaret.
Ashanti to Zulu: African Traditions.
Leo and Diane Dillon, Illustrators. New York: Dial, 1976. unpaged ISBN 0-8037-0358-9. A Caldecott award-winning book that describes

different African tribes through their distinctive lifestyles and dress.

N

595. Ness, Evaline.
Sam, Bangs & Moonshine.
New York: Henry Holt, 1966. unpaged ISBN 0-8050-0315-0. Sam learns to tell the difference between truth and "moonshine."

596. Nixon, Joan Lowery.
If You Were a Writer.
Bruce Degen, Illustrator. New York: Four Winds Press, 1988. Unpaged ISBN 0-02-768210-2. Nixon shows how a writer searches for the words that best tell her story—a story that should have a strong lead—through the use of a writer-mother describing how an author thinks to her aspiring writer-daughter.

597. Lowry, Lois,
Number the Stars.
Boston: Houghton Mifflin, 1989. 137 pages. ISBN 0-395-51060-0. The story of a group of courageous people during World War II and their attempt to smuggle Jewish citizens out of Nazi-held territories.

598 Noble, Trinka Hakes.
Apple Tree Christmas.
New York: Dial, 1984. unpaged ISBN 0-8037-0103-9. An apple tree gives a unique Christmas gift to a nineteenth-century family in rural America.

599. Noble, Trinka Hakes.
The Day Jimmy's Boa Ate the Wash.
Steven Kellogg, Illustrator. New York: Dial, 1980. unpaged ISBN 0-8037-0094-

6. A child tells about a very exciting field trip to a farm.

600. Numeroff, Laura.
If You Give a Mouse a Cookie.
Felicia Bond, Illustrator. New York: Harper & Row, 1985. unpaged ISBN 0-06-024587-5. An imagined domino effect stemming from the simple act of giving a little mouse a cookie. Great as a story starter.

601. Numeroff, Laura Joffe.
If You Give a Moose a Muffin.
Felicia Bond, Illustrator. New York: HarperCollins, 1991. unpaged ISBN 0-06-024405-4. The young host is run ragged by a surprise visit from a moose in the sequel to *If You Give A Mouse A Cookie.*

O

602. Oakes, Catherine.
The Middle Ages.
San Diego: Harcourt Brace Jovanovich, 1989. 64 pages. ISBN 0-15-200451-3. Exacting illustrations of life and possessions of the Middle Ages.

603. O'Dell, Scott.
Bright Star, Bright Dawn.
Boston: Houghton Mifflin, 1988. 144 pages. ISBN 0-395-47778-6. A young Eskimo girl decides to participate in the 1,197 mile-long Iditirod race.

604. O'Dell, Scott.
Island of the Blue Dolphins.
Boston: Houghton Mifflin, 1960. 161 pages. ISBN 0-395-06962-9. One of the most popular of the survival stories tells of a Native American girl stranded on an island for much of her life.

605. O'Dell, Scott.
Sarah Bishop.
Boston: Houghton Mifflin, 1980. 184 pages. ISBN 0-395-29185-2. The first-person account of what it was like for a young girl to live during the American Revolution.

606. O'Dell, Scott; Elizabeth Hall.
Thunder Rolling in the Mountains.
Boston: Houghton Mifflin, 1992. 128 pages. ISBN 0-395-59966-0. A chilling account of Chief Joseph's attempt to save the Nez Percé from the encroachment of white people told though the eyes of his daughter, Running Feet.

607. O'Dell Scott.
Streams to the River, River to the Sea: A Novel of Sacagawea.
Boston: Houghton Mifflin, 1986. 176 pages. ISBN 0-395-40430-4. The story of Sacagawea and her courage while traveling with Lewis and Clark on their famous exploratory journey through the western part of America in the early 1800s.

608. Oechsli, Helen; Kelly Oechsli.
In My Garden: A Child's Gardening Book.
Kelly Oechsli, Illustrator. New York: Macmillan, 1985. 32 pages. ISBN 0-02-768510-1. An entertaining look at an outdoor garden and all of the vegetables that can be grown in it.

609. Oppenheim, Joanne.
Left & Right.
Rosanne Litzinger, Illustrator San Diego: Harcourt Brace Jovanovich, 1989. 32 pages ISBN 0-15-200505-6. Two brothers, Left and Right, learn that they work better together than alone.

610. Ormerod, Jan.
The Frog Prince.
New York: Lothrop, 1990. unpaged ISBN 0-688-09568-2. The princess allows the frog to share her bed for three days as she had promised. During that time, she comes to love the frog, and he is transformed into a prince.

611. Osborne, Mary Pope.
American Tall Tales.
Michael McCurdy, Illustrator. New York: Knopf, 1991. 115 pages. ISBN 0-679-80089-1. Osborne presents the usual complement of tall tale characters—Johnny Appleseed, Pecos Bill, etc.—but also some not commonly seen, such as Mose from the Bowery, and Sally Ann Thunder Ann Whirlwind, who was Davy Crockett's wife.

612. Osborne, Mary Pope.
Favorite Greek Myths.
Troy Howell, Illustrator. New York: Scholastic, 1989. 81 pages. ISBN 0-590-41338-4. Sixteen Greek myths retold for younger readers.

613. Osborne, Will; Mary Pope Osborne.
The Deadly Power of Medusa.
New York: Scholastic, 1988. 92 pages. ISBN 0-590-41151-9. A retelling of this popular myth for young readers that describes the demise of the snake-haired monster whose gaze turns men to stone.

614. Osborne, Will; Mary Pope Osborne.
Jason and the Argonauts.
New York: Scholastic, 1988. 84 pages. ISBN 0-590-41152-7. A retelling of a popular myth for young readers that follows Jason and his fellow adventurers as they search for the golden fleece.

615. Otey, Mimi.
Daddy Has a Pair of Striped Pants.
New York: Farrar, Straus and Giroux, 1990. unpaged ISBN 0-374-31675-9. A touching first-hand look at a little girl's love for her father.

P

616. Pallotta, Jerry.
The Ocean Alphabet Book.
Frank Mazzola Jr., Illustrator. Watertown: Charlesbridge, 1986. unpaged ISBN 0-88106-458-0. A colorful school of ocean life that is found in the North Atlantic Ocean.

617. Parish, Peggy.
Amelia Bedelia.
Fritz Siebel, Illustrator. New York: Harper & Row, 1963. ISBN 0-06-024640-5. Amelia is a maid who is constantly getting into hilarious situations because she takes everything literally.

618. Parish, Peggy.
Good Hunting, Blue Sky.
James Watts, Illustrator. New York: HarperCollins, 1988. ISBN 0-06-024661-8 . A young Native American goes hunting, but ends up being brought back to the village by the animal he hunts.

619. Parker, Nancy Winslow; Joan Richards Wright.
Frogs, Toads, Lizards, and Salamanders.
Nancy Winslow Parker, Illustrator. New York: Greenwillow, 1990. 48 pages. ISBN 0-688-08680-2. Everything you wanted to

know about amphibians and reptiles.

620. Patent, Dorothy Hinshaw.
An Apple a Day:
From Orchard to You.
Photographs by William Munoz. New York: Dutton, 1990. 64 pages. ISBN 0-525-65020-2. A comprehensive look at apples and all of the work that goes into growing, picking, and processing them.

621. Patent, Dorothy Hinshaw.
Humpback Whales.
Photographs by Mark Ferrari and Deborah Glockner-Ferrari. New York: Holiday House 1989. 32 pages. ISBN 0-8234-0779-9. A photographic look at a rare member of the whale family.

622. Paterson, Katherine.
Bridge to Terabithia.
Donna Diamond, Illustrator. New York: Harper, 1977. 144 pages. ISBN 0-690-04635-9. Jess becomes good friends with the new girl in school only to lose her when she accidently drowns.

623. Paterson, Katherine.
Jacob Have I Loved.
New York: Crowell, 1980. ISBN 0-690-04078-4. Set in the Chesapeake Bay area, this story details the rivalry of two sisters, one a family favorite and the other taken-for-granted.

624. Paterson, Katherine.
Lyddie.
New York: Crowell, 1991. 160 pages. ISBN 0-525-67338-5. Lyddie's mother "hires her out" when the family is forced to break up. She becomes a mill girl, experiencing the hardships of

that life, and struggling to earn enough money to reunite the family, but she loses sight of real values.

625. Paterson, Katherine.
Park's Quest.
New York: Crowell, 1988. ISBN 0-525-67258-3. Park goes on a quest in search of the father he did not know and finds a crippled grandfather, a Vietnamese half-sister, and a stronger image of himself.

626. Paterson, Katherine.
The Tale of the
Mandarin Duck.
Leo and Diane Dillion, Illustrators. New York: Crowell, 1990. unpaged ISBN 0-525-67283-4. An old samurai warrior and a kitchen maid set a mandarin duck free only to be punished by their evil lord.

627. Paulsen, Gary.
Hatchet.
New York: Bradbury Press, 1987. 208 pages. ISBN 0-02-770130-1. A story of survival that pits a young boy, equipped with only a hatchet, against the northern Canadian wilderness. He finds that he has more resources than just the hatchet.

628. Paulsen, Gary.
The Island.
New York: Dell, 1990. 202 pages. ISBN 0-440-20632-4. A young boy searches for his personal identity while living alone on a deserted island.

629. Paulsen, Gary.
Tracker.
New York: Bradbury Press, 1984. 90 pages. ISBN 0-02-770220-0. A young boy searches for personal strength while attempting to look-down a deer.

630. Paulsen, Gary.
Woodsong.
New York: Scholastic, 1990. 132 pages. ISBN 0-590-45052-2. An almost autobiographical account of one of America's most popular young adult writers.

631. Peck, Ira.
The Life and Words of
Martin Luther King, Jr.
New York: Scholastic, 1968. 96 pages. ISBN 0-590-41309-0. The story of Martin Luther King,.Jr.

632. Peck, Robert Newton.
Soup.
New York: Dell, 1974. 96 pages. ISBN 0-440-48186-4. Stories of Peck's boyhood misadventures with his best friend, Soup. This is the first of the series.

633. Pfister, Marcus.
Penguin Pete's New Friends.
New York: North-South Books, 1988. unpaged ISBN 0-55858-025-5. The delightful journey of Penguin Pete on a fishing trip when he is introduced to a raft of new friends.

634. Phelps, Ethel Johnston.
The Maid of the North:
Feminist Folk Tales
from Around the World.
Lloyd Bloom, Illustrator. New York: Holt, Rinehart & Winston, 1981. 176 pages. ISBN 0-03-056893-5. A collection of folk tales with female protagonists.

635. Pine, Tillie S.;
Joseph Levine.
Magnets and How
to Use Them.
Bernice Myers, Illustrator. New York: Scholastic, 1965. 64 pages. An easy-to-read

explanation of magnets and some activities to try.

636. Pittman, Hellena Clare.
Once When I Was Scared.
Ted Rand, Illustrator. New York: Dutton, 1988. unpaged ISBN 0-525-44407-6. Young Daniel overcomes his fear of the woods after he is sent to the neighbor's house to fetch hot coals for the stove.

637. Polacco, Patricia.
Boat Ride with
Lillian Two Blossom.
New York: Philomel, 1987. unpaged ISBN 0-399-21470-4. A retelling of a family story in which an old Indian woman answers a young girl's questions, such as "What makes it rain?" and "How come the moon looks so cold?" It is a wild and magical boat ride that provides folklore-like answers.

638. Polacco, Patricia.
Mrs. Katz and Tush.
New York: Bantam, 1992. unpaged. ISBN 0-553-08122-5. A tale of friendship that grows between an old Polish, Jewish immigrant and a young, African American boy. A sense of warmth pervades the pictures and text as Mrs. Katz shares her culture with Larnel.

639. Polette, Nancy.
The Hole by the Apple Tree.
Nishan Akgulian, Illustrator. New York: Greenwillow, 1992. unpaged ISBN 0-688-105570-2. While digging by a tree, Harold and his friends weave a creative, imaginary story that incorporates all the letters of the alphabet.

640. Pollarck, Pamela.
The Random House
Book of Humor for Children.

Paul O. Zelinsky, Illustrator. New York: Random House, 1988. 311 pages. ISBN 0-394-88049-8. Humorous short stories and excerpts from children's fiction.

641. Porter-Gaylord, Laurel. *I Love My Daddy Because…* Ashley Wolff, Illustrator. New York: Dutton, 1991. unpaged ISBN 0-525-44624-9. A look through a preschooler's eyes at all of the wonderful things fathers do for their children with examples from the animal world.

642. Porter-Gaylord, Laurel. *I Love My Mommy Because…* Ashley Wolff, Illustrator. New York: Dutton, 1991. unpaged ISBN 0-525-44625-7. A look through a preschooler's eyes at all of the wonderful things mothers do for their children, with examples from the animal world.

643. Prelutsky, Jack. *It's Thanksgiving.* Marylin Hafner, Illustrator. New York: Greenwillow, ISBN 0-688-00441-5. Poems about Thanksgiving.

644. Prelutsky, Jack. *Ride a Purple Pelican.* Garth Williams, Illustrator. New York: Greenwillow, 1986. 64 pages. ISBN 0-688-04031-4. A collection of short verses and nonsense poetry that play on names of cities in the United States.

645. Prelutsky, Jack. *Something Big Has Been Here.* James Stevenson, Illustrator. New York: Scholastic, 1990. 160 pages. ISBN 0-590-45509-5. A whole bunch of new poems for children and

adults to laugh and giggle over.

646. Prelutsky, Jack. *Tyrannosaurus Was a Beast.* Arnold Lobel, Illustrator. New York: Greenwillow, 1988. 32 pages. ISBN 0-688-06442-6. A collection of short verses and nonsense poetry that play on names of dinosaurs.

647. Pringle, Laurence. *Twist, Wiggle, and Squirm: A Book about Earthworms.* Peter Parnall, Illustrator. New York: Crowell, 1964. 34 pages. ISBN 0-690-84155-8. Interesting information about earthworms.

648. Provensen, Alice Martin Provensen. *The Glorious Flight Across the Channel with Louis Blériot.* New York: Viking, 1983. unpaged ISBN 0-670-34259-9. The story of how Blériot became the first person to fly over the English Channel.

649. Provensen, Martin; Alice Provensen. *The Mother Goose Book.* New York: Random House, 1976. 60 pages. ISBN 0-394-92122-4. A wonderful interpretation of classic rhymes.

R

650. Rathburn, Elizabeth. *Exploring Your Solar System.* Washington, D.C.: National Geographic, 1989. 96 pages. ISBN 0-87044-708-4. A comprehensive look at the solar system and the various forces at work within it.

651. Reeder, Carolyn. *Shades of Gray.* New York: Macmillan, 1989. 165 pages. ISBN 0-02-775810-9. Young Will goes to live with his aunt and uncle after the Civil War and must cope with their pro-union sympathies.

652. Rees, Mary. *Ten in a Bed.* Boston: Little, Brown, 1988. unpaged ISBN 0-316-73708-9. A counting book that has a repeated refrain and is humorously engaging.

653. Reigot, Betty Polisar. *A Book about Planets and Stars.* New York: Scholastic, 1980. 48 pages. ISBN 0-590-40593-4. A student-friendly book about the universe that is packed with up-to-date information.

654. Roberts, Willo Davis. *Megan's Island.* New York: Aladdin, 1988. 187 pages. ISBN 0-689-31397-7. Meg and her family are being pursued by mysterious men for reasons of which she is unaware.

655. Robinson, Barbara. *The Best Christmas Pageant Ever.* Judith Gwyn Brown, Illustrator. New York: Harper, 1972. 81 pages. ISBN 0-380-00769-X. A wild story of how the Herdman family first disrupts and then brings new meaning to the Christmas Story.

656. Rockwell, Anne. *The Old Woman and Her Pig and 10 Other Stories.* New York: Crowell, 1979. unpaged ISBN 0-690-03927-1. An anthology aimed at the

early grades. It contains a few of the common but less well known tales—"Bremen Town Musicians," "The Fox and the Crow," "The Lad Who Went to the North Wind," and so on.

657. Rockwell, Anne. *Our Yard Is Full of Birds.* Lizzy Rockwell, Illustrator. New York: Macmillan, 1992. unpaged ISBN 0-02-777273-X. A colorful look at all of the birds a young boy sees on the lawn and in the flower garden.

658. Rockwell, Anne. *The Three Bears and 15 Other Stories.* New York: Crowell, 1975. 118 pages. ISBN 0-690-00597-0. Sixteen familiar tales retold and illustrated by Anne Rockwell. Includes "Red Riding Hood," "Gingerbread Man," "Three Billy Goats Gruff," "Three Bears." A must for pre-K and primary classrooms.

659. Rogers, Paul. *The Shapes Game.* Sian Tucker, Illustrator. New York: Henry Holt, 1989. unpaged ISBN 0-8050-1280-X. A rhythmic romp through simple geometric shapes.

660. Rosen, Michael. *We're Going on a Bear Hunt.* Helen Oxenbury, Illustrator. New York: Macmillan, 1989. unpaged ISBN 0-689-50476-4. The exciting adventure of a family that treks over hill and dale to find a bear that ends with a narrow escape from the new-found bruin.

661. Rounds, Glen. *I Know an Old Lady Who Swallowed a Fly.* New York: Holiday House, 1990. unpaged ISBN 0-8234-0814-0. A cumulative folk song telling of a lady who

keeps eating bigger animals to solve problems caused by earlier animal swallowings.

662. Ryder, Joanne.
Where Butterflies Grow.
Lynne Cherry, Illustrator. New York: Dutton, 1989. unpaged ISBN 0-525-67284-2. Enthralling descriptions coupled with brilliantly detailed illustrations of the metamorphosis of the black swallowtail butterfly.

663. Ryder, Joanne.
White Bear, Ice Bear.
Michael Rothman, Illustrator. New York: Morrow, 1989. unpaged ISBN 0-688-07174-0. A young boy lets his imagination run as he dreams of what it would be like if he were a polar bear in the cold arctic north.

664. Rylant, Cynthia.
Henry and Mudge and the Long Weekend.
Susie Stevenson, Illustrator. New York: Bradbury Press, 1992. 40 pages. ISBN 0-02-778013-9. Mom saves the the day in another Henry and Mudge adventure with her brilliant idea to turn a boring weekend into a fun one.

665. Rylant, Cynthia.
When I Was Young in the Mountains.
Diane Goode, Illustrator. New York: Dutton, 1982. unpaged ISBN 0-525-42525-X. Remembering life in the Appalachian Mountains. A very quiet, peaceful look at life.

S

666. Sadler, Catherine Edwards adapted by.
Sir Arthur Conan Doyle's The Adventures of Sherlock
Holmes: Volume I.
New York: Avon, 1981. 143 pages. ISBN 0-380-78089-5. Holmes and Watson are on the loose investigating crimes; especially adapted for younger readers.

667. Sadler, Marilyn.
Elizabeth and Larry.
Roger Bollen, Illustrator. New York: Simon & Schuster, 1990. unpaged ISBN 0-671-69189-9. A story of friendship between a woman and an alligator.

668. San Souci, Daniel.
North Country Night.
New York: Doubleday, 1990. unpaged ISBN 0-385-41319-3. In the falling snow, the reader takes a walk through a woodland encountering many of the birds and animals that live there.

669. San Souci, Robert.
The Talking Eggs.
Jerry Pickney, Illustrator. New York: Dial, 1989. unpaged ISBN 0-8037-0620-0. An African American folk tale of an ill-treated younger daughter being rewarded for her good deeds, while the greed and poor manners of the older daughter and mother result in their justly deserved punishment. Compare with *Mufaro's Beautiful Daughters* and "Cinderella."

670. San Souci, Robert D.
Young Merlin.
Daniel Horne, Illustrator. New York: Doubleday, 1990. unpaged ISBN 0-385-24800-8. San Souci tells about Merlin's childhood and how his mysterious parentage led to his encounter with King Vortigern and later with the rightful king of England, Aurelius, and his brother,
Uther (who is also King Arthur's father).

671. Sandburg, Carl; Lee Bennett Hopkins (selector).
Rainbows Are Made.
Fritz Eichenberg, Illustrator. New York: Harcourt Brace Jovanovich, 1982. ISBN 0-15-265481-X. A selection of Sandburg's poems in a picture book format.

672. Sara Stein.
The Evolution Book.
Photographs by Rona Beame. New York: Workman, 1986. 391 pages. ISBN 0-89480-927-X. A book loaded with information and projects about evolution, organized in a chronological fashion.

673. Sargent, William.
Night Reef: Dusk to Dawn on a Coral Reef.
New York: Franklin Watts, 1991. 41 pages. ISBN 0-531-15219-7. A captivating look at the abundance of action that takes place in and around a coral reef at night.

674. Sattler, Helen Roney.
Baby Dinosaurs.
Jean Day Zallinger, Illustrator. New York: Lothrop, Lee & Shepard, 1984. 32 pages. ISBN 0-688-03818-2. Sattler describes various baby dinosaurs that have been found and what life might have been like for them.

675. Sattler, Helen Roney.
The Book of Eagles.
Jean Day Zallinger, Illustrator. New York: Lothrop, 1989. 64 pages. ISBN 0-688-07021-3. A complete look at eagles from around the world.

676. Sattler, Helen Roney.
Dinosaurs of North America.
Anthony Rao, Illustrator. New
York: Lothrop, Lee & Shepard, 1981. 151 pages. ISBN 0-688-51952-0. Short descriptions of the common and not-so-common dinosaurs that have been found in North America

677. Sattler, Helen Roney.
The Illustrated Dinosaur Dictionary.
Pamela Carroll, Illustrator. New York: Lothrop, Lee & Shepard, 1983. 315 pages. ISBN 0-688-00479-2. Definitions include the dinosaur genuses, as well as families and other words of interest to the beginning paleontologist.

678. Sattler, Helen Roney.
Pterosaurs, the Flying Reptiles.
Christopher Santoro, Illustrator. New York: Lothrop, Lee & Shepard, 1985. 48 pages. ISBN 0-688-03995-2. Sattler describes what is known about these distant relatives of dinosaurs, from Euidimorphodon (the earliest) to the gigantic Quetzalcoatlus (one of the last).

679. Sattler, Helen Roney.
Tyrannosaurus Rex and Its Kin: The Mesozoic Monsters.
Joyce Powzyk, Illustrator. New York: Lothrop, 1989. 48 pages. ISBN 0-688-07747-1. A clear examination of the largest carnivorous dinosaurs.

680. Sattler, Helen R.
Whales, the Nomads of the Sea.
Jean Zallinger, Illustrator. New York: Lothrop, 1987. 128 pages. ISBN 0-688-05587-7. A comprehensive look at whales, with an extensive glossary and reference section.

681. Sawyer, Ruth.
Journey Cake, Ho!
Robert McCloskey, Illustrator.
New York: Viking, 1953.
unpaged ISBN 0-670-40943-X. A retelling of Johnny and his pursuit of a journey cake that taunts him as it rolls away.

682. Say, Allen.
Tree of Cranes.
Boston: Houghton Mifflin, 1991. unpaged ISBN 0-395-52024-X. A warm tale of a Japanese boy's remembrance of sharing an American Christmas with his American mother. It is a wonderful blending of two cultures.

683. Scheer, Julian.
Rain Makes Applesauce.
Marvin Bileck, Illustrator.
New York: Holiday House, 1964. unpaged ISBN 0-8234-0091-3. A book of poetry, humor, plays, pictures, and patterns.

684. Schneider, Herman; Nina Schneider.
Secret Magnets.
Talivaldis Stubis, Illustrator.
New York: Scholastic, 1979. 48 pages. An activity book about magnets.

685. Schwartz, Alvin, collected by.
Flapdoodle: Pure Nonsense from American Folklore.
John O'Brien, Illustrator. New York: Lippincott, 1980. 125 pages. ISBN 0-397-31919-3. A zany collection of American nonsense, spoonerisms, jokes, and riddles collected from all around the country.

686. Schwartz, Alvin collected by.
Scary Tales to Tell in the Dark.
Stephen Gammell, Illustrator.

New York: Harper & Row, 1981. unpaged ISBN 0-397-31927-4. Ghost stories collected from various regions of the United States.

687. Schwartz, Alvin, collected by.
Tomfoolery: Trickery and Foolery with Words.
Glen Rounds, Illustrator. New York: Lippincott, 1973. 125 pages. ISBN 0-397-31466-3. Recorded from the oral tradition, this is a collection of tricks and traps that are meant to stump the listener.

688. Schwartz, Alvin, collected by.
A Twister of Twists, A Tangler of Tongues.
Glen Rounds, Illustrator.
Philadelphia: Lippincott, 1972. 125 pages. ISBN 0-397-31387-X. A wonderful collection of tongue teasers that will stump even the most skilled elocutionist.

689. Schwartz, Amy.
Annabell Swift, Kindergartner.
New York: Orchard, 1988. unpaged ISBN 0-531-07027-1. In spite of her sisters best intentions, Annabelle's first day of school is a personal success.

690. Schwartz, David.
How Much Is a Million?
Steven Kellogg, Illustrator.
New York: Greenwillow, 1985. unpaged ISBN 0-590-43614-7. A whimsical look at how big a million, a billion, and a trillion really are.

691. Schwartz, Linda.
Earth Book for Kids.
Beverly Armstrong, Illustrator. Santa Barbara: The Learning Works, 1990. 184 pages. ISBN 0-88160-195-0.

Plenty of ideas and activities for students of all ages that promote healing the environment.

692. Scieszka, Jon.
The Frog Prince Continued.
Steve Johnson, Illustrator.
New York: Viking, 1991. unpaged ISBN 0-670-83421-1. Scieszka begins where most versions end—detailing the Frog Prince's unhappy adjustment to being human. He longs to be a frog again and searches for a witch to transform him, meeting several storied witches in the process.

693. Scieszka, Jon.
The True Story of the 3 Little Pigs.
Lane Smith, Illustrator. New York: Viking, 1989. unpaged ISBN 0-670-82759-2. The story of the three little pigs told from the wolf's point of view. It is interesting to debate whose version of the story is correct.

694. Seattle, Chief, adapted by Susan Jeffers.
Brother Eagle, Sister Sky.
Susan Jeffers, Illustrator. New York: Dial, 1991. unpaged ISBN 0-8037-0969-2. Breathtaking illustrations bring to life Chief Seattle's stirring message that is as important today as it was over 140 years ago.

695. Seddon, Tony; Jill Bailey.
The Living World.
Garden City: Doubleday, 1986. ISBN 0-385-23754-5. A nice overview of biology, especially zoology.

696. Seeger, Pete.
Abiyoyo: A South African Lullaby and Folk Story.

Michael Hayes, Illustrator.
New York: Macmillan, 1986. unpaged ISBN 0-02-781490-4. Adapted from an old South African folk tale, a father and his son combine to save a town from the dreaded monster Abiyoyo.

697. Settel, Joanne; Nancy Baggett.
Why Does My Nose Run? (And Other Questions Kids Ask about Their Bodies).
Linda Tunney, Illustrator. New York: Atheneum, 1985. 83 pages. ISBN 0-689-31078-1. One- and two-page answers to common questions about health and hygiene concerns.

698. Sewell, Anna; adapted by Robin McKinley.
Black Beauty.
Susan Jeffers, Illustrator. New York: Random House, 1986. 69 pages. ISBN 0-394-86575-8. An adaptation of a classic horse story that has been enriched through beautiful illustrations for younger readers.

699. Sharmat, Marjorie Weinman.
Nate the Great.
Marc Simont, Illustrator. New York: Coward-McCann, 1972. ISBN 0-698-30444-6. A young detective solves the mystery of the disappearing painting.

700. Shaw, Nancy.
Sheep in a Jeep.
Margot Apple, Illustrator. New York: Houghton Mifflin, 1986. unpaged ISBN 0-395-41105-X. The sheep jump in a jeep and end up mired in mud.

701. Shaw, Nancy.
Sheep in a Shop.
Margot Apple, Illustrator.
Boston: Houghton Mifflin,

1991. unpaged ISBN 0-395-53681-2. Sheep shop for a birthday present that will be simply shimmering.

702. Shaw, Nancy.
Sheep on a Ship.
Margot Apple, Illustrator. Boston: Houghton Mifflin, 1989. unpaged ISBN 0-395-48160-0. The sheep ship out on a rollicking rollercoaster ride over the ocean-blue.

703. Shulevitz, Uri.
The Magician.
New York: Macmillan, 1985. unpaged ISBN 0-02-782770-4. A poor old couple is rewarded for helping a stranger during Passover.

704. Siebert, Diane.
Heartland.
Wendell Minor, Illustrator. New York: Crowell, 1989. ISBN 0-690-04730-4. A poetic portrayal of the midwestern United States.

705. Simon, Norma.
I Am Not a Crybaby .
Helen Cogancherry, Illustrator. New York: Albert Whitman, 1989. unpaged ISBN 0-8075-3447-1. A heartfelt exploration of many of the actions and events that we encounter in life and how we react to them.

706. Simon, Seymour.
Big Cats.
New York: HarperCollins, 1991. unpaged ISBN 0-06-021647-6. An insightful look through photos of cats that are both fascinating and scary.

707. Simon, Seymour.
How to Be an Ocean Scientist in Your Own Home.
David A. Carter, Illustrator. New York: Harper, 1988. 144 pages. ISBN 0-397-32291-7.

Twenty-four experiments for young oceanographers.

708. Simon, Seymour.
Killer Whales.
New York: Harper Junior, 1989. unpaged ISBN 0-397-31784-0. A look at one of the most feared, yet least understood, members of the whale family.

709. Simon, Seymour.
The Largest Dinosaurs.
Pamela Carroll, Illustrator. New York: Macmillan, 1986. 32 pages. ISBN 0-02-782910-3. An exploration of six of the largest dinosaurs through pen-and- ink drawings.

710. Simon, Seymour.
Little Giants.
Pamela Carroll, Illustrator. New York: Morrow, 1983. unpaged ISBN 0-688-01727-2. A look at remarkable insects.

711. Simon, Seymour.
Saturn.
New York: Morrow, 1985. unpaged ISBN 0-688-05798-5. Stunning photos illustrate the story of the planet Saturn.

712. Simon, Seymour.
Snakes.
New York: HarperCollins, 1992. unpaged ISBN 0-06-022529-7. A photographic look at snakes highlighting their characteristics, attributes, and environmental importance.

713. Simon, Seymour.
Storms.
New York: Morrow, 1989. unpaged ISBN 0-688-07413-8. Remarkable photos and diagrams that help to explain the mysteries of storms.

714. Simon, Seymour.
Volcanoes.
New York: Morrow, 1988. unpaged ISBN 0-688-07411-1. Stunning photos of volcanoes and their destructive power.

715. Sloat, Teri.
The Eye of the Needle.
Teri Sloat, Illustrator. New York: Dutton, 1990. unpaged ISBN 0-525-44623-0. A Yupik legend that tells of a boy who goes hunting but keeps eating everything he finds, including a walrus and a whale.

716. Small, David.
Imogene's Antlers.
New York: Crown, 1985. unpaged ISBN 0-517-55564-6. Imogene wakes up one morning with antlers. and she learns how to use them in many creative ways.

717. Snape, Juliet; Charles Snape.
Frog Odyssey.
New York: Simon & Schuster, 1992. unpaged ISBN 0-671-74741-X. Forced to abandon their frog pond due to construction, a brave group of frogs explores the city looking for a new home.

718. Sneve, Virginia Driveing Hawk.
Dancing Teepees: Poems from American Indian Youth.
Steven Gammell, Illustrator. New York: Holiday House, 1989. 32 pages. Poems by Native Americans, some of which are traditional chants.

719. Snow, Nicholas.
The Monster Book of ABC Sounds.
New York: Dial, 1991. unpaged ISBN 0-8037-0935-

8. A delightful alphabet book that combines pictures and sounds to illustrate each letter.

720. Snyder, Zilpha Keatley.
And Condors Danced.
New York: Delacourt, 1987. 211 pages. ISBN 0-385-29575-8. A well-written story about life in California at the turn of the century.

721. Snyder, Zilpha Keatley.
Black and Blue Magic.
New York: Dell, 1966. ISBN 0-440-40053-8. Several adventures of a young boy who is given a gift of magic ointment that, when applied on his shoulder blades, gives him angel-like wings.

722. Snyder, Zilpha Keatly.
The Velvet Room.
New York: Dell, 1988. 216 pages. ISBN 0-440-40042-2. Robin finds a secret place of her own with the help of a friend.

723.Sorensen, Virginia.
Plain Girl.
New York: Scholastic, 1983. 151 pages. ISBN 0-590-43144-7. Esther is different and must learn to deal with being Amish while attending the local school, especially when her older brother rebels and runs away.

724.
Sorting.
New York: Random House, 1991. unpaged ISBN 0-679-81162-1. Photographic examples of a variety of initial math concepts.

725. Soto, Gary.
A Fire In My Hands: A Book of Poems.
James M. Cardillo, Illustrator. New York: Scholastic, 1990. 64 pages. ISBN 0-590-45021-2. Twenty-three poems

describing the author's youth as a Mexican American growing-up in the San Joaquin Valley in California, and his entry into parenthood. Each poem is preceded by a short explanation that sets the stage for the poem; at the back of the book are questions and answers about writing poetry.

726. Speare, Elizabeth George.
The Sign of the Beaver.
Boston: Houghton Mifflin, 1984. 135 pages. ISBN 0-395-33890-5. Finding help from an unexpected source, young Nat is left in the Maine woods to survive on his own until his father returns with the rest of the family.

727. Speare, Elizabeth George.
The Witch of Blackbird Pond.
Boston: Houghton Mifflin, 1987. 249 pages. ISBN 0-395-07114-3. Young Kit Tyler arrives in Wethersfield unannounced and unwanted only to become embroiled in a witch hunt.

728. Spector, Marjorie.
Pencil to Press: How This Book Came to Be.
New York: Lothrop, Lee & Shepard, 1975. 96 pages. ISBN 0-688-41713-2. Spector describes the production of a book. Emphasis is more on the book's production than on writing and editing.

729. Spier, Peter.
Noah's Ark.
New York: Doubleday, 1977. unpaged ISBN 0-385-09473-6. A wordless picture storybook of the biblical flood comes to life through Spier's detailed illustrations. It's always possible to find new

details in these illustrations, no matter how many times you look.

730. Spier, Peter.
Oh, Were They Ever Happy!
New York: Doubleday, 1978. unpaged ISBN 0-385-13175-5. An almost wordless book that shows how the Noonan children surprise their parents by painting their house—with humorous results.

731. Spier, Peter.
People.
New York: Doubleday, 1980. unpaged ISBN 0-385-13181-X. A picture book illustrating how all people are different, yet very much the same.

732. Spier, Peter.
Rain.
New York: Doubleday, 1982. unpaged ISBN 0-385-15484-4. A wordless story of a brother and sister and their adventures outside on a rainy day.

733. Spier, Peter.
To Market! To Market!
Peter Spier, Illustrator. New York: Doubleday, 1967. ISBN 0-385-09081-1. A collection of nineteen traditional rhymes from nineteenth-century America.

734. Spier, Peter.
We the People: The Constitution of the United States of America.
New York: Doubleday, 1987. unpaged ISBN 0-385-23589-5. The preamble to the American Constitution illustrated with watercolor paintings.

735. Spinelli, Jerry.
Maniac Magee.
Boston: Little, Brown, 1990. ISBN 0-316-80722-2. Magee

is a boy of mythical proportions who loses his parents, and runs away from his dysfunctional relatives to a racially divided community. His combination of naiveté and extraordinary skills helps to bring together this discordant community.

736. Stanley, Diane; Peter Vennema.
Shaka, King of the Zulus.
Diane Stanley, illustrator. New York: Morrow, 1988. unpaged ISBN 0-688-07342-5. A picture biography that tells how Shaka became the great leader of his people.

737. Steig, William.
Amos & Boris.
New York: Farrar, Straus and Giroux, 1971. unpaged ISBN 0-374-30278-2. Amos the mouse finds himself overboard and in the ocean, where he is rescued by Boris the whale. After many happy adventures together, Amos returns the favor years later.

738. Steig, William.
Brave Irene.
New York: Farrar, Straus and Giroux, 1986. unpaged ISBN 0-374-30947-7. Irene's bravery and super-human effort during a driving snow storm are rewarded after she delivers a dress to the Duchess down the mountain for her sick mother .

739. Steig, William.
Shrek!
New York: Farrar, Straus and Giroux, 1990. unpaged ISBN 0-374-36877-5. A humorous parody of an utterly repulsive creature that is sent out into the world, meets a witch, and accomplishes his quest to marry an equally repulsive princess.

740. Steig, William.
Sylvester and the Magic Pebble.
New York: Simon and Schuster, 1969. unpaged ISBN 0-13-881707-3. Sylvester finds a magic pebble that leads to pain and sorrow, and ultimately, to a happy ending.

741. Steptoe, John.
Mufaro's Beautiful Daughters: An African Tale.
New York: Lothrop, 1987. unpaged ISBN 0-688-04045-4. Two sisters set out to win a handsome king's heart; one by deceit and the other by honesty.

742. Steptoe, John (reteller).
The Story of Jumping Mouse.
New York: Lothrop, 1984. unpaged ISBN 0-688-01903-X. A richly detailed retelling of a young, selfless mouse who is justly rewarded for his kindness when he reaches the Far-Off Land where a mouse is never hungry.

743. Sterling, Dorothy.
Freedom Train The Story of Harriet Tubman.
New York: Scholastic, 1954. 191 pages. ISBN 0-590-40640-X. The story of an important American and her fight against slavery.

744. Stevenson, Robert Louis.
My Shadow.
Ted Rand, Illustrator. New York: Putnam, 1990. unpaged ISBN 0-399-22216-2. A retelling of a classic poem about young people that incorporates children from all over the world as they celebrate the joy of youth.

745. Stoutenburg, Adrien.
American Tall Tales.
Richard M. Powers, Illustrator. New York:

Penguin, 1966, 1969. 112 pages. ISBN 0-670-12032-4. Tales of eight legendary figures in American folklore.

746. Stratton, Barbara.
What Is a Fish.
New York: Franklin Watts, 1991. 33 pages. ISBN 0-531-15223-5. A comprehensive look at a variety of fish, including sharks and eels.

747. Sullivan, George.
The Day Pearl Harbor Was Bombed.
New York: Scholastic, 1991. 96 pages. ISBN 0-590-43449-7. A stunning photo history of the bombing of Pearl Harbor and the events leading up to it.

748. Sullivan, George.
The Day We Walked on the Moon.
New York: Scholastic, 1990. 72 pages. ISBN 0-590-42760-1. A photo story of an important time in the American space program.

749. Sullivan, Mary Beth; Linda Bourke.
A Show of Hands.
Linda Bourke, Illustrator. New York: Harper, 1980. 96 pages. ISBN 0-201-07456-7. A primer of signing, the language used by hearing-impaired people.

750. Surat, Michele Maria.
Angel Child, Dragon Child.
Vo-Dinh Mai, Illustrator. New York: Raintree, 1983. 35 pages. ISBN 0-940742-8. Ut, whose mother is still in Vietnam, teams up with her red-haired enemy to host a school fair to raise money to bring her mother home.

751. Sussman, Susan; Robert James.
Big Friend, Little Friend:

A Book about Symbiosis.
Boston: Houghton Mifflin, 1989. 30 pages. ISBN 0-395-49701-9. Excellent use of photos to illustrate a complex scientific phenomenon.

752. Sutcliff, Rosemary.
Flame-Colored Taffeta.
New York: Farrar, Straus and Giroux, 1989. 130 pages. ISBN 0-374-42341-5. Damaris, with the aid of a friend, helps a mysterious royal stranger in eighteenth-century England.

753. Sutcliff, Rosemary.
The Light Beyond the Forest: The Quest for the Holy Grail.
New York: Dutton, 1979. ISBN 0-525-33665-6. Another of Sutcliff's rich depictions of life in the Middle Ages.

754. Sutcliff, Rosemary.
Tristan and Iseult.
New York: Farrar, Straus and Giroux, 1991. 150 pages. ISBN 0-374-47982-8. A spirited retelling of one of the world's classic love stories by a master storyteller. Tristan defeats Ireland's champion warrior and gains a friend, only to lose his life and his love.

755. Swan, Robert.
Destination: Antarctica.
New York: Scholastic, 1988. unpaged ISBN 0-509-41285-X. An exciting narrative of three men and their 900-mile quest to cross Antarctica.

T

756. Taylor, Mildred D.
Roll of Thunder, Hear My Cry.
New York: Dial, 1976. 276 pages. ISBN 0-8037-7473-7. A family's struggle during the depression against racism,

poverty, and ignorance. Taylor tells us about a strong, proud family.

757. Tejima.
Swan Sky.
New York: Philomel, 1988. unpaged ISBN 0-399-21547-6. A poignant Japanese folk tale of a swan family's love for a member who was unable to fly north for the summer.

758. Terban, Marvin.
Mad as a Wet Hen! And Other Funny Idioms.
Giulio Maestro, Illustrator. New York: Clarion, 1987. unpaged ISBN 0-89919-478-8. An illustrated collection of idioms, what they mean, and where they came from.

759. Thomas, Dylan.
A Child's Christmas in Wales.
Edward Ardizzone, Illustrator. Boston: Godine, 1984. 45 pages. ISBN 0-87923-529-2. A warm recollection of the poet's childhood in Wales.

760. Thomas, Jane Resh.
The Comeback Dog.
Drawings by Troy Howell. New York: Clarion, 1983. 62 pages. ISBN 0-395-29423-0. Young Daniel's love for a stray dog is tested when it runs away soon after he had nursed it back to life.

761. Thurber, James.
Many Moons.
Louis Slobodkin, New York: Harcourt, 1944. unpaged ISBN 0-15-696264-0. A young princess wants the moon and an unlikely member of the king's court grants her wish.

762. Thurber, James.
Many Moons.
Marc Simot, Illustrator. San

Diego: Harcourt Brace Jovanovich, 1990. unpaged ISBN 0-15-251872-X. An engaging interpretation of a classic story of a young princess who would like the moon.

763. Titherington, Jeanne.
Pumpkin Pumpkin.
New York: Greenwillow, 1986. unpaged ISBN 0-688-05695-4. A beautifully illustrated story of Jamie, who plants a seed and watches it all through the summer as it grows into a pumpkin that he can carve for Halloween.

764. Tresselt, Alvin.
The Mitten.
Yaroslava, Illustrator. New York: Lorthrop, 1964. unpaged ISBN 0-688-51053-1. A Ukrainian folk tale of the animals who make a home out of a boy's lost mitten.

765. Tripp, Wallace, compiled by.
Granfa' Grig Had A Pig and other Rhymes Without Reason from Mother Goose.
Boston: Little Brown, 1976. 96 pages. ISBN 0-316-85284-8. Lively illustrations that accompany Mother Goose.

766. Tripp, Wallace, compiled by.
Marguerite, Go Wash Your Feet.
Boston: Houghton Mifflin, 1985. 48 pages ISBN 0-395-35392-0. A collection of poetry and nonsense from some famous authors.

767.
Trucks.
New York: Aladdin, 1991. 21 pages. ISBN 0-689-71405-X. A look at all kinds of trucks with their parts clearly labeled. A treat for the

younger reader who is enamored of large vehicles.

768. Tsuchiya, Yukio.
Faithful Elephants:
A True Story of Animals,
People and War.
Boston: Houghton, Mifflin, 1988. unpaged ISBN 0-395-46555-9. The story of how animals in the Tokyo Zoo had to be destroyed during World War II.

769. Turkle, Brinton.
Deep in the Forest.
New York: Dutton, 1976. unpaged ISBN 0-525-28617-9. A young bear invites himself into a vacant cabin, causing great havoc, in a clever twist of the Goldilocks folk tale.

770. Turner, Ann.
Dakota Dugout.
Ronald Himler, Illustrator. New York: Macmillan, 1985. unpaged ISBN 0-02-789700-1. A realistic account of a family's years homesteading on the prairie.

771. Turner, Ann.
Heron Street.
Lisa Desimini, Illustrator. New York: Harper, 1989. unpaged ISBN 0-06-026185-4. A pictorial history of human expansion in the United States and its effect on the surrounding environment.

772. Tyler, Linda Wagner.
The After-Christmas Tree.
Susan Davis, Illustrator. New York: Viking, 1990. unpaged ISBN 0-670-83045-3. A family, desiring to extend the Christmas season, plans a neighborhood party that includes redecorating the Christmas tree for birds and animals.

U

773. Untermeyer, Louis, (adaptor).
Aesop's Fables.
Ann and Martin Provensen, Illustrators. New York: Golden Press, 1965. 92 pages. Forty fables retold with beautiful illustrations.

V

774. Van Allsburg, Chris.
Just a Dream.
Boston: Houghton Mifflin, 1990. unpaged ISBN 0-395-53308-2. Young Walter is transported to a future where pollution has ravaged the earth and poisoned the environment, but finds that he can make a difference by being more aware of his actions.

775. Van Allsburg, Chris.
The Mysteries of
Harris Burdick.
Boston: Houghton Mifflin, 1984. unpaged ISBN 0-395-35393-9. A manuscript full of pictures, book titles, and captions supposedly submitted by an unpublished author-illustrator who never returned. The pictures and their provocative titles and captions challenge the reader to supply the rest of the story.

776. Van Allsburg, Chris.
Polar Express.
Boston: Houghton Mifflin, 1985. unpaged ISBN 0-395-38949-6. A young boy boards a mysterious train that takes him to the North Pole on Christmas Eve, where he receives the first gift of Christmas.

777. Van Laan, Nancy.
Possum Come a-Knockin'.
George Booth, Illustrator.

New York: Knopf, 1990. unpaged ISBN 0-394-82206-4. A folklike rhyme that will get your toes a-tappin'. Make sure you practice before you read it to a class, but once you do, it's a sure hit.

778. Van Leuwen.
Going West.
Thomas B. Allen, Illustrator. New York: Dial, 1992. unpaged ISBN 0-8037-1027-5. A nice picture book addition to the literature describing life on the Great Plains during the western migration. Told in the first person, it describes the hardships that were part of the daily life of these pioneering families.

779. Verdy, Violette.
Of Swans, Sugarplums,
and Satin Slippers.
Marcia Brown, New York: Scholastic, 1991. 90 pages. ISBN 0-590-43484-5. An accurate retelling of six famous ballets are accompanied by well written explanations of each ballet and sensational illustrations.

780. Viorst, Judith.
The Good-Bye Book.
Kay Charao, Illustrator. New York: Atheneum, 1988. unpaged ISBN 0-689-31308-X. Delicate illustrations that capture a young boy's reluctance to stay with a babysitter while his parents go out for the evening.

781. Viorst, Judith.
The Tenth Good Thing
about Barney.
Eric Blegvad, Illustrator. New York: Atheneum, 1971. unpaged ISBN 0-689-20688-7. A story about the death of a pet.

782. Voigt, Cynthia.
Dicey's Song.
New York: Atheneum, 1982. 196 pages. ISBN 0-689-30944-9. Dicey struggles to make her grandmother accept her and her siblings while she struggles with her own adolescence.

783. Vyner, Sue.
The Stolen Egg.
Tim Vyner, Illustrator. New York: Viking, 1993. unpaged ISBN 0-670-84460-8. Both educational and interesting. The reader is asked to guess who belongs to the egg the albatross stole.

W

784. Wadsworth, Olive A.
Over in the Meadow:
An Old Counting Rhyme.
David A. Carter, Illustrator. New York: Scholastic, 1992. unpaged ISBN 0-590-44498-0. An old favorite beautifully illustrated in collage with cut paper and other materials.

785. Walker, Barbara.
The Little House Cookbook.
New York: Scholastic, 1981. 240 pages. ISBN 0-590-45371-8. Over 100 authentic recipes of classic pioneer food gleaned from Laura Ingalls Wilder's books about herself and her family.

786. Walker, Paul Robert.
Bigfoot & Other
Legendary Creatures.
William Noonan, Illustrator. San Diego: Harcourt Brace Jovanovich, 1992. 56 pages. ISBN 0-15-207147-4. Does Bigfoot really exist? Based on reports from people who have witnessed Bigfoot and six other strange creatures, the author has created a story that describes each creature's

supposed encounters with modern beings.

787. Wallace, Bill.
Danger on Panther Peak.
New York: Holiday House, 1985. 155 pages. ISBN 0-8234-0715-2.

788. Ward, Leila.
I Am Eyes Ni Macho.
Nonny Hogrogian, New York: Scholastic, 1978. unpaged ISBN 0-590-40990-5. A young child leads the reader on a tour through Kenyan wildlife, celebrating what she sees.

789. Waters, Kate.
Sarah Morton's Day.
Photographs by Russ Kendall. New York: Scholastic, 1989. 32 pages. ISBN 0-590-42634-2. A historically accurate account of what young Sarah Morton's daily activities would have been during the early days of Plymouth Colony.

790. Waters, Kate.
The Story of the White House.
New York: Scholastic, 1991. 40 pages. ISBN 0-590-43335-0. A glimpse of the most famous building in the United States through carefully selected photos and informative text.

791. Waters, Kate; Madeline Slovenz-Low.
Lion Dancer: Ernie Wan's Chinese New Year.
Photographs by Martha Cooper. New York: Scholastic, 1990. unpaged ISBN 0-590-43046-7. A photographic look at Ernie, his family, and his very first Lion Dance during the Chinese New Year celebration.

792. Watson, Wendy.
Thanksgiving At Our House.
New York: Clarion, 1991. unpaged ISBN 0-395-53626-X. A sensitive look at a family Thanksgiving celebration, including traditional Thanksgiving poems.

793. Weinberg, Larry.
The Story of Abraham Lincoln, President for the People.
New York: Dell, 1991. 102 pages. ISBN 0-440-40411-8. A biography of Abraham Lincoln.

794. Westall, Robert.
Ghost Abby.
New York: Scholastic, 1988. 169 pages. ISBN 0-590-41692-8. Maggi and her family move to an old abandoned abbey with mysterious results.

795. Wexler, Jerome.
Wonderful Pussy Willows.
New York: Dutton, 1992. unpaged ISBN 0-525-44867-5. Accurate text and clear photography describe the life cycle of pussy willows.

796. Whelan, Gloria.
A Week of Raccoons.
Lynn Munsinger, Illustrator. New York: Knopf, 1988. unpaged ISBN 0-394-98396-3. Mr. Twerkle has big problems with raccoons! Each time he catches one after they have raided his home, he takes it out into the country and lets it go. Soon all of the captured raccoons find a new home in the country.

797. White, E. B.
Charlotte's Web.
Garth Williams, Illustrator. New York: Harper, 1952. 184 pages. ISBN 0-06-026385-7. A classic story of friendship

and the eternal cycle of life in the barnyard.

798. White, E. B.
The Trumpet of the Swan.
Edward Frascino, Illustrator. New York: Harper, 1970. 210 pages. ISBN 0-06-026397-0. Louis, a voiceless trumpeter swan, is helped by a human named Sam and ends up finding fame and fortune, and marrying the swan of his dreams. A classic story for all children.

799. White, Ellen Emerson.
Jim Abbot Against All Odds.
New York: Scholastic, 1990. 86 pages. ISBN 0-590-43503-5. The story of a man who overcame a childhood disability to pitch in the major leagues.

800. Whitfield, Dr. Philip; Joyce Pope.
Why Do the Seasons Change? Questions on Nature's Rhythms and Cycles.
New York: Viking, 1987. 96 pages. ISBN 0-670-81860-7. A comprehensive question-and-answer look at the why and what of seasonal changes in our world.

801. Wild, Margaret.
Mr. Nick's Knitting.
Dee Huxley, Illustrator. San Diego: Harcourt Brace Jovanovich, 1989. unpaged ISBN 0-15-200518-8. Mr. Nick and Mrs. Jolley knit while sitting on the train every day on their way to work. One day Mrs. Jolly isn't there, and Mr. Nick knits her a special gift to help her get well.

802. Wilde, Oscar.
The Selfish Giant.
Lisbeth Zwerger, Illustrator. Natchik: Picture Book Studio,

1984. unpaged ISBN 0-907234-30-5. A selfish giant, upon returning from a seven year visit with a Cornish ogre, sees children playing in his garden. Enraged, he banishes them and is punished when winter permanently takes over his garden. Eventually he sees the error in his ways and is rewarded in the end.

803. Wildsmith, Brian.
Brian Wildsmith's Mother Goose: Nursery Rhymes.
New York: Oxford, 1965. unpaged ISBN 0-19-279611-7. An eclectic collection of Mother Goose rhymes.

804. Wildsmith, Brian.
The Lazy Bear.
London: Oxford University Press, 1973. unpaged ISBN 0-19-279693-3. Bear takes advantage of his friends by being a bully, but ends up receiving his just desserts.

805. Willard, Nancy.
East of the Sun & West of the Moon.
Barry Moser, Illustrator. San Diego: Harcourt Brace Jovanovich, 1989. 64 pages. ISBN 0-15-224750-5. The story of a beautiful young princess who sets out to find her prince and save him before he marries a troll. Set in the form of a play.

806. Willard, Nancy.
Pish, Posh, Said Hieronymus Bosch.
Leo & Diane Dillon, Illustrators. San Diego: Harcourt Brace Jovanovich, unpaged.15 Hieronymus Bosch is an artist who collects odd creatures that are taken care of by his housekeeper until she gets fed up and quits. A humorous story told in verse with a happy ending.

807. Willard, Nancy.
A Visit to William Blake's Inn: Poems for the Innocent & Experienced Travelers.
Alice and Martin Provensen, Illustrators. San Diego: Harcourt Brace Jovanovich, 1981. 44 pages. ISBN 0-15-293822-2. Easy- to-read poems that celebrate renowned author William Blake and are set in his imaginary inn.

808. Williams, Linda.
The Little Old Lady Who Was Not Afraid of Anything.
Megan Lloyd, Illustrator. New York: Harper & Row, 1986. unpaged ISBN 0-690-04584-0. The imaginary sounds of the night come alive as a little old lady walks home after sunset.

809. William, Sue.
I Went Walking.
Julie Vivas, Illustrator. San Diego: Harcourt Brace Jovanovich, 1989. unpaged ISBN 0-15-200471-8. A young boy goes for a walk and discovers a variety of animals along the way.

810. Williams, Vera.
A Chair for My Mother.
New York: Greenwillow, 1982. unpaged ISBN 0-688-00915-8. After suffering from a devastating fire, a young girl, her grandmother, and her mother, who is a waitress, save money to purchase a comfortable chair for their new home.

811. Winter, Jeanette.
Follow the Drinking Gourd.
New York: Knopf, 1988. unpaged ISBN 0-394-89694-7. A story of how slaves on the Underground Railroad were taught to follow the drinking gourd (the Big Dipper) and go north to freedom.

812. Winthrop, Elizabeth.
The Castle in the Attic.
New York: Holiday House, 1986. 179 pages. ISBN 0-8234-0579-6. Given a mysterious castle, William meets Sir Simon, a miniature knight, who tells him of magic and evil deeds. William leaves on a quest that is twofold; first to keep his best friend in the world, Mrs. Phillips, from going home to England, and second, to help Sir Simon retrieve his rightful throne.

813. Winthrop, Elizabeth.
Vasilissa the Beautiful.
Alexander Koshkin, Illustrator. New York: HarperCollins, 1991. unpaged ISBN 0-06-021662-X. This is a Russian Cinderella tale. A doll from her mother acts as the fairy godmother, while her obedience and industriousness protect her from Baba Yaga, the Russian witch, and earn her a "happily- ever-after" reward.

814. Wood, Audrey.
King Bidgood's in the Bathtub.
Don Wood, Illustrator. New York: Harcourt Brace Jovanovich, 1985. unpaged ISBN 0-15-242730-9. King Bidgood won't come out of the bathtub, no matter what.

815. Wood, Audrey.
Little Penguin's Tale.
San Diego: Harcourt Brace Jovanovich, 1989. unpaged ISBN 0-15-246475-1. As Granny tells of the little penguin who didn't listen to her stories; a little penguin sneaks away and experiences each of the adventures. The illustrations tell of the new penguin's adventures, while the text describes the earlier ones.

816. Woodruff, Elvira.
George Washington's Socks.
New York: Scholastic, 1991. 166 pages. ISBN 0-590-44035-7. Five children are transported from their Kansas campsite back in time to the revolutionary war and learn of its associated cruelties.

817. Wright, Betty Ren.
A Ghost in the Window.
New York: Holiday House, 1987. 152 pages. ISBN 0-8234-0661-X. Sent to her aunt's for the summer, Meg helps her cousin solve a mystery concerning the disappearance of her uncle and money from a bank robbery.

818. Wyndham, Robert.
The Chinese Mother Goose Rhymes.
Ed Young, Illustrator. New York: Putnam, 1982. 48 pages ISBN 0-399-21718-5. A collection of traditional riddles, rhymes, and games that have been taught to Chinese children

Y

819. Yagawa, Sumiko.
The Crane Wife.
Suekichi Akaba, Illustrator. New York: Morrow, 1981, 1979. unpaged ISBN 0-688-07048-5. One of the most popular of Japanese folk tales, this story is about a shape-changer who becomes the wife of a peasant. When times are difficult, she weaves a marvelous cloth. Unfortunately, her husband's greed results in an unhappy ending.

820. Yep, Laurence.
The Rainbow People.
David Wiesner, Illustrator. New York: Harper & Row, 1989. 194 pages. ISBN 0-06-026760-7. Twenty Chinese American folk tales that were collected in Oakland, CA, during the 1930s and artfully retold by Yep.

821. Yolen, Jane.
The Devil's Arithmetic.
New York: Viking Kestrel, 1988. ISBN 0-670-81027-4. A girl is transported back to a World War II German concentration camp. She takes the place of her grandmother in the death chamber.

822. Yolen, Jane.
Dove Isabeau.
San Diego: Harcourt Brace Jovanovich, 1989. unpaged ISBN 0-15-224131-0. A love story in which the hero must overcome the spell of the wicked stepmother to save his beautiful princess.

823. Yolen, Jane.
Dragon's Boy.
New York: Harper & Row, 1990. 120 pages. ISBN 0-06-026790-9. Young Arthur meets a dragon who becomes his mentor in an interesting variation of the King Arthur legend.

824. Yolen, Jane (editor).
The Lap-Time Song and Play Book.
Musical arrangements by Margot Tomes and Adam Stemple. San Diego: Harcourt Brace Jovanovich, 1989. 32 pages. ISBN 0-15-243588-3. A collection of British and American rhymes that are set to music with beautiful illustrations.

825. Yolen, Jane.
Owl Moon.
John Schoenherr, Illustrator.
New York: Philomel, 1987.
unpaged ISBN 0-399-21457-7. Father and daughter go for a special night in the winter woods.

826. Yolen, Jane.
Ring of Earth.
John Wallner, Illustrator. San Diego: Harcourt Brace Jovanovich, 1986. unpaged ISBN 0-15-267-140-4. A combination of verse and illustrations that describe the seasons for older readers.

827. Yolen, Jane.
Sky Dogs.
Barry Moser, Illustrator. San Diego: Harcourt Brace Jovanovich, 1990. unpaged ISBN 0-15-275480-6. The story of how horses came to the Plains Indians.

828. Yolen, Jane (reteller).
Tam Lin.
Charles Mikolaycak, Illustrator. San Diego: Harcourt Brace Jovanovich, 1990. unpaged ISBN 0-15-284261-6. Jennet, against the wishes of her parents, braves the wrath of the Faery Queen to win back her true love.

829. Yorinks, Arthur.
Ugh.
Richard Egielski, Illustrator. New York: Farrar, Straus and Giroux, 1990. unpaged ISBN 0-374-38028-7. A retelling of Cinderella with a Stone-Age boy as the protagonist. He escapes his servitude by inventing a bicycle and astonishing his peers who elect him king. Told in a wonderful tongue-in-cheek style.

830. Yoshida, Toshi.

Elephant Crossing.
New York: Philomel, 1989. unpaged ISBN 0-399-21745-2. A first-hand look at a herd of elephants and the deadly perils they face.

831. Young, Ed.
Lon Po Po.
New York: Philomel, 1989. unpaged ISBN 0-399-21619-7. The Chinese version of the classic Red Riding Hood story.

832. Young, Ed (adaptor).
Seven Blind Mice.
Ed Young, Illustrator. New York: Philomel, 1992. unpaged ISBN 0-399-22261-8. Adapted from "The Blind Men and The Elephant," this is a humorous fable illustrated in paper-collage of seven mice who take turns trying to figure out what the Something is!

Z

833. Zelinsky, Paul O.
Rumplestiltskin.
New York: Dutton, 1986. unpaged ISBN 0-525-44265-0. Lush illustrations make this a good addition to any collection.

834. Zemach, Harve.
Duffy and the Devil.
Margot Zemach, Illustrator. New York: Farrar, Straus and Giroux, 1973. unpaged ISBN 0-374-41897-7. The story of a devil who helps Duffy with her spinning, but threatens to take her away unless she can guess his name. Compare this tale to "Rumpelstiltskin" and "Tom Tit Tot."

835. Zemach, Harve.
*Mommy, Buy Me
a China Doll.*
Margot Zemach, Illustrator.
New York: Farrar, Straus and

Giroux, 1975. ISBN 0-374-45286-5. Eliza Lou has a plan to trade her father's feather bed for a china doll that she would like.

836. Zemach, Harve.
Salt.
Margot Zemach, Illustrator. Chicago: Follett, 1965. unpaged ISBN 0-374-36385-4. A Russian folk tale about Ivan the Fool who goes to sea to make his fortune. He discovers a mountain of salt that he takes as his cargo. He later trades for a fortune and a bride.

837. Zemach, Margot.
*It Could Always Be Worse:
A Yiddish Folk Tale.*
New York: Farrar, Straus and Giroux, 1976. 32 pages. ISBN 0-374-33650-4. Following the Rabbi's advice, a poor man learns that things can always be worse.

838. Zemach, Margot.
The Three Little Pigs.
New York: Farrar, Straus and Giroux, 1988. 32 pages. ISBN 0-374-37527-5. A wonderful retelling of a classic folk tale that stays true to the original version.

839. Zhensun, Zheng;
Alice Low.
A Young Painter.
New York: Scholastic, 1991. 80 pages. ISBN 0-590-44906-0. The life of a remarkable young Chinese artist is chronicled in a beautifully written photo-story.

840. Zolotow, Charlotte.
*The Bunny Who
Found Easter.*
Betty Peterson, Illustrator. Boston: Houghton Mifflin, 1959. unpaged ISBN 0-395-27677-2. A little bunny,

thinking that Easter is a place, finds the true meaning of Easter during his search.

841. Zolotow, Charlotte.
River Winding.
Regina Shekerjian, Illustrator. New York: Crowell, 1970. 32 pages. ISBN 0-690-03867-4. Graceful poems written for young children, illustrated with delicate drawings.

The Index of **AWARDS**

THE CALDECOTT MEDAL

1938
Animals of the Bible
by Helen Dean Fish, illustrated by Dorothy P. Lathrop, Lippincott
Honor Books: *Seven Simeons* by Boris Artzybasheff, Viking; *Four and Twenty Blackbirds* by Helen Dean Fish, illustrated by Robert Lawson, Stokes

1939
Mei Li
by Thomas Handforth, Doubleday
Honor Books: *The Forest Pool* by Laura Adams Armer, Longmans; *Wee Gillis* by Munro Leaf, illustrated by Robert Lawson, Viking; *Snow White and the Seven Dwarfs* by Wanda Gág, Coward; *Barkis* by Clare Newberry, Harper;   by James Daugherty, Viking

1940
Abraham Lincoln
by Ingri and Edgar Parin D'Aulaire, Doubleday
Honor Books: *Cock-A-Doodle Doo* by Berta and Elmer Hader, Macmillan; *Madeline* by Ludwig Bemelmans, Viking; *The Ageless Story* illustrated by Lauren Ford, Dodd

1941
They Were Strong and Good
by Robert Lawson, Viking
Honor Book: *April's Kittens* by Clare Newberry, Harper

1942
Make Way for Ducklings
by Robert McCloskey, Viking
Honor Books: *An American ABC* by Maud and Miska

Petersham, Macmillan; *In My Mother's House* by Ann Nolan Clark, illustrated by Velino Herrera, Viking; *Paddle-to-the-Sea* by Holling C. Holling, Houghton; *Nothing at All* by Wanda Gág, Coward

1943
The Little House
by Virginia Lee Burton, Houghton
Honor Books: *Dash and Dart* by Mary and Conrad Buff, Viking; *Marshmallow* by Clare Newberry, Harper

1944
Many Moons
by James Thurber, illustrated by Louis Slobodkin, Harcourt
Honor Books: *Small Rain: Verses from the Bible* selected by Jessie Orton Jones, illustrated by Elizabeth Orton Jones, Viking; *Pierre Pigeon* by Lee Kingman, illustrated by Arnold E. Bare, Houghton; *The Mighty Hunter* by Berta and Elmer Hader, Macmillan; *A Child's Good Night Book* by Margaret Wise Brown, illustrated by Jean Charlot, W. R. Scott; *Good Luck Horse* by Chih-Yi Chan, illustrated by Plao Chan, Whittlesey

1945
Prayer for a Child
by Rachel Field, illustrated by Elizabeth Orton Jones, Macmillan
Honor Books: *Mother Goose*, illustrated by Tasha Tudor, Walck; *In the Forest* by Marie Hall Ets, Viking; *Yonie Wondenose* by Marguerite de Angeli, Doubleday; *The Christmas Anna Angel* by Ruth Sawyer, illustrated by Kate Seredy, Viking

1946
The Rooster Crows…
selected and illustrated by

Maud and Miska Petersham, Macmillan
Honor Books: *Little Lost Lamb* by Golden MacDonald, illustrated by Leonard Welsgard, Doubleday; *Sing Mother Goose* by Opal Wheeler, illustrated by Marjorie Torrey, Dutton; *My Mother Is the Most Beautiful Woman in the World* by Becky Reyher, illustrated by Ruth Gannett, Lothrop; *You Can Write Chinese* by Kurt Wiese, Viking

1947
The Little Island
by Golden MacDonald, illustrated by Leonard Weisgard, Doubleday
Honor Books: *Rain Drop Splash* by Alvin Tresselt, illustrated by Leonard Weisgard, Lothrop; *Boats on the River* by Marjorie Flack, illustrated by Jay Hyde Barnum, Viking; *Timothy Turtle* by Al Graham, illustrated by Tony Palazzo, Viking; *Pedro, The Angel of Olvera Street* by Leo Politi, Scribners; *Sing in Praise: A Collection of the Best Loved Hymns* by Opal Wheeler, illustrated by Marjorie Torrey, Dutton

1948
White Snow, Bright Snow
by Alvin Tresselt, illustrated by Roger Duvoisin, Lothrop
Honor Books: *Stone Soup* by Marcia Brown, Scribners; *McElligot's Pool* by Dr. Seuss, Random; *Bambino the Clown* by George Schreiber, Viking; *Roger and the Fox* by Lavinia Davis, illustrated by Hildegard Woodward, Doubleday; *Song of Robin Hood* edited by Anne Malcolmson, illustrated by Virginia Lee Burton, Houghton

1949
The Big Snow
by Berta and Elmer Hader, Macmillan
Honor Books: *Blueberries for Sal* by Robert McCloskey, Viking; *All Around the Town* by Phyllis McGinley, illustrated by Helen Stone, Lippincott; *Juanita* by Leo Politi, Scribners; *Fish in the Air* by Kurt Wiese, Viking

1950
Song of the Swallows
by Leo Politi, Scribners
Honor Books: *America's Ethan Allen* by Stewart Holbrook, illustrated by Lynn Ward, Houghton; *The Wild Birthday Cake* by Lavinia Davis, illustrated by Hildegard Woodward, Doubleday; *The Happy Day* by Ruth Krauss, illustrated by Marc Simont, Harper; *Bartholomew and the Oobleck* by Dr. Seuss, Random; *Henry Fisherman* by Marcia Brown, Scribners

1951
The Egg Tree
by Katherine Milhous, Scribners
Honor Books: *Dick Whittington and His Cat* by Marcia Brown, Scribners; *The Two Reds* by William Lipkind, illustrated by Nicholas Mordvinoff, Harcourt; *If I Ran the Zoo* by Dr. Seuss, Random; *The Most Wonderful Doll in the World* by Phyllis McGinley, illustrated by Helen Stone, Lippincott; *T-Bone, the Baby Sitter* by Clare Newberry, Harper

1952
Finders Keepers
by William Lipkind, illustrated by Nicholas Mordvinoff, Harcourt
Honor Books: *Mr. T. W. Anthony Woo* by Marie Hall

Ets, Viking; *Skipper John's Cook* by Marcia Brown, Scribners; *All Falling Down* by Gene Zion, illustrated by Margaret Bloy Graham, Harper; *Bear Party* by William Pene du Bois, Viking; *Feather Mountain* by Elizabeth Olds, Houghton

1953
The Biggest Bear
by Lynn Ward, Houghton
Honor Books: *Puss in Boots* by Charles Perrault, illustrated and translated by Marcia Brown, Scribners; *One Morning in Maine* by Robert McCloskey, Viking; *Ape in a Cape* by Fritz Eichenberg, Harcourt; *The Storm Book* by Charlotte Zolotow, illustrated by Margaret Bloy Graham, Harper; *Five Little Monkeys* by Juliet Kepes, Houghton

1954
Madeline's Rescue
by Ludwig Bemelmans, Viking
Honor Books: *Journey Cake, Ho!* by Ruth Sawyer, illustrated by Robert McCloskey, Viking; *When Will the World Be Mine?* by Miriam Schlein, illustrated by Jean Charlot, W. R. Scott; *The Steadfast Tin Soldier* by Hans Christian Andersen, illustrated by Marcia Brown, Scribners; *A Very Special House* by Ruth Krauss, illustrated by Maurice Sendak, Harper; *Green Eyes* by A. Birnbaum, Capitol

1955
Cinderella, or the Little Glass Slipper
by Charles Perrault, translated and illustrated by Marcia Brown, Scribners
Honor Books: *Books of Nursery and Mother Goose Rhymes*, illustrated by Marguerite de Angeli,

Doubleday; *Wheel on the Chimney* by Margaret Wise Brown, illustrated by Tibor Gergely, Lippincott; *The Thanksgiving Story* by Alice Dalgliesh, illustrated by Helen Sewell, Scribners

1956
Frog Went A-Courtin'
edited by John Langstaff, illustrated by Feodor Rojankovsky, Harcourt
Honor Books: *Play with Me* by Marie Hall Ets, Viking; *Crow Boy* by Taro Yashima, Viking

1957
A Tree Is Nice
by Janice May Udry, illustrated by Marc Simont, Harper
Honor Books: *Mr. Penny's Race Horse* by Marie Hall Ets, Viking; *1 Is One* by Tasha Tudor, Walck; *Anatole* by Eve Titus, illustrated by Paul Galdone, McGraw; *Gillespie and the Guards* by Benjamin Elkin, illustrated by James Daugherty, Viking; *Lion* by William Pene du Bois, Viking

1958
Time of Wonder
by Robert McCloskey, Viking
Honor Books: *Fly High, Fly Low* by Don Freeman, Viking; *Anatole and the Cat* by Eve Titus, illustrated by Paul Galdone, McGraw

1959
Chanticleer and the Fox
adapted from Chaucer and illustrated by Barbara Cooney, T. Crowell
Honor Books: *The House That Jack Built* by Antonio Frasconi, Harcourt; *What Do You Say, Dear?* by Sesyle Joslin, illustrated by Maurice Sendak, W. R. Scott;

Umbrella by Taro Yashima, Viking

1960
Nine Days to Christmas
by Marie Hall Ets and Aurora Labastida, illustrated by Marie Hall Ets, Viking
Honor Books: *Houses from the Sea* by Alice E. Goudey, illustrated by Adrienne Adams, Scribners; *The Moon Jumpers* by Janice May Udry, illustrated by Maurice Sendak, Harper

1961
Babushka and the Three Kings
by Ruth Robbins, illustrated by Nicolas Sidjakov, Parnassus
Honor Book: *Inch by Inch* by Leo Lionni, Obolensky

1962
Once a Mouse
retold and illustrated by Marcia Brown, Scribners
Honor Books: *The Fox Went Out on a Chilly Night* by Peter Spier, Doubleday; *Little Bear's Visit* by Else Holmelund Minarik, illustrated by Maurice Sendak, Harper; *The Day We Saw the Sun Come Up* by Alice E. Goudey, illustrated by Adrienne Adams, Scribners

1963
The Snowy Day
by Ezra Jack Keats, Viking
Honor Books: *The Sun Is a Golden Earring* by Natalia M. Belting, illustrated by Bernarda Bryson, Holt; *Mr. Rabbit and the Lovely Present* by Charlotte Zolotow, illustrated by Maurice Sendak, Harper

1964
Where the Wild Things Are
by Maurice Sendak, Harper &

Row
Honor Books: *All in the Morning Early* by Sorche Nic Leodhas, illustrated by Evaline Ness, Holt, Rinehart & Winston; *Mother Goose and Nursery Rhymes* by Philip Reed, Atheneum; *Swimmy* by Leo Lionni, Pantheon

1965
May I Bring a Friend?
by Beatrice Schenk de Regniers, Atheneum
Honor Books: *A Pocketful of Cricket* by Rebecca Caudill, illustrated by Evaline Ness, Holt, Rinehart & Winston; *Rain Makes Applesauce* by Julian Scheer, illustrated by Marvin Bileck, Holiday; *The Wave* by Margaret Hodges, illustrated by Blair Lent, Houghton Mifflin

1966
Always Room for One More
by Sorche Nic Leodhas, illustrated by Nonny Hogrogian, Holt, Rinehart & Winston
Honor Books: *Hide and Seek Fog* by Alvin Tresselt, illustrated by Roger Duvoisin, Lothrop, Lee & Shepard; *Just Me* by Marie Hall Ets, Viking; *Tom Tit Tot* edited by Joseph Jacobs, illustrated by Evaline Ness, Scribners

1967
Sam, Bangs & Moonshine
by Evaline Ness, Holt, Rinehart & Winston
Honor Book: *One Wide River to Cross* by Barbara Emberley, illustrated by Ed Emberley, Prentice-Hall

1968
Drummer Hoff
by Barbara Emberley, illustrated by Ed Emberley, Prentice-Hall
Honor Books: *Frederick* by

Seashore Story by Taro Yashima, Viking; *The Emperor and the Kite* by Jane Yolen, illustrated by Ed Young, Harcourt Brace Jovanovich

1969
The Fool of the World and the Flying Ship
by Arthur Ransome, illustrated by Uri Shulevitz, Farrar, Straus & Giroux
Honor Book: *Why the Sun and the Moon Live in the Sky: An African Folk tale* by Elphinstone Dayrell, illustrated by Blair Lent, Houghton Mifflin

1970
Sylvester and the Magic Pebble
by William Steig, Windmill/Simon & Schuster
Honor Books: *Alexander and the Wind-Up Mouse* by Leo Lionni, Pantheon; *Goggles!* Ezra Jack Keats, Macmillan; *The Judge: An Untrue Tale* by Harve Zemach, illustrated by Margot Zemach, Farrar, Straus & Giroux; *Pop Corn and Ma Goodness* by Edna Mitchell Preston, illustrated by Robert Andrew Parker, Viking; *Thy Friend, Obadiah* by Brinton Turkle, Viking

1971
A Story, A Story
by Gail E. Haley, Atheneum
Honor Books: *The Angry Moon* by William Sleaton, illustrated by Blair Lent, Atlantic-Little; *Frog and Toad Are Friends* by Arnold Lobel, Harper & Row; *In the Night Kitchen* by Maurice Sendak, Harper & Row

1972
One Fine Day
by Nonny A. Hogrogian, Macmillan

Honor Books: *Hildilid's Night* by Cheli Duran Ryan, illustrated by Arnold Lobel, Macmillan; *If All the Seas Were One Sea* by Janina Domanska, Macmillan; *Moja Means One: Swahili Counting Book* by Muriel Feelings, illustrated by Tom Feelings, Dial

1973
The Funny Little Woman
by Arlen Mosel, illustrated by Blair Lent, E. P. Dutton
Honor Books: *Hosie's Alphabet* by Tobias Hosea, and Lisa Baskin, illustrated by Leonard Baskin, Viking; *Snow-White and the Seven Dwarfs*, translated by Randall Jarrell from *The Brothers Grimm*, illustrated by Nancy Ekholm Burkert, Farrar, Straus & Giroux; *When Clay Sings* by Byrd Baylor, illustrated by Tom Bahti, Scribners

1974
Duffy and the Devil
by Harve and Margot Zemach, Farrar, Straus & Giroux
Honor Books: *Cathedral: The Story of Its Construction* by David Macaulay, Houghton; *The Three Jovial Huntsmen* by Susan Jeffers, Bradbury Press

1975
Arrow to the Sun
by Gerald McDermott, Viking
Honor Book: *Jambo Means Hello: A Swahili Alphabet Book* by Muriel Feeings, illustrated by Tom Feelings, Dial

1976
Why Mosquitoes Buzz in People's Ears
by Verna Aardema, illustrated by Leo and Diane Dillon, Dial
Honor Books: *The Desert Is*

Theirs by Byrd Baylor, illustrated by Peter Parnall, Scribners; *Strega Nona* by Tomie de Paola, Prentice-Hall

1977
Ashanti to Zulu
by Margaret Musgrove, illustrated by Leo and Diane Dillon, Dial
Honor Books: *The Amazing Bone* by William Steig, Farrar, Straus & Giroux; *The Contest* by Nonny Hogrogian, Greenwillow; *Fish for Supper* by M. B. Goffstein, Dial; *The Golem: A Jewish Legend* by Beverly Brodsky McDermott, Lippincott; *Hawk I'm Your Brother* by Byrd Baylor, illustrated by Peter Parnall, Scribners

1978
Noah's Ark: The Story of the Flood
by Peter Spier, Doubleday
Honor Books: *Castle* by David Macaulay, Houghton; *It Could Always Be Worse* by Margot Zemach, Farrar, Straus & Giroux

1979
The Girl Who Loved Wild Horses
by Paul Goble, Bradbury Press
Honor Books: *Freight Train* by Donald Crews, Greenwillow; *The Way to Start a Day* by Byrd Baylor, illustrated by Peter Parnall, Scribners

1980
Ox-Cart Man
by Donald Hall, illustrated by Barbara Cooney, Viking
Honor Books: *Ben's Trumpet* by Rachel Isadora, Greenwillow; *The Garden of Abdul Gasazi* by Chris Van Allsburg, Houghton; *The Treasure* by Uri Shulevitz, Farrar, Straus & Giroux

1981
Fables
by Arnold Lobel, Harper & Row
Honor Books: *The Bremen-Town Musicians* by Ilse Plume, Doubleday; *The Grey Lady and the Strawberry Snatcher* by Molly Bang, Four Winds; *Mice Twice* by Joseph Low, Atheneum; *Truck* by Donald Crews, Greenwillow

1982
Jumanji
by Chris Van Allsburg, Houghton Mifflin
Honor Books: *On Market Street* by Arnold Lobel, illustrated by Anita Lobel, Greenwillow; *Outside Over There* by Maurice Sendak, Harper & Row; *A Visit to William Blake's Inn: Poems for Innocent and Experienced Travelers* by Nancy Willard, illustrated by Alice and Martin Provensen, Harcourt; *Where the Buffaloes Begin* by Olaf Baker, illustrated by Stephen Gammell, Warne

1983
Shadow
by Blaise Cendrars, translated and illustrated by Marcia Brown, Scribners
Honor Books: *A Chair for My Mother* by Vera B. Williams, Greenwillow; *When I Was Young in the Mountains* by Cynthia Rylant, illustrated by Diane Goode, E. P. Dutton

1984
The Glorious Flight Across the Channel with Louis Bleriot by Alice and Martin Provensen, Viking
Honor Books: *Little Red Riding Hood* by Trina Schart Hyman, Holiday; *Ten, Nine, Eight* by Molly Bang,

Leo Lionni, Pantheon; Greenwillow

1985
Saint George and the Dragon
by Margaret Hodges, illustrated by Trina Schart Hyman, Little, Brown
Honor Books: *Hansel and Gretel* by Rika Lesser, illustrated by Paul O. Zelinsky, Dodd, Mead; *Have You Seen My Duckling?* by Nancy Tafuri, Greenwillow; *The Story of Jumping Mouse* by John Steptoe, Lothrop, Lee & Shepard

1986
The Polar Express
by Chris Van Allsburg, Houghton Mifflin
Honor Books: *King Bidgood's in the Bathtub* by Audrey Wood, illustrated by Don Wood, Harcourt Brace Jovanovich; *The Relatives Came* by Cynthia Rylant, Bradbury Press

1987
Hey, Al
by Arthur Yorinks, illustrated by Richard Egielski, Farrar, Straus & Giroux
Honor Books: *Alphabatics* by Suse MacDonald, Bradbury Press; *Rumplestiltskin* retold and illustrated by Paul O. Zelinsky, E. P. Dutton; *The Village of Round and Square Houses* by Anne Grifalconi. Little, Brown

1988
Owl Moon
by Jane Yolen, illustrated by John Schoenherr, Philomel
Honor Book: *Mufaro's Beautiful Daughters: An African Tale* by John Steptoe, Morrow

1989
Song and Dance Man
by Karen Ackerman, illustrated by Stephen Gammell, Knopf
Honor Books: *The Boy of the Three Year Nap* by Dianne Snyder, illustrated by Allen Say, Houghton Mifflin; *Free Fall* by David Wiesner, Lothrop, Lee, & Shepard; *Goldilocks and the Three Bears* by James Marshall, Dial; *Mirandy and Brother Wind* by Patricia C. McKissack, illustrated by Jerry Pinkney, Knopf

1990
Lon Po Po: A Red Riding Hood Story from China
translated and illustrated by Ed Young, Putnam
Honor Books: *Bill Peet: An Autobiography* written and illustrated by Bill Peet, Houghton Mifflin; *Color Zoo* written and illustrated by Lois Ehlert, Harper & Row; *Hershel and the Hanukkah Goblins* by Eric A. Kimmel, illustrated by Trina Schart Hyman, Holiday; *The Talking Eggs* by Robert San Souci, illustrated by Jerry Pinkney, Doubleday

1991
Black and White
by David Macauley, Houghton Mifflin
Honor Books: *"More More, More," said the Baby* written and illustrated by Vera Williams, Greenwillow

1992
Tuesday
by David Wiesner, Lothrop, Lee, & Shepard
Honor Books: *Tar Beach* written and illustrated by Faith Ringgold, Crown.

1993
Mirette on the High Wire
by Emily Arnold McCully, Putnam
Honor Books: *Seven Blind Mice* written and illustrated by Ed Young, Philomel; *The Stinky Cheese Man and Other Fairly Stupid Tales* by John Scieszka, illustrated by Lane Smith, Viking; *Working Cotton* by Sherley Anne Williams, illustrated by Carole Byard, Harcourt

---

THE CORETTA SCOTT KING AWARD

AUTHORS

1970
Lillie Patterson
Dr. Martin Luther King, Jr., Man of Peace
by Lillie Patterson, Garrard

1971
Charlemae Rollins
Langston Hughes,
by Charlemae Rollins, Rand McNally
Honor Books: I Know Why the Caged Bird Sings by Maya Angelou, Random; *Unbought and Unbossed* by Shirley Chisolm, Houghton; *I Am a Black Woman* by Mari Evans, Morrow; *Every Man Heart Lay Down* by Lorenz Graham, Crowell; *The Voice of Children* by June Jordan and Terry Bush, Holt; *Black Means* by Gloom Grossman, Hill & Wang; *Ebony Book of Black Achievement*, Johnson Publishing; *Mary Jo's Grandmother* by Janice May Udry, Whitman

1972
Elton C. Fax
17 Black Artists
by Elton C. Fax, Dodd

1973
Alfred Duckett
I Never Had It Made: The Autobiography of Jackie Robinson
by Alfred Duckett, Putman

1974
Sharon Bell Mathis
Ray Charles
by Sharon Bell Mathis, Crowell
Honor Books: A Hero Ain't Nothing But a Sandwich by Alice Childress, Coward-McCann; *Don't You Remember?* by Lucille Clifton, Dutton; *Ms. Africa: Profiles of Modern African Women* by Louise Crane, Lippincott; *Guest in the Promised Land* by Kristin Hunter, Scribner; *Musasa* by John Nagenda, Macmillan

1975
Dorothy Robinson
The Legend of Africania
by Dorothy Robinson, Johnson Publishing

1976
Pearl Bailey
Duey's Tale
by Pearl Bailey, Harcourt
Honor Books: Julius K. Nyerere: Teacher of Africa by Shirley Graham, Messner; *Paul Robeson* by Eloise Greenfield, Crowell; *Fast Sam, Cool Clyde and Stuff* by Walter Dean Myers, Viking; *Song of the Trees* by Mildred Taylor, Dial.

1977
James Haskins
The Story of Stevie Wonder
by James Haskins, Lothrop
Honor Books: Everett Anderson's Friend by Lucille Clifton, Holt; *Roll of Thunder,*

Hear My Cry by Mildred Taylor; *Quiz Book on Black America* by Clarence N. Blake and Donald F. Martin, Houghton

1978
Eloise Greenfield
Africa Dream
by Eloise Greenfield, Crowell
Honor Books: The Days When the Animals Talked: Black Folk Tales and How They Came to Be by William J. Faulkner, Follett; *Marvin and Tige* by Frankcine Glass, St. Martin's; *Mary McCleod Bethune* by Eloise Greenfield, Crowell; *Barbara Jordan* by James Haskins, Dial; *Coretta Scott King* by Lillie Patterson, Garrard; *Portia: The Life of Portia Washington Pittman, The Daughter of Booker T. Washington* by Ruth Ann Stewart, Doubleday

1979
Ossie Davis
Escape From Freedom: A Play About Federick Douglass
by Ossie Davis, Viking
Honor Books: Skates From Uncle Richard by Carol Fenner, Random; *Justice and Her Brothers* by Virginia Hamilton, Greenwillow; *Benjamin Banneker* by Lillie Patterson, Abingdon Press; *I Have a Sister, My Sister Is Deaf* by Jeanne W. Peterson, Harper

1980
Walter Dean Myers
The Young Warlords
by Walter Dean Myers, Viking
Honor Books: Movin' Up by Berry Gordon, Harper; *Childtimes: A Three-Generation Memoir* by Eloise Greenfield and Lessie Jones Little, Harper; *Andrew Young:*

Young Man with A Mission by James Haskins, Lothrop; *Let the Lion Eat Straw* by Ellease Southerland, Scribners

1981
Sidney Poitier
This Life
by Sidney Poitier, Knopf
Honor Books: Don't Explain: A Song of Billie Holiday, by Alexis De Veaux, Harper

1982
Mildred Taylor
Let The Circle Be Broken
by Mildred Taylor, Dial
Honor Books: Rainbow Jordan by Alice Childress, Coward-McCann *Lou in the Limelight* by Kristin Hunter, Scribners; *Mary: An Autobiography* by Mary E. Mebane, Viking

1983
Virginia Hamilton
Sweet Whispers, Brother Rush
by Virginia Hamilton, Philomel
Honor Books: This Strange New Feeling by Julius Lester, Dial

1984
Lucille Clifton
Everett Anderson's Goodbye
by Lucille Clifton, Holt
Honor Books: The Magical Adventures of Pretty Pearl by Virginia Hamilton, Harper; *Lena Horn* by James Haskins, Coward-McCann; *Bright Shadow* by Joyce Carol Thomas, Avon; *Because We Are* by Mildred Pitts Walter, Lothrop
Special Citation: The Words Of Martin Luther King, Jr. compiled by Coretta Scott King, Newmarket Press

1985
Walter Dean Myers
Motown and Didi

by Walter Dean Myers, Viking
Honor Books: Circle of Gold by Candy Dawson Boyd, Apple/Scholastic; *A Little Love* by Virginia Hamilton, Philomel

1986
Virginia Hamilton
The People Could Fly: American Black Folktales
by Virginia Hamilton, Knopf
Honor Books: Junius Over Far by Virginia Hamilton, Harper; *Trouble's Child* by Mildred Pitts Walter, Lothrop

1987
Mildred Pitts Walter
Justin and the Best Biscuits in the World
by Mildred Pitts Walter, Lothrop
Honor Books: Lion and the Ostrich Chicks and Other African Folk Tales by Ashley Bryan, Atheneum; *Which Way Freedom?* by Joyce Hansen, Walker

1988
Mildred Taylor
The Friendship
by Mildred Taylor, Dial
Honor Books: An Enchanted Hair Tale by Alexis De Veaux, Harper; *The Tales of Uncle Remus: The Adventures of Brer Rabbit*, by Julius Lester, Dial

1989
Walter Dean Myers
Fallen Angels
by Walter Dean Myers, Scholastic
Honor Books: The Thief in the Villiage and Other Stories by James Berry, Orchard: *Anthony Burns: The Defeat and Triumph of a Fugitive Slave*, Knopf

1990
Patricia and Fred McKissack
A Long Hard Journey: The Story of the Pullman Porter
by Patricia and Fred McKissack, Walker
Honor Books: Nathaniel Talking by Eloise Greenfield, Black Butterfly; *The Bells of Christmas* by Virginia Hamilton, Harcourt; *Martin Luther King Jr., and the Freedom Movement*, Facts on File

1991
Mildred Taylor
The Road to Memphis
by Mildred Taylor, Dial
Honor Books: Black Dance in America: A History Through Its People by James Haskins, Crowell; *When I Am Old With You* by Angela Johnson, Orchard

1992
Walter Dean Myers
Now Is Your Time: The African American Struggle for Freedom
by Walter Dean Myers, Harper Collins
Honor Books: Night in the Neighborhood by Eloise Greenfield, illustrated by Jan Spivey Gilchrist, Dial

1993
Patricia McKissick
The Dark Thirty: Southern Tales of the Supernatural
by Patricia McKissick, illustrated by Jerry Pinkney, Knopf
Honor Books: Mississippi Challenge by Mildred Pitts Walter, Bradbury Press; *Sorjourner Truth: Ain't I A Woman* by Patricia McKissack, Scholastic; *Somewhere in Darkness* by Walter Dean Myers, Scholastic

ILLUSTRATORS

1974
George Ford
Ray Charles
by Sharon Bell Mathis,
illustrated by George Ford,
Crowell

1979
Tom Feelings
Something on My Mind
by Nikki Grimes, illustrated
by Tom Feelings, Dial

1980
Carole Byard
Cornrows
by Camille Yarbough,
illustrated by Carole Byard,
Coward-McCann

1981
Ashley Bryan
Beat the Story
Drum Pum-Pum
by Ashley Bryan, Atheneum
Honor Books: Grandmama's
Joy by Eloise Greenfield,
illustrated by Carole Byard,
Philomel; *Count On Your*
Fingers African Style by
Claudia Zaslavsky, illustrated
by Jerry Pickney

1982
John Steptoe
Mother Crocodile: An Uncle
Amadou Tale from Senegal
translated by Rosa Guy,
illustrated by John Steptoe,
Delacorte
Honor Books: Daydreams by
Eloise Greenfield, illustrated
by Tom Feelings, Dial

1983
Peter Magubane
Black Child
by Peter Magubane, Knopf
Honor Books: All The Colors
of the Race by Arnold Adoff,
illustrated by John Steptoe,
Lothrop; *I'm Going to Sing:*
Black American Spirituals by

Ashley Bryan, Atheneum; *Just*
Us Women by Jeannette
Caines, illustrated by Pat
Cummings, Harper

1984
Pat Cummings
My Mama Needs Me by
Mildred Pitts Walter,
illustrated by Pat Cummings,
Lothrop

1986
Jerry Pinkney
The Patchwork Quilt
by Valerie Flournoy,
illustrated by Jerry Pinkney,
Dial
Honor Books: The People
Could Fly: American Black
Folktales told by Virginia
Hamilton, illustrated by Leo &
Diane Dillon

1987
Jerry Pinkney
Half Moon and
One Whole Star
by Crescent Dragonwagon,
illustrated by Jerry Pickney,
Macmillan
Honor Books: Lion and the
Ostrich Chicks and Other
African Folk Tales by Ashley
Bryan, Atheneum;
C.L.O.U.D.S. by Pat
Cummings, Lothrop

1988
John Steptoe
Mufaro's Beautiful
Daughters
by John Steptoe, Lothrop
Honor Books: What A
Morning! The Christmas Story
of Black Spirituals selected by
John Langstaff, illustrated by
Ashley Bryan, Macmillan;
The Invisible Hunters: A
Legend from the Miskito
Indians of Nicaragua
compiled by Harriet Rohmer,
et al., illustrated by Joe Sam,
Children's Book Press

1989
Jerry Pickney
Mirandy and Brother Wind
by Patricia C. McKissack,
illustrated by Jerry Pickney,
Knopf
Honor Books: Under the
Sunday Tree by Eloise
Greenfield, illustrated by
Amos Ferguson, Harper;
Storm in the Night by Mary
Stoltz, illustrated by Pat
Cummings, Harper

1990
Jan Spivey Gilchrist
Nathaniel Talking
by Eloise Greenfield,
illustrated by Jan Spivey
Gilchrist, Black Butterfly
Honor Books: The Talking
Eggs by Robert D. San Souci,
illustrated by Jerry Pickney,
Dial

1991
Leo and Diane Dillon
Aida
edited by Bonnie Ingbar,
illustrated by Leo and Diane
Dillon, Harcourt

1992
Faith Ringgold
Tar Beach
written and illustrated by Faith
Ringgold, Crown
Honor Books: Night in the
Neighborhood by Eloise
Greenfield, illustrated by Jan
Spivey, Dial; *All Night, All*
Day: A Child's First Book of
African Spirituals, selected
and illustrated by Ashley
Bryan

1993
Kathleen Atkins Wilson
The Origin of Life on Earth:
A Yoruba Creation Myth
retold by David A. Anderson
and Sankofa, illustrated by
Kathleen Atkins Wilson,
Sights Publications
Honor Books: Little Eight

John by Jim Wahl, illustrated
by Wil Clay, Lodestar; *Sukey*
and the Mermaids by Robert
San Souci, illustrated by Jerry
Pinkney, Four Winds;
Working Cotton by Sherley
Anne Williams, illustrated by
Carole Byard, Harcourt

THE NEWBERY MEDAL

1922
The Story of Mankind
by Hendrik Willem van Loon,
Liveright
Honor Books: *The Great*
Quest by Charles Hawes,
Little; *Cedric the Forester* by
Bernard Marshall, Appleton;
The Old Tobacco Shop by
William Bowen, Macmillan;
The Golden Fleece and the
Heroes Who Lived Before
Achilles by Padraic Colum,
Macmillan; *Windy Hill* by
Cornelia Meigs, Macmillan

1923
The Voyages of
Doctor Dolittle
by Hugh Lofting, Lippincott
Honor Books: No record

1924
The Dark Frigate
by Charles Hawes,
Atlantic/Little
Honor Books: No record

1925
Tales from Silver Lands
by Charles Finger, Doubleday
Honor Books: *Nicholas* by
Anne Carroll Moore, Putnam;
Dream Coach by Anne
Parrish, Macmillan

1926
Shen of the Sea
by Arthur Bowie Chrisman,
Dutton
Honor Book: *Voyagers* by

Padraic Colum, Macmillan

1927
Smoky, the Cowhorse
by Will James, Scribners
Honor Books: No record

1928
Gayneck,
The Story of a Pigeon
by Dhan Gopal Mukerji,
Dutton
Honor Books: *The Wonder Smith and His Son* by Ella Young, Longmans; *Downright Dencey* by Caroline Snedeker, Doubleday

1929
The Trumpeter of Krakow
by Eric P. Kelly, Macmillan
Honor Books: *Pigtail of Ah Lee Ben Loo* by John Bennett, Longmans; *Millions of Cats* by Wanda Gág, Coward; *The Boy Who Was* by Grace Hallock, Dutton; *Clearing Weather* by Cornelia Meigs, Little; *Runaway Papoose* by Grace Moon, Doubleday; *Tod of the Fens* by Elinor Whitney, Macmillan

1930
Hitty, Her First
Hundred Years
by Rachel Field, Macmillan
Honor Books: *Daughter of the Seine* by Jeanette Eaton, Harper; *Pran of Albania* by Elizabeth Miller, Doubleday; *Jumping Off Place* by Marian Hurd McNeely, Longmans; *Tangle-Coated Horse and Other Tales* by Ella Young, Longmans; *Vaino* by Julia Davis Adams, Dutton; *Little Blacknose* by Hildegarde Swift, Harcourt

1931
The Cat Who Went to Heaven
by Elizabeth Coatsworth, Macmillan
Honor Books: *Floating Island*

by Anne Parrish, Harper; *The Dark Star of Itza* by Alida Malkus, Harcourt; *Queer Person* by Ralph Hubbard, Doubleday; *Mountains Are Free* by Julia Davis Adams, Dutton; *Spice and the Devil's Cave* by Agnes Hewes, Knopf; *Meggy Macintosh* by Elizabeth Janet Gray, Doubleday; *Garram the Hunter* by Herbert Best, Doubleday; *Ood-Le-Uk the Wanderer* by Alice Lide and Margaret Johansen, Little

1932
Waterless Mountain
by Laura Adams Armer, Longmans
Honor Books: *The Fairy Circus* by Dorothy P. Lathrop, Macmillan; *Calico Bush* by Rachel Field, Macmillan; *Boy of the South Seas* by Eunice Tietjens, Coward; *Out of the Flame* by Eloise Lownsbery, Longmans; *Jane's Island* by Marjorie Allee, Houghton; *Truce of the Wolf and Other Tales of Old Italy* by Mary Gould Davis, Harcourt

1933
Young Fu of
the Upper Yangtze
by Elizabeth Foreman Lewis, Winston
Honor Books: *Swift Rivers* by Cornelia Meigs, Little; *The Railroad to Freedom* by Hildegarde Swift, Harcourt; *Children of the Soil* by Nora Burglon, Doubleday

1934
Invincible Louisa
by Cornelia Meigs, Little
Honor Books: *The Forgotten Daughter* by Caroline Snedeker, Doubleday; *Swords of Steel* by Elsie Singmaster, Houghton; *ABC Bunny* by Wanda Gág, Coward; *Winged Girl of Knossos* by Erik Berry,

Appleton; *New Land* by Sarah Schmidt, McBride; *Big Tree of Bunlahy* by Padraic Colum-Macmillan; *Glory of the Seas* by Agnes Hewes, Knopf; *Apprentice of Florence* by Anne Kyle, Houghton

1935
Dobry
by Monica Shannon, Viking
Honor Books: *Pageant of Chinese History* by Elizabeth Seeger, Longmans; *Davy Crockett* by Constance Rourke, Harcourt; *Day on Skates* by Hilda Van Stockum, Harper

1936
Caddie Woodlawn
by Carol Brink, Macmillan
Honor Books: *Honk, The Moose* by Phil Stong, Dod; *The Good Master* by Kate Seredy, Viking; *Young Walter Scott* by Elizabeth Janet Gray, Viking; *All Sail Set* by Armstrong Sperry, Winston

1937
Roller Skates
by Ruth Sawyer, Viking
Honor Books: *Phebe Fairchild: Her Book* by Lois Lenski, Stokes; *Whistler's Van* by Idwal Jones, Viking; *Golden Basket* by Ludwig Bemelmans, Viking; *Winterbound* by Margery Bianco, Viking; *Audubon* by Constance Rourke, Harcourt; *The Codfish Musket* by Agnes Hewes, Doubleday

1938
The White Stag
by Kate Seredy, Viking
Honor Books: *Pecos Bill* by James Cloyd Bowman, Little; *Bright Island* by Mabel Robinson, Random; *On the Banks of Plum Creek* by Laura Ingalls Wilder, Harper

1939
Thimble Summer
by Elizabeth Enright, Rinehart
Honor Books: *Nino* by Valenti Angelo, Viking; *Mr. Popper's Penguins* by Richard and Florence Atwater, Little; *"Hello the Boat!"* by Phyllis Crawford, Holt; *Leader by Destiny: George Washington, Man and Patriot* by Jeanette Eaton, Harcourt; *Penn* by Ellzabeth Janet Gray, Viking

1940
Daniel Boone
by James Daugherty, Viking
Honor Books: *The Singing Tree* by Kate Seredy, Viking; *Runner of the Mountain Tops* by Mabel Robinson, Random; *By the Shores of Silver Lake* by Laura Ingalls Wilder, Harper; *Boy with a Pack* by Stephen W. Meader, Harcourt

1941
Call It Courage
by Armstrong Sperry, Macmillan
Honor Books: *Blue Willow* by Doris Gates, Viking; *Young Mac of Fort Vancouver* by Mary Jane Carr, T. Crowell; *The Long Winter* by Laura Ingalls Wilder, Harper; *Nansen* by Anna Gertrude Hall, Viking

1942
The Matchlock Gun
by Walter D. Edmonds, Dodd
Honor Books: *Little Town on the Prairie* by Laura Ingalls Wilder, Harper; *George Washington's World* by Genevieve Foster, Scribners; *Indian Captive: The Story of Mary Jemison* by Lois Lenski, Lippincott; *Down Ryton Water* by Eva Roe Gággin, Viking

1943
Adam of the Road
by Elizabeth Janet Gray,

Viking
Honor Books: *The Middle Moffat* by Eleanor Estes, Harcourt; *Have You Seen Tom Thumb?* by Mabel Leigh Hunt, Lippincott

1944
Johnny Tremain
by Esther Forbes, Houghton
Honor Books: *These Happy Golden Years* by Laura Ingalls Wilder, Harper; *Fog Magic* by Julia Sauer, Viking; *Rufus M.* by Eleanor Estes, Harcourt; *Mountain Born* by Elizabeth Yates, Coward

1945
Rabbit Hill by Robert Lawson, Viking
Honor Books: *The Hundred Dresses* by Eleanor Estes, Harcourt; *The Silver Pencil* by Alice Dalgliesh, Scribners; *Abraham Lincoln's World* by Genevieve Foster, Scribners; *Lone Journey: The Life of Roger Williams* by Jeanette Eaton, Harcourt

1946
Strawberry Girl
by Lois Lenski, Lippincott
Honor Books: *Justin Morgan Had a Horse* by Marguerite Henry, Rand; *The Moved-Outers* by Florence Crannell Means, Houghton; *Bhimsa, The Dancing Bear* by Christine Weston, Scribners; *New Found World* by Katherine Shippen, Viking

1947
Miss Hickory
by Carolyn Sherwin Bailey, Viking
Honor Books: *Wonderful Year* by Nancy Barnes, Messner; *Big Tree* by Mary and Conrad Buff, Viking; *The Heavenly Tenants* by William Maxwell, Harper; *The Avion My Uncle Flew* by Cyrus

Fisher, Appleton; *The Hidden Treasure of Glaston* by Eleanore Jewett, Viking

1948
The Twenty-one Balloons
by William Pene du Bois, Viking
Honor Books: *Pancakes-Paris* by Claire Huchet Bishop, Viking; *Li Lun, Lad of Courage* by Carolyn Treffinger, Abingdon; *The Quaint and Curious Quest of Johnny Longfoot* by Catherine Besterman, Bobbs; *The Cow-Tail Switch, and Other West African Stories* by Harold Courlander, Holt; *Misty of Chincoteague* by Marguerite Henry, Rand

1949
King of the Wind
by Marguerite Henry, Rand
Honor Books: *Seabird* by Holling C. Holling, Houghton; *Daughter of the Mountains* by Louise Rankin, Viking; *My Father's Dragon* by Ruth S. Gannett, Random; *Story of the Negro* by Arna Bontemps, Knopf

1950
The Door in the Wall
by Marguerite de Angeli, Doubleday
Honor Books: *Tree of Freedom* by Rebecca Caudill, Viking; *The Blue Cat of Castle Town* by Catherine Coblentz, Longmans; *Kildee House* by Rutherford Montgomery, Doubleday; *George Washington* by Genevieve Foster, Scribners; *Song of the Pines* by Walter and Marion Havighurst, Winston

1951
Amos Fortune, Free Man
by Elizabeth Yates, Aladdin
Honor Books: *Better Known*

as Johnny Appleseed by Mabel Leigh Hunt, Lippincott; *Gandhi, Fighter Without a Sword* by Jeanette Eaton, Morrow; *Abraham Lincoln, Friend of the People* by Clara Ingram Judson, Follett; *The Story of Appleby Capple* by Anne Parrish, Harper

1952
Ginger Pye
by Eleanor Estes, Harcourt
Honor Books: *Americans Before Columbus* by Elizabeth Baity, Viking; *Minn of the Mississippi* by Holling C. Holling, Houghton; *The Defender* by Nicholas Kalashnlkoff, Scribners; *The Light at Tern Rock* by Julia Sauer, Viking; *The Apple and the Arrow* by Mary and Conrad Buff, Houghton

1953
Secret of the Andes
by Ann Nolan Clark, Viking
Honor Books: *Charlotte's Web* by E. B. White, Harper; *Moccasin Trail* by Eloise McGraw, Coward; *Red Sails to Capri* by Ann Weil, Viking; *The Bears on Hemlock Mountain* by Alice Dalgliesh, Scribners; *Birthdays of Freedom, Vol. 1* by Genevieve Foster, Scribners

1954
... and now Miguel
by Joseph Krumgold, T. Crowell
Honor Books: *All Alone* by Claire Huchet Bishop, Viking; *Shadrach* by Meindert DeJong, Harper; *Hurry Home Candy* by Meindert DeJong, Harper; *Theodore Roosevelt, Fighting Patriot* by Clara Ingram Judson, Follett; *Magic Maze* by Mary and Conrad Buff, Houghton

1955
The Wheel on the School
by Meindert DeJong, Harper
Honor Books: *The Courage of Sarah Noble* by Alice Dalgliesh, Scribners; *Banner in the Sky* by James Ullman, Lippincott

1956
Carry on, Mr. Bowditch
by Jean Lee Latham, Houghton
Honor Books: *The Secret River* by Marjorie Kinan Rawlings, Scribners; *The Golden Name Day* by Jennie Lindquist, Harper; *Men, Microscopes, and Living Things* by Katherine Shippen, Viking

1957
Miracles on Maple Hill
by Virginia Sorensen, Harcourt
Honor Books: *Old Yeller* by Fred Gipson, Harper; *The House of Sixty Fathers* by Meindert DeJong, Harper; *Mr. Justice Holmes* by Clara Ingram Judson, Follett; *The Corn Grows Ripe* by Dorothy Rhoads, Viking; *Black Fox of Lorne* by Marguerite de Angeli, Doubleday

1958
Rifles for Watie
by Harold Keith, T. Crowell
Honor Books: *The Horsecatcher* by Mari Sandoz, Westminster; *Gone-Away Lake* by Elizabeth Enright, Harcourt; *The Great Wheel* by Robert Lawson, Viking; *Tom Paine, Freedom's Apostle* by Leo Gurko, T. Crowell

1959
The Witch of Blackbird Pond
by Elizabeth George Speare, Houghton
Honor Books: *The Family under the Bridge* by Natalie S.

Carlson, Harper; *Along Came a Dog* by Meindert DeJong, Harper; *Chucaro: Wild Pony of the Pampa* by Francis Kalnay, Harcourt; *The Perilous Road* by William O. Steele, Harcourt

1960
Onion John
by Joseph Krumgold, T. Crowell
Honor Books: *My Side of the Mountain* by Jean George, Dutton; *America Is Born* by Gerald W. Johnson, Morrow; *The Gammage Cup* by Carol Kendall, Harcourt

1961
Island of the Blue Dolphins
by Scott O'Dell, Houghton
Honor Books: *America Moves Forward* by Gerald W. Johnson, Morrow; *Old Ramon* by Jack Schaefer, Houghton; *The Cricket in Times* Square by George Selden, Farrar

1962
The Bronze Bow
by Elizabeth George Speare, Houghton
Honor Books: *Frontier Living* by Edwin Tunis, World; *The Golden Goblet* by Eloise McGraw, Coward; *Belling the Tiger* by Mary Stolz, Harper

1963
A Wrinkle in Time
by Madeleine L'Engle, Farrar
Honor Books: *Thistle and Thyme* by Sorche Nic Leodhas, Holt; *Men of Athens* by Olivia Coolidge, Houghton

1964
It's Like This, Cat
by Emily Cheney Neville, Harper
Honor Books: *Rascal* by Sterling North, Dutton; *The Loner* by Esther Wier, McKay

1965
Shadow of a Bull
by Maia Wojciechowska, Atheneum
Honor Book: *Across Five Aprils* by Irene Hunt, Follett

1966
I, Juan de Pareja
by Elizabeth Borten de Trevino, Farrar
Honor Books:
The Black Cauldron by Lloyd Alexander, Holt; *The Animal Family* by Randal Jarrel, Pantheon; *The Noonday Friends* by Mary Stolz, Harper

1967
Up a Road Slowly
by Irene Hunt, Follett
Honor Books: *The King's Fifth* by Scott O'Dell, Houghton; *Zlateh the Goat and Other Stories* by Isaac Bashevis Singer, Harper; *The Jazz Man* by Mary H. Weik, Atheneum

1968
From the Mixed-Up Files of Mrs. Basil E. Frankweiler
by E. L. Konigsburg, Atheneum
Honor Books: *The Black Pearl* by Scott O'Dell, Houghton Mifflin; *The Egypt Game* by Zilpha Keatley Snyder, Atheneum; *The Fearsome Inn* by Isaac Bashevis Singer, Scribners; *Jennifer, Hecate, Macbeth, William McKinley, and Me, Elizabeth* by E. L. Konigsburg, Atheneum

1969
The High King
by Lloyd Alexander, Holt, Rinehart & Winston
Honor Books: *To Be a Slave* by Julius Lester, Dial; *When Shlemiel Went to Warsaw and Other Stories* by Isaac

Bashevis Singer, Farrar, Straus & Giroux

1970
Sounder
by William Armstrong, Harper & Row
Honor Books: *Journey Outside* by Mary Q. Steele, Viking; *Our Eddie* by Sulamith Ish-Kishor, Pantheon; *The Many Ways of Seeing: An Introduction to the Pleasures of Art* by Janet Gaylord Moore, Harcourt Brace Jovanovich

1971
The Summer of the Swans
by Betsy Byars, Viking
Honor Books: *Enchantress from the Stars* by Sylvia Louise Engdahl, Atheneum; *Kneeknock Rose* by Natalie Babbitt, Farrar, Straus & Giroux; *Sing Down the Moon* by Scott O'Dell, Houghton Mifflin

1972
Mrs. Frisby and the Rats of Nimh
by Robert C. O'Brien, Atheneum
Honor Books: *Annie and the Old One* by Miska Miles, Atlantic-Little; *The Headless Cupid* by Zilpha Keatley Snyder, Atheneum; *Incident at Hawk's Hill* by Allan W. Eckert, Little, Brown; *The Planet of Junior Brown* by Virginia Hamilton, Macmillan; *The Tombs of Atuan* by Ursula K. LeGuin, Atheneum

1973
Julie of the Wolves
by Jean C. George, Harper & Row
Honor Books: *Frog and Toad Together* by Arnold Lobel, Harper & Row; *The Upstairs Room* by Johanna Reiss,

Crowell; *The Witches of Worm* by Zilpha Keatley Snyder, Atheneum

1974
The Slave Dancer
by Paula Fox, Bradbury Press
Honor Book: *The Dark Is Rising* by Susan Cooper, Atheneum

1975
M. C. Higgins, the Great
by Virginia Hamilton, Macmillan
Honor Books: *Figgs and Phantoms* by Ellen Raskin, E. P. Dutton; *My Brother Sam Is Dead* by James Lincoln Collier and Christopher Collier, Four Winds; *The Perilous Guard* by Elizabeth Marie Pope, Houghton Mifflin; *Philip Hall Likes Me, I Reckon Maybe* by Bette Greene, Dial

1976
The Grey King
by Susan Cooper, Atheneum
Honor Books: *Dragonwings* by Laurence Yep, Harper & Row; *The Hundred Penny Box* by Sharon Bell Mathis, Viking

1977
Roll of Thunder, Hear My Cry
by Mildred Taylor, Dial
Honor Books: *Abel's Island* by William Steig, Farrar, Straus & Giroux; *A String in the Harp* by Nancy Bond, Atheneum

1978
Bridge to Terabithia
by Katherine Paterson, Crowell
Honor Books: *Anpao: An American Indian Odyssey* by Jamake Highwater, Lippincott; *Ramona and Her Father* by Beverly Cleary, Morrow

1979
The Westing Game
by Ellen Raskin, Dutton
Honor Book: *The Great Gilly
Hopkins* by Katherine
Paterson, Crowell

1980
*A Gathering of Days:
A New England Girl's
Journal, 1830–32*
by Joan W. Blos, Scribners
Honor Book: *The Road from
Home: The Story of an
Armenian Girl* by David
Kerdian, Greenwillow

1981
Jacob Have I Loved
by Katherine Paterson,
Crowell
Honor Books: *The Fledgling*
by Jane Langton, Harper &
Row; *A Ring of Endless Light*
by Madeleine L'Engle, Farrar,
Straus & Giroux

1982
*A Visit to William Blake's
Inn: Poems for Innocent
and Experienced Travelers*
by Nancy Willard, Harcourt
Brace Jovanovich
Honor Books: *Ramona
Quimby, Age 8* by Beverly
Cleary, Morrow; *Upon the
Head of the Coat: A
Childhood in Hungary, 1933-
1944* by Aranka Siegal,
Farrar, Straus & Giroux

1983
Dicey's Song
by Cynthia Voigt, Atheneum
Honor Books: *The Blue
Sword* by Robin McKinley,
Greenwillow; *Doctor DeSoto*
by William Steig, Farrar,
Straus & Giroux; *Graven
Images* by Paul Fleischman,
Harper & Row; *Homesick: My
Own Story* by Jean Fritz,
Putnam; *Sweet Whispers,
Brother Rush* by Virginia
Hamilton, Philomel

1984
Dear Mr. Henshaw
by Beverly Cleary, Morrow
Honor Books: *The Sign of the
Beaver* by Elizabeth George
Speare, Houghton Mifflin; *A
Solitary Blue* by Cynthia
Voigt, Atheneum; *Sugaring
Time* by Kathryn Lasky,
Macmillan; *The Wish Giver*
by Bill Brittain, Harper &
Row

1985
The Hero and the Crown
by Robin McKinley,
Greenwillow
Honor Books: *Like Jake and
Me* by Mavis Jukes, Alfred A.
Knopf; *The Moves Make the
Man* by Bruce Brooks, Harper
& Row; *One-Eyed Cat* by
Paula Fox, Bradbury Press

1986
Sarah, Plain and Tall
by Patricia MacLachlan,
Harper & Row
Honor Books: *Commodore
Perry in the Land of the
Shogun* by Rhoda Blumberg,
Lothrop, Lee & Shepard;
Dogsong by Gary Paulsen,
Bradbury Press

1987
The Whipping Boy
by Sid Fleischman,
Greenwillow
Honor Books: *A Fine White
Dust* by Cynthia Rylant,
Bradbury Press; *On My Honor*
by Marion Dane Bauer,
Clarion; *Volcano: The
Eruption and Healing of
Mount St. Helen's* by Patricia
Lauber, Bradbury Press

1988
Lincoln: A Photobiography
by Russell Freedman, Clarion
Honor Books: *After the Rain*
by Norma Fox Mazer,
Morrow; *Hatchet* by Gary
Paulsen, Bradbury Press

1989
*Joyful Noise:
Poems for Two Voices*
by Paul Fleischman,
Harper & Row
Honor Books: *In the
Beginning: Creation Stories
from Around the World* by
Virginia Hamilton, Harcourt
Brace Jovanovich; *Scorpions*
by Walter Dean Myers,
Harper & Row

1990
Number the Stars
by Lois Lowry, Houghton
Mifflin
Honor Books: *Afternoon of
the Elves* by Janet Taylor
Lifle, Watts; *Shabanu:
Daughter of the Wind* by
Suzanne Fisher Staples,
Knopf; *The Winter Room* by
Gary Paulsen, Watts

1991
Maniac Magee
by Jerry Spinelli, Little Brown
Honor Books: *True
Confessions of Charlotte
Doyle* by Avi, Orchard;
Marshmallow by Newberry,
Harper & Row

1992
Shilo
by Phyllis Reynolds Naylor,
Honor Books: *Nothing but the
Truth* by Avi, Orchard;
*Wright Brothers: How They
Invented the Plane* by Russell
Freedman, Holiday House

1993
Missing May
by Cynthia Rylant, Orchard
Honor Books: *The Dark
Thirty: Southern Tales of the
Supernatural* by Patricia
McKissick, illustrated by Jerry
Pinkney, Knopf; *Somewhere
in the Darkness* by Walter
Dean Myers; *What Hearts* by
Bruce Brooks, HarperCollins

THE LAURA INGALLS WILDER AWARD

Sponsored by the Association
for Library Service to
Children of the American
Library Association, this
award is given to a U.S.
author or illustrator whose
body of work has made a
lasting contribution to
children's literature.

1954 Laura Ingalls Wilder

1960 Clara Ingram Judson

1965 Ruth Sawyer

1970 E. B. White

1975 Beverly Cleary

1980 Theodor Geisel

1983 Maurice Sendak

1986 Jean Fritz

1989 Elizabeth George Speare

1992 Marcia Brown

NATIONAL COUNCIL OF TEACHERS OF ENGLISH AWARD FOR EXCELLENCE IN POETRY FOR CHILDREN

Sponsored by the National
Council of Teachers of
English, this award is given to
a U.S. poet in recognition of
his or her total body of work
written for ages 3 through 13.

1977 David McCord

1978 Aileen Fisher

1979 Karla Kuskin

1980 Myra Cohn Livingston

1981 Eve Merriam

1982 John Ciardi

1985 Lilian Moore

1988 Arnold Adoff

1991 Valerie Worth

THE HANS CHRISTIAN ANDERSEN AWARD

This award is given every two years to a living author and, since 1966, illustrator. Sponsored by the International Board on Books for Young People, it is given as recognition of a person's complete work that has made an important international contribution to children's literature.

1956
Eleanor Farjeon
(Great Britain)

1958
Astrid Lindgren (Sweden)

1960
Erich Kastner (Germany)

1962
Meindert DeJong (U.S.A.)

1964
Rene Guillot (France)

1966
Author: Tove Jansson
(Finland)
Illustrator: Alois Carigiet
(Switzerland)

1968
Authors: James Kruss
(Germany),

Jose Maria Sanchez-Silva
(Spain)
Illustrator: Jiri Trnka
(Czechoslovakia)

1970
Author: Gianni Rodari (Italy)
Illustrator: Maurice Sendak
(U.S.A.)

1971
Author: Scott O'Dell (U.S.A.)
Illustrator: Ib Spang Olsen
(Denmark)

1974
Author: Maria Gripe (Sweden)
Illustrator: Farshid Mesghali
(Iran)

1976
Author: Cecil Bodker
(Denmark)
Illustrator: Tatjana Mawrina
(U.S.S.R.)

1978
Author: Paula Fox (U.S.A.)
Illustrator: Otto S. Svend
(Denmark)

1980
Author: Bohumil Riha
(Czechoslovakia)
Illustrator: Suekichl Akaba
(Japan)

1982
Author: Lygia Bojunga Nunes
(Brazil)
Illustrator:
Zbigniew Rychlicki
(Poland)

1984
Author: Christine Nostlinger
(Austria)
Illustrator: Mitsumasa Anno
(Japan)

1986
Author: Patricia Wrightson
(Australia)
Illustrator: Robert Ingpen
(Australia)

1988
Author: Annie M. G. Schmidt
(Netherlands)
Illustrator: Dusan Kallay
(Czechoslovakia)

1990
Author: Tormod Haugen
(Norway)
Illustrator: Lisbeth Zwerger
(Austria)

1992
Author:
Virginia Hamilton
(USA)
Illustrator: Kveta Pacovska
(Czechoslovakia)

The
Index
of
TEACHER
RESOURCES

Allison, Christine.
*I'll Tell You a Story,
I'll Sing You a Song: A
Parent's Guide to the Fairy
Tales, Fables, Songs, and
Rhymes of Childhood.*
New York: Delacorte Press;
1987; ISBN: 0-385-29569-3.
This is really an anthology of
childhood "classics" along
with some background
information and suggestions
as to when and how to use the
stories and rhymes. It is a
good addition to any early
elementary teacher's
bookshelf, and would not go
unused even in upper
elementary grades. Of
particular use might be the
section on "Motion Songs and
Finger Plays".

Bauer, Caroline Feller.
Celebrations.
Bronx, New York: W. H.
Wilson Company; 1985;
ISBN: 0-8242-0708-4.
Bauer has put together sixteen
celebrations centered on
children's books and poems.
Arranged alphabetically, they
range from celebrating art to
Valentine's Day. Many are a
bit offbeat (a favorite is
"National Nothing Day").
Each celebration contains
prose and poetry selections,
activities, writing ideas,
bulletin boards, and a
bibliography.

Bauer, Caroline Feller.
This Way to Books.
New York, New York: H. W.
Wilson Company; 1983;
ISBN: 0-8242-0678-9.
While this book might be
aimed at librarians, the
activities could be used
effectively in many settings.
The avowed aim of the book
is to bring children and books
together in interesting ways.
The sections in the book on

booktalking and storytelling
may be the most helpful. The
section on poetry has many
exciting ideas for presenting
poetry to children. If you're
looking for ideas to stimulate
interest in books and/or to
extend some of your lessons,
this book can help.

Bosma, Bette.
*Fairy Tales, Fables, Legends,
and Myths: Using Folk
Literature in Your
Classroom.*
New York, New York:
Teachers College Press; 1987;
ISBN: 0-8077-2827-6.
This is an excellent resource
for anyone teaching folk
literature in elementary
grades, especially the upper
elementary. Bosma begins
with a justification for using
folk literature with children
but the majority of the book is
devoted to ideas and activities
for involving children in this
rich branch of literature. She
has also included an extensive
bibliography.

Bromley, Karen D'Angelo.
*Webbing with Literature:
Creating Story Maps with
Children's Books.*
Boston: Allyn & Bacon; 1991;
ISBN: 0-205-12610-3.
Bromley provides background
for teachers on how they can
use mapping to help children
explore literature. The book
includes semantic mapping,
story mapping, and webbing
activities for writing. In
addition, she provides
information on using literature
effectively in classrooms and
a bibliography of children's
books that includes ideas for
using them in the classroom.

Carroll, Frances Laverne;
Mary Meacham.
Exciting, Funny, Scary,

*Short, Different, and Sad
Books Kids Like About
Animals, Science, Sports,
Families, Songs and
Other Things.*
Chicago: American Library
Association; 1984; ISBN: 0-
8389-1423-8.This book was
written in response to
children's requests to librarians
for books on popular topics.
Librarians were surveyed for
their most requested book
topics and the books they could
provide for children on these
topics. The selection is quite
eclectic, but may help to give
some insight into what children
want to read. The annotated
lists of books for each topic are
helpful, too.

Children's Book Council;
International Reading
Association.
*Kid's Favorite Books:
Children's Choices
1989-1991.*
Newark, Delaware:
International Reading
Association; 1992; ISBN: 0-
87207-370-X.
Over 300 titles and brief
annotations of books chosen
by children in the "Children's
Choices" project. The
purpose of the project is for
students from across the
United States to evaluate new
books and vote on the titles
they like best. The
annotations include suggested
reading levels and
bibliographic information. It
is certainly a great place to
look if you want to find books
that children will respond to in
positive ways. It is interesting
to compare their picks with
those of the major reviewers
of children's books.

Cullinan, Bernice E.; Editor
*Children's Literature in the
Reading Program.*

Newark:DE: International
Reading Association; 1987;
ISBN: 0-87207-782-9.
A comprehensive guide to
implementing children's
literature into the regular
reading program.

Farrell, Catharine.
*Storytelling:
A Guide For Teachers.*
New York: Scholastic; 199;
ISBN: 0-590-49139-3.
A guide for teachers interested
in the craft of storytelling in
the classroom. It includes
eight stories, each of which is
already scripted for telling.

Freeman, Judy; Editor.
*Books Kids Will Sit Still For:
The Complete Read-Aloud
Guide, Second Edition.*
New York: Bowker; 1990;
ISBN: 0-8352-3010-4.
Another large reference book
for school libraries. Freeman
provides hundreds of book
titles categorized by subject
and by grade level. Excellent
indexes make book finding
easy. The introductory
chapters provide a good
background or review of
reasons to read aloud, and
practices to enhance reading
aloud.

Gallo, Donald R.; Editor.
*Speaking for Ourselves:
Autobiographical Sketches
by Notable Authors of Books
for Young Adults.*
Urbana, Illinois: National
Council of Teachers of
English; 1990; ISBN: 0-8141-
4625-2.
While this book is aimed
primarily at middle school and
above, upper elementary
grades will find some of their
favorite authors here too.
These sketches are written by
the authors themselves and
provide very nice insights.

There is also a sequel to this edition.

Gensler, Kinereth; Nina Nyhart,
The Poetry Connection: An Anthology of Contemporary Poems with Ideas to Stimulate Children's Writing.
New York: Teachers and Writers Collaborative; 1978; ISBN: 0-915924-08-0.
The beginning sections cover ideas to help children explore poetry as well as their own feelings and thoughts. They also cover some of the attributes of poems. The remainder of the book is given to poems including an extensive selection of poems written by children.

Gillespie, John T.; Corinne J. Naden, Editors.
Best Books for Children: Preschool through Grade 6.
New York: Bowker; 1990; ISBN: 0-8352-2668-9.
This is one of those resources that should be in every school library. It is probably too expensive to put on every teacher's bookshelf. It is a great book finder, allowing the teacher to look for books on a particular subject. It is thoroughly indexed to make finding books fairly easy.

Hearne, Betsy; Marilyn Kaye.
Celebrating Children's Books
New York: Lothrop; 1981; ISBN: 0-688-00676-0.
An anthology of writers who talk about their craft, providing insight into their work.

Hopkins, Lee Bennett.
Books are by People.
New York: Citation Press; 1969.
This book is out of print and is

becoming dated. However, it is a good resource for finding out about the author or illustrator. These are interviews by Hopkins with 104 authors and illustrators. Another book in the series was More Books by More People, also by Hopkins using the same format.

Hopkins, Lee Bennett.
Pass the Poetry Please, Revised Edition.
New York: Harper & Row; 1987; ISBN: 0-06-446062-2.
Hopkins presents short biographies and insights into many writers of children's poetry along with ideas for using that poetry with children. He provides many ways to incorporate poetry into every child's life. He also shows ways to help children write their own poetry.

Jett-Simpson, Mary; Editor.
Adventuring with Books: A Booklist for Pre-K—Grade 6, Ninth Edition.
Urbana, Illinois: National Council of Teachers of English; 1989; ISBN: 0-8141-0078-3.
Every few years the NCTE issues a new booklist for elementary students with this title. They should be in every school. The format makes in helpful in putting together literature for thematic units as well as finding the book that will put the crowning touch on a unit. While each edition covers only a few years (this edition covers primarily 1985-1988), having previous editions allows one to go back and find books that are most likely still in the school and public libraries. Upper grade teachers may want to get Your Reading: A Booklist for

Junior High and Middle School Students.

Johnson, Terry D.; Daphne R. Louis.
Bringing it all Together.
Portsmouth:NH: Heinemann; 1990; ISBN: 0-435-08502-6.
A primer on how to incorporate a literature-based language program into any K-8 classroom.

Kimmel, Margaret Mary; S, Elizabeth Segel,.
For Reading Out Loud!
A Guide to Sharing Books with Children.
New York, New York: Delacorte; 1983; ISBN: 0-440-02711-X.
This is an excellent resource for classrooms. Kimmel and Segel have included long annotations on their book selections as well as some lists to help select books by topics. Some will find their "book places" list helpful in that they list books by the places in which they are set. This could be helpful for a teacher who wants to "visit" a place being studied in class.

Kobrin, Beverly.
Eyeopeners! How to Choose and Use Children's Books About Real People, Places and Things.
New York, New York: Penguin; 1988; ISBN: 0-14-046830-7.
Kobrin has put together a well indexed, annotated guide to over 500 children's informational books. She has also included many ideas for extending topics in the classroom. While the annotated guide is the major part of the book, teachers and parents will also find the beginning chapters helpful. These help to lay a foundation

for evaluating and using informational books with children.

Kovacs, Deborah; James Preller.
Meet The Authors and Illustrators: 60 Creators of Favorite Children's Books Talk About Their Work.
New York: Scholastic; 1991; ISBN: 0-590-49097-4.
Sixty authors share ideas about their craft as writers and illustrators. The book is divided equally between picture books and intermediate books. Each author annotation is accompanied by a variety of books.

Lima, Carolyn W.; John A Lima
A to Zoo: Subject Access to Children's Picture Books, Third Edition.
New York: Bowker; 1989; ISBN: 0-8352-2599-2.
This is another resource that should be in every school. Using this book teachers should be able to find picture book resources for most thematic units. Teachers at all levels, including upper grades, will find this a useful book finding tool.

Lukens, Rebecca J.
A Critical Handbook of Children's Literature, Fourth Edition.
New York: HarperCollins; 1990; ISBN: 0-673-38773-9.
An easy to read and complete guide to children's literature with plenty of examples.
Lynch, Priscilla. Using Big Books and Predictable Books.
New York: Scholastic; 1986; ISBN: 0-590-71368-X.
A book that is full of suggestions for teachers looking for practical ideas for implementing Big Books and

predictable books in their classroom

Moen, Christine Boardman. *Teaching with Caldecott Books: Activities Across the Curriculum.* New York: Scholastic; 1991; ISBN: 0-590-49079-6. Fifteen Caldecott Medal winners are used to illustrate a variety of teaching strategies for incorporating award-winning literature in any classroom.

Moss, Joy F. *Focus Units in Literature: A Handbook for Elementary School Teachers.* Urbana Illinois: National Council of Teachers of English; 1984; ISBN: 0-8141-1756-2. Moss has created thirteen literature units centered around themes ranging from first and second grade through fifth and sixth. What makes the book so valuable is not the themes that are covered (although they are excellent) but rather the example that she sets. Teachers will feel comfortable using her units to begin to use literature in classrooms and then develop their own units following her patterns. She also includes a great "Guidelines for Questioning" chapter.

Reasoner, Charles F *Releasing Children to Literature.* New York: Dell; 1976. An excellent classroom companion for any teacher interested in incorporating literature in the classroom. Although the example books are dated, the process and procedures of using trade-book literature in the classroom is still very usable.

Reasoner, Charles F. *Where the Readers Are: The Second Teacher's Guide to Yearling Books.* New York: Dell; 1972. ISBN: 0-685-29120-0. Similar to the First Teacher's Guide, this edition offers newer books and activities.

Rothlein, Liz; Anita Meyer Meinbach. *The Literature Connection.* Glenview:IL: Scott, Foresman and Company; 1991; ISBN: 0-673-38450-0. An excellent resource for any classroom teacher, this book incorporates information about children's literature with a variety of activities and examples that can be used in any classroom.

Rudman, Masha Kabakow; Editor. *Children's Literature: Resource for the Classroom.* Christopher Gordon; 1989; ISBN: 0-926842-01-3. This collection of twelve articles about children's literature and its use in the classroom serves as both a resource for developing a philosophy for presenting literature and a guide for its implementation. Rudman's chapter alone: "Children's Literature in the Reading Program," would be worth the purchase. Adding to it chapters by Nancy Larrick, Donna Norton, Anita Silvey, Jane Yolen, Eileen Tway, and Julius Lester makes this a must-have for a reading teacher's bookshelf.

Somers, Albert B.; Janet Evens Worthington, *Response Guides for Teaching Children's Books.* Urbana, Illinois: National Council of Teachers of

English; 1979; ISBN: 0-8141-4086-6. This is an older resource but still popular. The guide covers 27 highly-used children's books covering all the elementary grades. Each book guide is two to five pages in length and provides a summary, ideas to begin the book, discussion questions, and follow-up activities. The activities include ideas for art, dramatization, and writing. It is a guide well worth having in every elementary classroom.

Stewig, John Warren; Sam Leaton Sebesta; Editors. *Using Literature in the Elementary Classroom, Revised Edition.* Urbana, Illinois: National Council of Teachers of English; 1989; ISBN: 0-8141-5618-5. This collection of seven articles both addresses the reasons children's literature should be used in classrooms and gives ideas on its effective presentation. The topics range from using books for supporting artistic literacy, to vocabulary development. The "how to" element is valuable to the classroom teacher. Each article contains a bibliography of children's books.

Sutherland, Zena. *The Best in Children's Books:* The University of Chicago Guide to Children's Literature 1979-1984. Chicago, Illinois: University of Chicago Press; 1986; ISBN: 0-226-78060-0. This is a continuing series that presents the better children's books reviewed in The Bulletin of the Center for Children's' Books. The

reviews are helpful in choosing quality books. (Following the Bulletin's convention, especially noteworthy books are starred.) There is also a subject index and a "Type of Literature" index.

Thompson, Gare. *Teaching Through Themes.* New York: Scholastic; 1991; ISBN: 0-590-49129-6. A user-friendly collection of thematic units for students of all ages that can be adapted to classroom use. The themes for younger students are people, friendship, and habitats. The themes for older readers are survival, mystery, and courage.

Trelease, Jim. *The New Read-Aloud Handbook.* New York: Penguin; 1989; ISBN: 0-14-046.881-1. This book has quickly become something of a classic. Trelease provides both a justification for reading aloud as well as solid guidelines for doing so. He provides a bibliography including annotations and suggested levels for use. We feel that reading aloud should be part of every classroom, especially literature-based classrooms.

Zinsser, William. *The Art and Craft of Writing For Children.* Boston:MA: Houghton Mifflin; 1990; ISBN: 0-395-51425-8. Six prominent writers talk about their craft. The writers are Jean Fritz, Maurice Sendak, Jill Krementz, Jack Prelutsky, Rosemary Wells, and Katherine Paterson. Journals

PERIODICALS

Elleman, Barbara; Editor.
Book Links.
Chicago, Il: American Library Association; bi-monthly.
This is the best new publication about children's books. It provides thematic booklists on several topics in each issue in addition to articles about authors and illustrators and "how to" articles. This magazine should be accessible to every teacher.

Hearne, Betsy; Editor.
The Bulletin of the Center for Children's Books.
Urbana, Illinois: University of Illinois; bi-monthly.
This journal contains only book reviews. It reviews books both good and not-so-good. This can be helpful. Its viewpoint is often different from that of the Horn Book and so can provide another voice.

Silvey, Anita; Editor.
The Horn Book Magazine.
Boston; bi-monthly.
This is one magazine that should be available in every school library. The reviews are excellent but the best part is the articles by authors and interpreters of children's literature. It is a great way to keep up with happenings in the world of children's books.

Taxel, Joel; Editor.
The New Advocate.
Boston: Christopher Gordon; quarterly
This book is centered on using children's books. The philosophy is very literature- and whole-language-based. It provides articles to develop a philosophy and background about children's books as well as articles on how they can be used in the classroom. There is also a review of children's books in each issue. This is a good teacher resource.